D1180850

MENTORING

MENTORING

A Henley Review of Best Practice

Jane Cranwell-Ward, Patricia Bossons
and Sue Gover

First published 2004 by
PALGRAVE MACMILLAN
Houndmills, Basingstoke, Hampshire RG21 6XS and
175 Fifth Avenue, New York, N.Y. 10010
Companies and representatives throughout the world

PALGRAVE MACMILLAN is the global academic imprint of the Palgrave Macmillan division of St. Martin's Press, LLC and of Palgrave Macmillan Ltd. Macmillan® is a registered trademark in the United States, United Kingdom and other countries. Palgrave is a registered trademark in the European Union and other countries.

ISBN 1–4039–3568–8

This book is printed on paper suitable for recycling and made from fully managed and sustained forest sources.

A catalogue record for this book is available from the British Library.

A catalog record for this book is available from the Library of Congress.

10 9 8 7 6 5 4 3 2 1
13 12 11 10 09 08 07 06 05 04

Printed and bound in Great Britain by
Creative Print & Design (Wales), Ebbw Vale

To our co-contributors, husbands, family, friends and colleagues for their support and tolerance

Contents

List of Figures and Tables

Tables

Foreword

Mentors are people who help others to reach their potential. Organisations in the private and, increasingly, the public sectors are beginning to recognise the growing importance of the role mentors can play in offering advice and direction and acting as a sounding board to employees. These organisations are also seeing how the relationship between mentor and mentee can bring benefits to their business. When staff have the opportunity to seek confidential feedback and guidance on their careers, the result, in many cases, is a more engaged employee.

Mentors work with individuals and teams from a diverse range of organisations, from men and women running small local businesses through to the directors of some of the world's largest organisations.

At Microsoft, we believe that great people make great companies. It is a truism that applies to any industry, but is especially meaningful for a software company, where creativity, ideas and the energy behind those ideas are the driving forces behind great products.

But what are great people and how can we develop them? At Microsoft, we believe great people have six core traits:

▶ Honesty and integrity

▶ Openness and respect for others

▶ Willingness to take on big challenges

▶ Passion for customers, partners and technology

▶ Accountability

▶ Self-criticism.

Microsoft's mission – to enable people and businesses throughout the world to realise their full potential – begins by enabling employees to realise their own potential. Our ability to achieve this mission depends on the individual decisions and actions of every Microsoft employee around the world.

As a company we want, and need, our people to be willing to ask for and constructively use feedback about their strengths and weaknesses. We encourage employees to seek opportunities for personal and professional growth, which is why we use mentors to help individuals and teams at Microsoft.

Staff are encouraged to choose mentors who work well for them. Both internal and external mentors are helpful in developing talent. Internal mentors offer the benefit of internal and applicable industry knowledge, whilst external mentors can help to bring a fresh perspective to an issue or problem.

Whatever the situation, it is always possible to include mentoring as part of maximising the performance of individuals and organisations. *Mentoring: A Henley Review of Best Practice* is the perfect practical guide for those involved in any aspect of mentoring. The authors have succeeded in presenting the shared experiences of many different individuals and organisations in a comprehensive and easily accessible format.

I believe mentoring will continue to help Microsoft to stay at the leading edge – both in running the business and in providing an inspiring environment for our people.

STEVE HARVEY
Senior director of people and culture,
Microsoft UK

Acknowledgements

We would like to thank the following participants of the Henley Mentoring Focus Group for their contributions to this book, either in the form of actual materials and case studies or by contributing to our discussions in the Focus Group meetings or by agreeing to be interviewed.

Abbey
Avaya
B&Q plc
Barclaycard
British Airways plc
Canon (UK) Ltd
Christies
David Clutterbuck
David Megginson
Debenhams plc
Department for Work & Pensions
Dixons Group plc
EDS
Eric Parsloe
Group 4 Falck

Henley Management College
  (Maureen George, Richard McBain)
Marks & Spencer plc
Merrill Lynch Europe plc
National Air Traffic Services Ltd
Orange plc
Tarmac
The Prince's Trust
RWE Thames Water plc
Smiths Group
Virgin Money Ltd
Vodafone Ltd
YELL Ltd
Yorkshire Water Services Ltd
Zurich

ROYALTIES

The authors have agreed that royalties from sales of this book will be donated to The Prince's Trust *Mentoring for Care Leavers* network, a mentoring programme aimed at helping young people who are leaving the care system. We are indebted to Will Large for this suggestion.

The authors and publisher wish to thank the following for permission to use copyright materials and also for waiving their fees in favour of The Prince's Trust:

Material from *Making Sense of Emotional Intelligence*, Higgs & Dulewicz (2002) is printed with permission of the publisher nferNelson, The Chiswick Centre, 414 Chiswick High Road, London, W4 5TF; Material taken from *Everyone Needs a Mentor*, David Clutterbuck, 3rd edition (2001), is printed with the permission of the publisher, the Chartered Institute of Personnel and Development, London; Material taken from *Mentoring Executives & Directors*, Clutterbuck & Megginson, copyright (1999), is printed with permission from Elsevier; Quotations from *Coaching for Performance*, John Whitmore, 2nd edition (1996) are reproduced with the permission of Nicholas Brealey Publishing, London; Material taken from *Transformational Mentoring*, Julie Hay (1999) is reproduced with the permission of Sherwood Publishing; Material taken from *The Art of Mentoring*, Mike Pegg (2003) is printed with the permission of Management Books 2000 Ltd; Material taken from *The Mentoring Pocketbook*, Alred, Garvey & Smith (1998) is printed with permission of Management Pocketbooks Ltd; Definition of 'mentor' is taken from *Oxford English Reference Dictionary* edited by Pearsall, Judy & Trumble, Bill (2002). By permission of Oxford University Press, www.oup.com. Free permission.

The authors would also like to thank Richard McBain at Henley Management College, for allowing us to use his materials (including evaluation of mentoring) prepared for the Henley e-learning programme on mentoring.

PART I

Overview of the Book and Business Context

1 Introduction

The Henley Learning Partnership was set up by Henley Management College in 1995. Its objective is to provide an arena in which organisations can benefit from the synergy of working together to share and explore development issues. There are now around 40 member organisations in the Partnership and managers from these organisations attend over 30 events at Henley each year. These events include specialist forums, conferences and a number of focus groups looking at particular development areas. One of these is the Mentoring Focus Group, which has been running in its present form since 1999. It is one of the most popular of the focus groups and the level of interest in mentoring amongst the member population seems to get stronger each year.

The underpinning philosophy behind the Mentoring Focus Group has been a strongly held view that 'the world could use more mentoring'. Particularly in business, the traditional approach to mentoring has been to target specific groups within the business, such as graduate trainees or fast-track management candidates. The range of applications and programmes that the member organisations are now developing make it clear that mentoring can be more a state of mind, rather than just a specific activity for the chosen few. The more that mentoring can move to be seen as a central part of an organisation's functionality, rather than a peripheral activity, the better.

This book is designed to help readers to share the Group's experience and enthusiasm. The book replicates the experience of attending a Focus Group meeting, where any aspect of mentoring, in its broadest sense, can come up for discussion. When this happens, a wealth of ideas and examples are shared, often from the least likely sources. Whatever the issue, some form of mentoring solution can always help. The spin-offs from incorporating mentoring as a core part of a strategic solution can be far-reaching. The improvement in communication and cross-divisional networking alone can address problems which have been subversively rumbling around an organisation, or department, for years and the challenges to 'the way we do things around here' thinking can be very significant.

Apart from sharing the organisational case studies and experiences, David Clutterbuck and David Megginson, two leading European mentoring gurus, regularly attended meetings of the Focus Group to share their expertise. At one meeting they were part of an expert panel and their replies to questions from the Group appear throughout the book. Good practice from a review of the literature has also been included to complement lessons from the Focus Group.

One of the main advantages mentoring has over many other types of corporate 'development' initiative is that it is intrinsically deeply personal. It is about a relationship between two people, which focuses on issues of specific and personal importance to one, or both, parties. A successful mentoring relationship, therefore, is one of the most motivating situations an individual can find themselves in as part of their working life. If an organisation can harness and tap into the energy that can come from this motivation, then many performance-linked problems could disappear without any further direct company involvement.

This may seem rather idealistic, but it does reflect the increased focus on work–life balance concerning many working people, and the need for there to be 'something for me' in the ongoing experience of going to work. Personal development is now a much more common interest for many people in these days of 'portfolio careers' and personal responsibility for their own direction – the redesigning (or, as far as many people are concerned, the destruction) of the psychological contract at work now means that individuals are driven to look after themselves more than ever before. A stable structure and a job for life are no longer concepts that occur to the majority of people in the workforce. A mentoring relationship can address this need, by acknowledging the needs of the individual and supplying a much-needed thread of consistency in a climate of constant change, ambiguity and uncertainty.

How to Use the Book

This book has been written to enable the different readers to take the lessons drawn from sharing experience in the Mentoring Focus Group and apply these lessons to their own specific mentoring situation. It does not need to be read from cover to cover. The main sections of the book have been written as stand-alone parts, with different levels of importance for different readership groups.

Table 1.1 at the end of this section will focus readers on the parts that will most meet their needs. It is likely that, at some stage, scheme managers, trainers and consultants will find the whole book of relevance to them. There are summaries at the end of each chapter to ensure that lessons learned are readily accessible to readers.

The book is divided into five parts.

PART I – OVERVIEW OF THE BOOK AND BUSINESS CONTEXT

All target groups should read Part I. It has been written to put mentoring within a broader development and business framework. Readers will appreciate the growing importance of mentoring and some of the key business drivers for its use in business. The background will be particularly helpful for those required to take a business decision on whether to invest in a mentoring solution within their own organisation. It will also give a context for those embarking on a mentoring relationship: both mentor and mentee, whether the mentor is internal or external to the particular organisation.

PART II – WHAT IS MENTORING? DEFINITION AND CONTEXT

Part II will clarify what mentoring is, the differences between mentoring and coaching and factors influencing the decision to introduce a mentoring scheme or take part in a mentoring relationship. Once more, all target groups should read this part. It will help those deciding on the introduction of a mentoring scheme to be clearer in their own minds of exactly what mentoring is and what it is not. It will also help readers to understand some of the differences between coaching and mentoring, as seen through the eyes of a group of professionals.

Mentors and mentees will also benefit from understanding exactly what is meant by mentoring and, if given a choice, how to decide whether or not to take part in a mentoring relationship. Line managers should focus carefully on the differences between mentoring and coaching. They may act as a coach to a member of their team who could, at the same time, be mentored by someone else. This section will also help readers to clarify whether to go the mentoring or coaching route by way of a development intervention.

PART III – SETTING UP AND RUNNING A MENTORING SCHEME

Part III gives detailed knowledge and frameworks for those seeking to introduce their own mentoring scheme and/or evaluate their own scheme. It gives all the necessary information, from setting up a scheme, including gaining buy-in and influencing key stakeholders and marketing the scheme, to setting it up and establishing processes and procedures. It helps the scheme manager to match up mentoring pairs, train participants, run and monitor the scheme and, finally, to evaluate it. As the title of this part suggests, it will be particularly helpful for those readers wishing to set up or review their own scheme and should be read in depth.

Decision makers who are considering setting up a mentoring scheme should skim-read Part III to understand what is involved. Mentors, mentees and line managers will also benefit from skim-reading this part to gain an overview of how a mentoring scheme is set up and run.

PART IV – TAKING PART IN A MENTORING RELATIONSHIP

The purpose of Part IV is to give the reader an understanding of how to get the best out of a mentoring relationship. It will be particularly helpful for those about to embark on, or who are already involved in, a mentoring relationship. Mentors and mentees need to read this part of the book thoroughly in order to develop ways of making their mentoring relationships even more effective. It helps mentors and mentees to get started in a mentoring relationship, with advice on how to build rapport and then an even deeper relationship. An overview of mentoring skills is included. Finally, mentors and mentees are given guidance on how to evaluate the mentoring relationship and bring it to a close.

Those who run schemes will find this section of the book useful if they are planning to provide training for their mentors and mentees. Finally, those taking a decision on implementing mentoring would find it helpful if they skim-read this section to extend their understanding of mentoring and what is required to make the relationship a success.

PART V – LESSONS LEARNED AND CONCLUSIONS

This final part of the book brings together the conclusions and lessons learned which have been summarised throughout the book. It will provide useful reference in the future for all readers, and includes lessons learned by specific organisations. A final section provides further reading, useful websites and information about networking.

We hope that you will feel a part of the discussions that took place in collecting the material for this book and become as passionate as we are about the value of mentoring as an important element of any development process.

Table 1.1 gives guidance on the parts of the book to be given high priority by each category of reader.

Table 1.1 **Priorities for categories of reader: X indicates the part is high priority**

Part	Scheme manager	Mentor	Mentee	Line manager	Trainer/ consultant	Decision-maker
Introduction	X	X	X	X	X	X
What is Mentoring?	X	X	X	X	X	X
Setting Up and Running a Mentoring Scheme	X				X	
Taking Part in a Mentoring Relationship	X	X	X		X	
Lessons Learned and Conclusions	X	X	X	X	X	X

2 The Business Context and Organisational Drivers for Mentoring

Introduction

All those involved with the mentoring process need to be aware of the broader business environment and drivers for mentoring. This chapter helps to explain why many organisations are adopting mentoring as part of the development of the capability of their workforces. It will help those setting up mentoring schemes to make the business case for mentoring. For those taking part in a mentoring relationship, the chapter will provide the context and rationale for mentoring.

The business context and organisational drivers can be divided into two categories: external and internal influences. These influences are summarised in Table 2.1. Key influences will be outlined in this chapter to help the reader to understand the relevance of mentoring for meeting the different drivers.

Table 2.1 **Summary of the external and internal influences for mentoring**

External influences	Internal influences
Business environment	Developing organisational capabilities
Globalisation	Succession planning
Technological change	War for talent
Restructuring of organisations	Focus on business performance
Mergers and acquisitions	Increased motivation
Diversity	Encouraging teamwork and productivity
Changing shape of development	Change management initiatives
Corporate social responsibility	Knowledge management
Changing psychological contract	Individual development and continuous improvement
Managing stress at work	
Work–life balance and flexible working	

External Influences

There are a number of external factors that have influenced the rising popularity of mentoring as a development tool. These range from large-scale changes in the businesses environment, globalisation and technology, through to changes at organisational level such as corporate social responsibility, restructuring of organisations and increase in the number of mergers and acquisitions. The impact of issues such as stress, work–life balance and diversity also affect the use of mentoring.

THE BUSINESS ENVIRONMENT

The start of the 21st century can best be described as challenging, changing, turbulent and unpredictable. What does this mean for organisations and their people? It requires both to become more flexible and innovative and, in turn, demands that people develop a different skill set. In this uncertain and changing world mentoring provides an excellent option for people to develop themselves in order to keep ahead of the game.

In tough economic times organisations need to plan for the unexpected and will, in turn, find opportunities where others see threats. Cowan (2002) suggested that in an economic downturn managers and executives prepare to be able to reap the benefits of recovery. Their companies anticipate change instead of simply reacting to it and are more likely to prosper as a result, as do the careers of managers and their executives. Those planning for the unexpected find opportunity where others see threat. This behaviour is particularly valued among the hi-tech industries of southern California. Biotech, information technology and software companies all operate in highly volatile markets where new products surface very suddenly. Survival under these conditions means having flexibility and the capability to change direction quickly.

Faced with uncertainties in the external environment, Mockler (2003) suggested that managers can either adopt a structured approach to formulating strategy or act intuitively. Mockler felt that the best approach was a balance of the two. Managers need to be able to spot the risks as well as emerging and changing trends. In the US airline industry Southwest and JetBlue have managed to achieve the right balance between structure and innovative thinking. Mentoring can be a useful way to develop the broader business perspective needed to develop the right strategy.

In tough economic conditions there is an expectation on staff to achieve more with fewer resources. This has an implication for mentoring where the emphasis switches to flexibility rather than specialisation.

GLOBALISATION

Globalisation, not technology, is the fundamental driver of the real new economy, according to Eisenhardt (2002) writing in *Sloan Management Review*. Globalisation is the deep interrelationship among countries, companies and individuals. The connections may be cultural, as in the case of global brands like Sony, or environmental, with global warming and over-fishing of the oceans. The connections are technical, for example the inter-net and wireless communication, or financial, for example the linking of major stock exchanges and the growth of NAFTA-like trade agreements.

As organisations increasingly are competing in a global marketplace, employees need to develop their skills and become second to none. With the right investment in staff, people will be able to develop to their full poten-tial and increase the profitability of the organisation. In particular globalisa-tion requires people to be able to work across cultural boundaries, handle the pace of doing business and deal with the scale and speed of change that is unpredictable.

Carrington (2003) discusses the career of Claire Thompson. She has had an international HR career, moving from being European HR Manager with Unilever, based in Brussels, to becoming Vice-president Human Resources, Unilever de Mexico. Thompson emphasises that business and national cultures are very different beasts. As well as helping to develop a cohesive business culture within the bigger Unilever de Mexico, Thompson had to get to grips with living and working in a foreign land. Building trust and confidence takes time and to become part of the team requires a step change. Mentoring was important in coming to terms with the Mexican culture and Thompson used people from her own team, as well as friends who had worked in Mexico.

Globalisation also impacts on mentoring by requiring more mentoring to take place electronically and mentoring schemes need to become aligned with a range of different cultures. It may also necessitate the translation of mentoring materials into a range of different languages.

TECHNOLOGICAL CHANGE

There has been unprecedented growth and change in technology, the hi-tech industry and the way organisations do business over the last few years. Managing in the new economy requires different ways of working and doing business. Different ways of learning have also been made possible including e-learning. Mentoring can help people to take advantage of the available technology and manage the necessary changes with technological advances.

A survey conducted by Henley Management College (2000) found that traditional organisations have now recognised the importance of strategic planning, e-business knowledge and leadership to help to cope with the demands of the new economy. Four key needs were identified for leaders to help their organisations stay ahead of the competition:

1   To cope with change in highly uncertain environments

2   To develop skills in leadership and relationship-building

3   To become more risk-aware and take more risks

4   To adopt new working practices and be less detached from subordinates.

Additional skills and attributes were also identified:

1   To develop a 'can-do attitude'

2   To have a broader business perspective to cope with broader responsibilities

3   To be on the look out for new business opportunities which become possible with advancing technology.

RESTRUCTURING OF ORGANISATIONS

In the past organisations were designed for efficiency in a stable environment. Typically organisations were large and people worked within their own functional areas, with a command and control style of leadership. In the 1980s and 90s several drivers for change emerged:

▶ Increased competition and the need to respond quickly to changes in the marketplace.

▶ A tougher economic environment and the need to drive down costs.

▶ Organisations competing globally and the need to keep ahead to stay in business.

▶ A greater demand for people to be more innovative.

▶ Technological change giving more access to information quicker.

As a result of these changes in the environment, organisations downsized dramatically to help to become more competitive and more cost-effective. The new-style organisations were flatter and more boundaryless, as a result of partnerships, outsourcing and more people moving towards short-term contracts and portfolio careers.

Changes in the structure of organisations have had a profound effect on the working lives of managers. In particular, they have greater accountability for performance, are required to develop a broader business perspective and have the capability to work across functional boundaries. For many managers, the downsizing has resulted in working longer hours, with more work and fewer people to deliver business results.

Ellis (2003), reporting in *Sloan Management Review* on the research of Rajan & Wulf, believes that, with flatter hierarchies and improved information technology, lower level managers can handle decisions effectively and CEOs are much closer to operational details. Mentoring is an excellent development tool to help managers to adjust to the changes.

MERGERS AND ACQUISITIONS

In the late 1990s and early 21st century there has been rapid growth in the number of mergers and acquisitions, as a response to increased competition and globalisation. Many mergers are doomed to failure because they do not conduct proper due diligence of their people. They often fail to deliver the predicted financial benefits and lose their most talented staff.

Not enough regard is given to understanding the risks associated with the members of the top teams or how the organisations will work together. The best balance sheet in the world is meaningless if the people cannot or will not deliver. Organisations could manage the risk more carefully; instead they invariably confine their judgements of synergies and fit to ratios and financial models.

It is important to find a mechanism for managing the integration of the businesses and aligning their cultural fit, for transferring and sharing knowledge and developing the new organisation's capabilities. Using mentoring across the merging companies can be a useful intervention to help to integrate the culture of the merged organisation.

DIVERSITY

Changes in demographics and a chronic skill shortage are forcing companies in the UK, the USA and throughout the world to employ and develop a much more diverse workforce. To make the best use of resources, many organisations are using mentoring as a way of ensuring minority groups are given the best opportunity to realise their full potential.

The Fair Play Consortium (2003) stated: 'promoting equal opportunities is of crucial importance to all companies regardless of size, sector or location'. New and changing equality legislation, European directives related to equality, the changing composition of the labour market and greater international competition mean that businesses need to ensure that they are able to respond to the requirements of a diverse market, in addition to being able to recruit and retain staff of the highest calibre.

As a way of increasing the number of companies with active equal opportunities and related policies, the Fair Play Consortium is offering mentoring to a range of companies to support them in promoting specific developments in equality policy and practice.

Oracle (2003) cultivates a work environment that is inclusive of all employees. Individual differences enrich Oracle's agile work atmosphere and present it with opportunities to examine business issues from varying perspectives. It offers a suite of training products and courses to enhance the personal development of all employees in a diverse workplace. Tailored to meet the needs of its distributed, global organisation, a range of development methods are used, including mentoring.

Oracle actively encourages mentoring, as it sees it as a way of transferring skills from seasoned employees to those entering new skill areas. Oracle Diversity promotes corporate-wide mentoring in job groups where women and ethnic minorities are underrepresented. It also has a programme called Women Unlimited: an in-company mentoring programme that provides executive development for high-performing, first-line managers who are matched with external mentors.

Ambrose (2003) emphasised the importance of developing women as the leaders of the future in the healthcare industry. Engaging in a mentoring programme that encourages diversity will help to empower the mentees. It will also help leaders to appreciate the value of a culturally diverse environment.

CHANGING SHAPE OF DEVELOPMENT

In the 1980s and 90s organisations embarked on large management development initiatives. By the end of the 1990s the pressure from increased competition and a tough economy forced organisations to make development interventions shorter and more flexible. Development programmes by this stage were often modular. By 2001, organisations were beginning to realise the importance of helping managers to take responsibility for their own learning. At this stage, many organisations turned to mentoring to supplement traditional management development programmes. This approach helped to consolidate learning back at work and ensured that managers were focusing on their own development.

At the very senior level, directors and managers are likely to have external mentors or executive coaches. Mentoring can help with gaining a broader business focus and direction career-wise; coaching can help to plug any specific skill gaps. At this executive level, the distinction between mentoring and coaching can become rather blurred. Mentoring, however, takes a more holistic approach. It is particularly suitable for senior executives – allowing them to learn from working on real business issues.

Weinstein & Schuele (2003) cited an interesting example of mentoring being used at college to encourage more students to major on the accounting programme. At the time enrolment for the accounting programmes was falling and students were assigned practitioners as mentors. They were in a better position to describe what it was like to have a career in accountancy. Whilst the number of students majoring in accounting did not greatly increase, the response to the mentoring programme was very positive. The students found the mentoring relationship very fulfilling and that it helped them to gain broader business awareness.

CORPORATE SOCIAL RESPONSIBILITY (CSR)

Starck & Kruckeberg (2003) define CSR as a concept whereby business voluntarily contributes towards building a better society. Increasingly, corporations make decisions that affect large numbers of people. More and more people are expressing the need to hold large organisations accountable for their actions. As markets are increasingly driven by competition, this requires values to shift from a bottom-line mentality to thinking also of environmental and social issues on a global basis.

In seeking to be a socially responsible organisation, mentoring offers an excellent opportunity to build bridges between organisations and the community. The mentoring process used in this context is equally beneficial for both parties. Managers are given the opportunity to practise valuable skills in a safer environment, thus benefiting the organisation. The community and society benefit from having access to resources: the expertise of mentors and the skills, experience and other resources that come with the mentor, particularly technology.

Oracle has set up the Oracle and Portway School E-Pals scheme in Newham, one of London's most vibrant and ethnically diverse boroughs. It is an area of high unemployment and low academic achievement and the scheme's objectives are to raise the educational achievements of young people in terms of literacy and IT skills through regular correspondence with their mentor via e-mail. It also aims to raise the aspirations of Newham's young people through contact and feedback from their mentor. Oracle has volunteered six employees as mentors to participate in this scheme.

IBM has set up an e-mentoring programme called IBM MentorPlace. This is a key component of IBM's overall commitment to public education and raising student achievement. Through this corporate volunteer programme, IBM employees provide students with academic assistance and career counselling, whilst letting them know that adults care about their issues and concerns. IBM employees work with teachers, offering technological advice and other assistance. IBM MentorPlace programmes are under way in sites around the world. IBM aims to reach thousands of students and is continuing to grow the scheme.

THE CHANGING PSYCHOLOGICAL CONTRACT

In the past employees joined an organisation with an expectation of a job for life, career progression and, in turn, to be rewarded for their service. This resulted in a workforce that was highly committed and had a strong work ethic. In recent years, employers can no longer offer a job for life and, with flatter organisations, there are fewer opportunities for career progression.

This has put considerable pressure on employers, as they fight to attract and retain talented staff. They need to consider the level of satisfaction and involvement of their staff: whether they feel recognised for their effort, fulfilled in their work and have the opportunity for development.

Generation X employees, born between 1965 and 1975, represent a considerable proportion of the working population and have a very different approach to work:

▶ There is a decline of trust in terms of relationships and security of employment.

▶ They are self-reliant and look after themselves.

▶ Independent and wanting choice, they are prepared to leave their jobs if they are unhappy with the situation.

▶ They value their leisure time.

Generation Y, who came after Generation X, are goal-orientated and motivated. They are able to multitask and are very skilled technologically. They are strong team players, unlike Generation X, and need regular recognition.

In the absence of jobs for life, development assumes far greater importance. Mentoring would appeal to the self-reliance of Generation X and the motivated, goal-directed Generation Y.

MANAGING STRESS AT WORK

At a time when the Health and Safety Executive (HSE) in the UK estimates that 13.4 million days were lost through stress-related illness in 2001 (HSE, 2001), at a cost of at least £3.8 billion (some estimates put the figure as high as £11 billion), few can afford the impact of stress on the productivity and wellbeing of staff. To quote *Personnel Today* (2003):

> Stress is a complex phenomenon that is blighting British business and working life. At its best it delivers incredible performance and results. At its worst, it can have a devastating impact on the individual, the team or the organisation as a whole. (p. 27)

Throughout 2003, the HSE threatened to adopt a much tougher approach towards employers who fail to take appropriate steps to address stress. In particular, organisations are now obligated to undertake a risk assessment that addresses the mental wellbeing of their employees. The HSE advises that the key areas representing the factors that put individuals at risk are:

▶ **Factor 1:** Culture – level of communication and consultation, hours worked and approach to stress.

▶ **Factor 2:** Demands of the job – for example workload and physical hazards.

▶ **Factor 3:** Control – how much say the person has.

▶ **Factor 4:** Relationships – relationships with managers, bullying and harassment.

▶ **Factor 5:** Change – the way it is managed and communicated, level of uncertainty and insecurity.

▶ **Factor 6:** Role – understanding role and avoiding conflicting roles.

▶ **Factor 7:** Support, training and factors unique to the individual.

Whilst the first six factors are generic to particular job categories, factor 7 is quite individual in nature and includes the support and training needed. Mentoring is a good intervention for helping an individual to address many of the issues that are likely to be identified by a risk assessment.

One of the issues that many organisations are facing today is the high workload of staff and the associated long hours culture to get the work done. Currently the UK has the longest working hours in Europe, but still less than hours worked in the USA.

Mentoring gives people the opportunity to step back, assess the ways they are approaching work and consider issues of work–life balance. It can also be useful in helping people deal with change and manage transitions in their careers.

WORK–LIFE BALANCE AND FLEXIBLE WORKING

The Campaign for Work–Life Balance, launched in the UK by the government in 2000, was described as being designed to encourage employers to introduce arrangements that will enable employees to achieve a better balance between work and the rest of their life. The campaign sits within the Department for Trade and Industry, alongside policy and legislation on employment rights, and its issues are closely linked to stress.

According to The Work Foundation (2003), British business has accepted that work–life balance policies are here to stay and do provide business benefits such as:

▶ Improved employee commitment and motivation

▶ Higher retention rates

▶ Improved employee relations.

In a recent survey released by The Work Foundation, 68 per cent of employers accepted organisational responsibility to help staff to achieve a healthy work–life balance; that, in turn, gives them a feeling of control over their lives. The public and voluntary sectors and utility firms are particularly supportive of this view and their policies apply to all staff, not just working parents. However, approximately 28 per cent offer these policies only to working parents, largely as a result of management resistance to change. Measures used to create a better work–life balance included:

▶ part-time working

▶ family/emergency leave

▶ general unpaid leave.

At this stage the survey showed that only a small minority of staff took advantage of these measures.

Work can now be done any time, anywhere, with the growth in use of technology including portable computers, the internet and mobile phones, and the shift from manufacturing work to knowledge work. Increasingly managers are required to lead dispersed teams. This raises issues of integrating and developing the team. Mentoring is a good way to ensure that members of the team feel committed to the organisation and part of the team.

Internal Influences

At the organisational level there is a need constantly to ensure that staff have the right skills and capabilities to meet the challenges of today's world. Development is taking a much more individual route and needs to address the issue of attracting and retaining talent. There is a particular need to acquire and share knowledge and all organisations need to ensure that people are performing at the highest possible level.

DEVELOPING ORGANISATIONAL CAPABILITIES

In this challenging and changing world, organisations need constantly to ensure that staff have the right skills and capabilities to deliver the organisation's strategy. The mentoring relationship provides a cost-effective way for individuals to develop the skills and capabilities to achieve goals.

Bhatta & Washington (2003) reported that mentoring is now widely accepted as a useful tool for helping individuals to develop their careers and for organisations to enhance their human resource capability. Their study focused on the New Zealand Public Service. At the time of the survey in 2000, women, specifically women managers, were more likely to have mentors than their male counterparts. Evidence from qualitative data suggests that this might reflect both the greater need for a mentor and/or deliberate attempts by women to seek extra support for their career advancement, particularly at the management level.

The restaurant industry is taking advantage of the benefits provided by mentoring to develop staff in general, but also its leaders for tomorrow. Yudd (2003) commented that organisations could work towards becoming the employer of choice and put an end to recruitment and retention problems. Those restaurants in the industry who have achieved this always have a real-life mentor in their midst. They may come from different jobs or be at different levels in the organisation, but each focuses on helping others to succeed. They help to develop basic skills and create an environment where others can learn and grow. People are more likely to stay when they receive genuine care and concern.

SUCCESSION PLANNING

At some time, most organisations are faced with senior managers who are approaching retirement age and have to find replacements for them. There is sometimes merit from recruiting externally, but equally organisations are often keen to recruit from within. High-potential development programmes to address succession issues are common at present. Often mentoring is set up, and run in parallel, to ensure that the knowledge and wisdom of senior managers is captured before they leave the company. Sometimes mentoring helps to identify high-potential people who can then be developed to fill future vacancies.

WAR FOR TALENT

The challenge today is to attract and retain the best staff. Even in a tough economy it is essential to have the right people strategies in place to ensure that talented people are attracted to the organisation in the first place and then are retained. Attention needs to be directed to all levels of staff, from graduate recruits to high potentials and high flyers to senior managers. Mentoring is an excellent way to show staff that their contribution to the organisation is recognised and valued. Mentoring also offers challenge to mentors, so it works for both mentors and mentees. Graduates, particularly, are often attracted to those organisations who offer mentoring in support of a graduate training programme.

FOCUS ON BUSINESS PERFORMANCE

In today's competitive environment, organisations need to have a constant focus on business performance. Having people with the right skills and capabilities can make the difference between success and failure. Organisations are meeting the skill gaps by developing individual training programmes. Mentoring is a particularly effective method of development as it encourages individuals to take some responsibility for their own development. Even after a mentoring relationship has ended, individuals are likely to seek continuously to improve their skills and capabilities, thus contributing to business performance.

Horn (2003) stated that Random House Group Ltd believes that training can make a fundamental difference to its bottom line and is investing in a top-down training programme. In the past the publishing industry has had a reputation for relying on training on the job. Random House is planning an ambitious new training scheme through which each member of staff will receive an individual training programme. Given the level of expertise in-house, part of the development is to enhance the capability of managers to mentor others. Using mentoring as a means of development complements the strategy of individualised development plans. Random House hopes that the expenditure on training and development, already more than four times what it would normally spend, will produce results. In particular, it hopes that this will establish it as an employer of choice in an increasingly competitive environment, reduce staff turnover through motivation and development and ultimately strengthen its bottom line.

Kellam (2003), President and CEO of a consultancy affiliate of Baker and Daniels, a law firm in Indianapolis, stated that mentoring is a key factor in individual and organisational growth leading to the successful development of managers and leaders. Organisations with active mentoring programmes note lower turnover, increased loyalty and happier people.

Tyler (1998) also highlighted the place of mentoring in the productivity of the organisation through improved retention, nurturing promising employees and bringing new recruits up to speed much faster. This was noted by the Director of Diversity and Staffing Services for Texas Instruments in Dallas, Texas. It had a mentoring programme for new staff and found that they were able to contribute much faster: they understood how to get things done in the system.

INCREASED MOTIVATION

Investment in individuals is likely to have a motivating effect on staff, by making them feel valued and recognised by the organisation. The mentoring relationship itself is also likely to be motivational, providing support and guidance to the mentee. Neuborne (2003: 16) reported the words of Lois

Zachary, President of Leadership Development Services, Phoenix, Arizona, who said:

> We are living in tough times and more people are realising that the key to getting through and building success is through relationships. It can help you to feel anchored and that is a key to remaining motivated.

Neuborne reported two company examples, IKEA and Intel, both using mentoring as a strategy for motivating employees and producing top performers. At IKEA US, based in Pennsylvania, one objective is to improve diversity. The company learning and development manager wanted to address the company profile of old Swedish and predominantly male staff. In the pilot programme, 50 employee pairs were brought together, with no two pairs from the same department. They went through a three-day training session and then started a one-year mentoring relationship, using a combination of e-mentoring and at least three face-to-face meetings in the year. Mentees addressed personal goals such as improving communication skills, rather than specific business goals.

At Intel mentees select a skill-related goal and, via a web-based tool, the mentee is matched with a person with a higher level of the skill to help them. The goal might relate to career progression to a specific job. Mentoring relationships lasted about six to nine months. Whilst Intel has not specifically tracked the success of its mentoring programme, there is a tendency for those progressing their careers within the company to have taken part in a mentoring programme.

The survey conducted in the New Zealand Public Service by Bhatta & Washington (2003) showed that staff with mentors differed from other staff members, in terms of what they valued in the workplace and how they rated their jobs and organisations (as good, average or poor) on these factors. They were more likely to consider as highly important:

▶ opportunities for advancement

▶ challenging work

▶ reputation of the organisation.

They felt more positive about:

▶ access to challenging work

▶ opportunities for advancement

▶ accomplishment in their jobs.

Bhatta & Washington concluded from their study that the results suggested that staff with a mentor were more likely to want to move ahead, look for stretch in their work and realise the extent to which a good organisational reputation can reflect positively on them.

ENCOURAGING TEAMWORK AND IMPROVED PRODUCTIVITY

As organisations have become flatter and there is a greater need for working in a range of different teams and situations, more people are being appointed as team leaders. Often leadership is distributed or the teams are self-managed. If teams are to work productively together, interpersonal skills and relationship skills assume far greater importance. Having a mentor who can develop these essential skills will help teams become far more effective.

CHANGE MANAGEMENT INITIATIVES

Every organisation is undergoing continuous change in terms of:

▶ Culture

▶ Strategy

▶ Organisation structures

▶ Processes and procedures.

Often these changes occur in parallel and are accompanied by changes for individuals in their roles and responsibilities and the way they carry out their jobs. Change can give rise to anxiety and uncertainty. Even if an individual feels positive and motivated by the changes taking place, he or she still needs a strategy for dealing with change.

For those fearing the changes, mentoring can provide excellent support and help them to move forward to manage the change in the best way possible. Those who are stimulated by the change can be helped to develop a vision and strategy to deal with the changes. Change usually requires a change in mindset and mentoring is a good development tool for effecting this.

KNOWLEDGE MANAGEMENT

The acquisition, development and sharing of knowledge are key components of competitive advantage. Organisations need to ensure that their managers have the right skill set for the knowledge economy. In particular they need to be entrepreneurial, flexible and able to make good business decisions, sometimes with limited information. They must be able to collaborate in cross-functional, cross-organisational teams and have a mindset of sharing information, rather than seeing information as power.

Mentoring is an excellent development initiative to help to address the challenges thrown up by the knowledge economy. Knowledge can be shared both ways between mentors and mentees and helps to ensure that less knowledge is lost when senior managers resign or retire from the organisation.

INDIVIDUAL DEVELOPMENT AND CONTINUOUS IMPROVEMENT

It was indicated earlier in this chapter that development is changing, with a move towards more focused development of the individual. Mentoring is particularly advantageous as it approaches learning in an integrated way, developing the whole person in both their work and home lives. The philosophy behind mentoring encourages the mentee to take responsibility for his or her learning. The person does, however, need to be committed to the mentoring process in order to gain maximum benefit.

Summary

This chapter has provided an overview of the influences that have raised the profile of mentoring in organisations. The external influences are quite interlinked: the competitive, uncertain and changing environment provides a background for organisations becoming global; size helps to make organisations more competitive, resulting in the growth of mergers and acquisitions; and people need to keep abreast of these changes. Mentoring integrates the achievement of strategic goals with the career development of the individual.

Internally, organisations have to face issues of managing succession and the war for talent. Demands on individuals are changing, with the rise of the knowledge worker, an increase in teamwork and the drive for productivity and performance. Mentoring prepares individuals well in career terms and stops essential skills being lost. It also offers a good support mechanism for individuals constantly needing to adapt to change.

PART II

What is Mentoring? Definition and Context

3 Introduction

Part II of the book explores the various definitions which abound around mentoring and clarifies where the boundaries would be drawn by the practitioners who were involved in the Henley Mentoring Focus Group. As can be seen in the general developmental arena, 'mentoring' can have many different interpretations, depending upon the background and context in which it is being used.

This book is based primarily upon a Western and, even within that, European corporate background for mentoring. This is also specifically within the context of development schemes for particular management groups. There are some references to a wider background for the development of the discussion, as many useful and interesting new ideas can be drawn from casting the net more widely. For example, the work of The Prince's Trust, referred to in Chapter 4, gives an excellent model of a disseminated scheme, with high levels of responsibility being taken by local centres and only the structure of the scheme being controlled centrally. This model could well be useful for organisations where the original scheme has been successful and promoted requests for replication from other areas of the business, but where the original operators are not able to run additional schemes themselves.

In the first chapter of this section, the original model of categorisation of mentoring schemes devised by the Focus Group in its first meeting is presented. This definition seemed to summarise participants' experiences pretty accurately and helps to address the initial question of 'What is Mentoring?' Various illustrations of different types of schemes, with a range of backgrounds and contexts, are then given. This includes some of the wider applications of mentoring explored in the Group, such as peer mentoring, cross-company mentoring and mentoring to support diversity.

The next chapter in this section looks at the differences between mentoring and coaching – a subject about which there is much debate. Interestingly, the Focus Group members found it fairly straightforward to come up with a consistent set of differentiators, which also helped to define important boundaries when setting expectations with the participants of mentoring schemes.

Finally, the actual decision of whether to go ahead and introduce a mentoring scheme or not is explored. This gives an essential 'reality check' to the various critical success factors that help prospective mentees and mentors and also scheme managers to decide whether it is right to proceed.

4 What is Mentoring?

This chapter examines what is meant by the term 'mentoring' and leads the reader through a number of definitions and approaches that can be taken when considering setting up or participating in a mentoring scheme. Different models of mentoring are explored, as well as the reasons why mentoring may be introduced in the first place. A number of different case studies illustrate the variety of types of scheme that the Henley Mentoring Focus Group has come across.

Definitions of Mentoring

Understanding of the term 'mentoring' varies widely and is often used interchangeably with the word 'coaching'. It is important to start by being able to give a definition of what is meant by mentoring in the context of what is being attempted. The following are some examples of definitions of mentoring from a variety of organisations and some of the classic generic definitions:

> *Mentoring is a term used to help, advise and guide employees through the complexities of the business.* Avaya
>
> *Mentoring at EDS is a mutual learning partnership in which individuals assist each other with personal and career development through coaching, role modeling, counseling, sharing knowledge and providing emotional support.* EDS
>
> *Creating possibilities and providing guidance and support to others in a relationship of trust; it includes facilitating, bringing visions to life and enabling people to achieve.* Henley Management College 2000
>
> *Offline help by one person to another in making significant transitions in knowledge, work or thinking.* Megginson & Clutterbuck 1995
>
> *A relationship, not just a procedure or activity, where one person professionally assists the development of another outside of the normal manager/subordinate relationship.* Abbey
>
> *A mentor is that person who achieves a one-to-one developmental relationship with a learner; and one whom the learner identifies as having enabled personal growth to take place.* Bennetts 1994

> *Behind every successful person, there is one elementary truth:*
> *somewhere, somehow, someone cared about their growth and*
> *development. This person was their mentor.*   Quoted in the ANZABI,
>   BEC and NNA National Conference 2003 and elsewhere
>
> *mentor n. experienced and trusted adviser [F f. L f. Gk Mentor adviser of*
> *the young Telemachus in Homer's* Odyssey *and Fénelon's* Télémaque]
>   Definition of 'mentor' from *Oxford English Reference Dictionary*
>   edited by Pearsall, Judy & Trumble, Bill (2002).
>   By permission of Oxford University Press

Models of Mentoring

The Focus Group started with this issue of defining mentoring. Chapter 5
focuses on the importance of clarifying the difference in understanding
between mentoring and coaching. It is
equally important to ensure that there is a
common understanding as to whether the
scheme is intended to focus on career sponsorship, as in the US, or whether it has
greater emphasis on learning and development, which is the model found more
commonly elsewhere.

> **Mentoring models**
>
> *USA:* the focus is primarily
> on sponsoring an individual's
> career.
>
> *Europe:* the emphasis is on
> growth and development.

THE HENLEY FOCUS GROUP MODEL OF MENTORING

After a review of the various schemes represented in the Group at the time,
the Henley Focus Group Model of Mentoring was developed (see Figure 4.1).
This represented all the main categories of mentoring schemes which were
familiar to organisational scheme managers. It also allowed for progression
from one type of scheme to another, as a programme matured or the organisational requirements changed. In addition, it was found that in some organisations, several different types of scheme were operating simultaneously – and
perfectly effectively. The differences occurred due to the explicit purposes of
the schemes, and as long as there was agreement about this, each type of
scheme had an equally good chance of success. Mutual agreement and understanding of the common purpose and terms of engagement is a core theme in
terms of success which will be found throughout this book, both from the
perspective of the scheme manager and the mentors and mentees.

The Henley Focus Group Model (Figure 4.1) is useful as it allows for a
broadbrush categorisation of schemes, each with their own organisational
issues to manage. Once it is clear which type of scheme best meets a particular organisational requirement, it is much simpler to begin to map out the
implementation process required to make it work.

	Informal	Formal
Structured	**Self-help**	**Embedded**
Unstructured	**Social**	**Ad hoc**

Figure 4.1 **The Henley Focus Group Model of Mentoring**

The model is based around two axes, one of which looks at whether the mentoring scheme is *structured* or *unstructured*, and the other looks at whether the scheme is *formal* or *informal*. The four categories highlighted in the matrix may be understood from the following characteristics:

1 *Embedded:* These are the formal, structured, schemes found in organisations such as the ones in the Focus Group. Such schemes are clearly linked into the organisation's development strategies and/or performance management processes. They will have specific, stated objectives, often targeted at specific groups such as graduates or high flyers and usually run for a defined timeframe of, say, 12 or 24 months.

2 *Ad hoc:* These schemes frequently follow on from successful embedded schemes. Ad hoc programmes are official, but uncontrolled, that is, started by the organisation, but left to run pretty much by themselves. Databases of mentors, which can be accessed via an intranet/internet site, allow for self-selection by mentors according to their needs.

3 *Social:* Both informal and unstructured, this type of mentoring is driven by the learner and goes largely unrecognised as being 'mentoring'. Prefaced by phrases such as 'Can you help me with ...', learners approach colleagues or friends for help with a problem. It occurs on a haphazard, needs-driven basis.

4 *Self-help:* This is a more structured method of informal mentoring, where the learner recognises a specific development need and requests help from an 'expert'. This can also move over into the coaching category and away from a true mentoring relationship – this will be discussed more fully in the next chapter. While there are some ground rules set around the relationship, such as more regular meetings, it retains a more social style.

This book is based primarily upon the embedded scheme examples being run by the members of the Henley Group. However, practically all Group members would also say that there were examples of the other three scheme types running in various ways in their organisations at the same time. The difference tended to be that a formal mentoring scheme manager was only appointed for the most formal of mentoring schemes.

When considering introducing a mentoring scheme into an organisation, it is helpful to think not only about who it will be aimed at, but also about which model of mentoring will be best suited to that organisation. As well as the Henley Focus Group Model of categorisation shown above, the Focus Group identified a further dimension along which any of the above categories could be placed. This dimension is one around whether a mentoring scheme is centralised or decentralised.

This aspect looks at the difference between all mentoring activities in an organisation being controlled from a central hub, such as the HR department, versus schemes being run regionally, based upon a central initiative.

A CENTRALISED MENTORING MODEL (FIGURE 4.2)

This is where all activities to do with the mentoring scheme are developed and handled by a central department, usually HR or training and development. This was the approach most commonly used by organisations in the Focus Group.

The main advantage of using a centralised model is that decision-making is relatively quick and, usually, rests with the scheme manager. The risk is that the resource level required to manage the scheme on a day-to-day basis is often insufficient. In many of the Focus Group organisations, mentoring was only one of many responsibilities carried by the scheme managers and they found it challenging to devote sufficient time to keep on top of events.

HR/TRAINING DEPT

Process and goal definition

Organisational commitment

Stakeholder identification and management

Administration

Budget management

Marketing

Training and support

Review/evaluation

Continuous improvement

Figure 4.2 **A centralised model of mentoring**

A DECENTRALISED MENTORING MODEL

This is a less commonly seen model for mentoring (Figure 4.3), where key policy decisions on minimum standards and guidance are made centrally, but the implementation of the mentoring scheme is the responsibility of a local group or organisation. It may be that this model suits the organisation from the outset, as with The Prince's Trust; alternatively, it may be one that is adopted once the concept of mentoring has been successfully introduced and the scheme begins to grow.

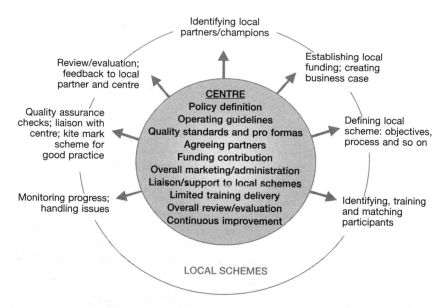

Figure 4.3 **A model of decentralised mentoring**

Decentralised mentoring allows interpretation of common frameworks and guidelines to suit local circumstances. Once principles have been agreed, funding arrangements made and a partner (or partners) found, the implementation and decision-making is the responsibility of the local partnership. Through quality checks and evaluation systems, the centre is able to keep an overall view of all the local schemes that are operating.

B&Q operated a model which lay somewhere between the two of these whereby the centre (HR) provided most of the required 'services' and ownership and responsibility for the success of the scheme lay with the line function and the local mentoring champions.

The following case study illustrates how a decentralised model of mentoring has worked within The Prince's Trust.

DECENTRALISED MENTORING

Under the umbrella of The Prince's Trust Mentoring for Care Leavers (MCL) programme, Surrey County Council's Youth Support Service partnered with Rainer to put in place a mentoring scheme for local young people leaving care.

The scheme was set up at short notice and so a wide trawl was made of all Surrey County Council's departments for potential mentors via an initial e-mail. This request for mentors was cascaded out by e-mail and word of mouth to approximately 7,000 employees and resulted in over 100 responses. Following initial telephone conversations, 80 people asked for briefing packs and 25 were interviewed. Part of the selection process was an open evening, following which interviewing and natural selection culled the numbers to the 15 aimed for. An essential part of the selection process was a police check – mandatory for working with young people in this situation. Of the final 12 mentors, there was a 25:75 per cent male:female split and one was non-white.

The mentees were to be drawn from young people soon to be leaving care. Colleagues and care workers were consulted and, again, word of mouth resulted in a lot of referrals.

The objectives of the scheme were that it would run for 12–18 months and be primarily task-focused, based on the young people's agendas. Matching was carried out using forms completed by both parties, where mentors outlined their skills and what they could offer and mentees indicated what help they wanted, their age and the type of person they were looking for. The process was a simple 'wants and offers' one: mentees' wants were linked with what mentors could offer. However, an overlay of the complex needs of the young people also had to be made: these potentially included substance misuse, learning difficulties, single parenthood and so on.

Funding was given jointly by MCL, Rainer and Surrey CC to cover the running costs of recruitment, training and supervision. This was used for the extensive training programme, which included 3 x one-day sessions of formal training (sourced from the central MCL) and group meetings. Supervision, in the form of one-to-one sessions with a core team member, as well as group sessions, was also included and provided mentors with an opportunity to talk about the issues they were dealing with and how they were helping the young person resolve them.

Practical guidance given to participants included: always meet in public places and never in each other's home, that the mentor should travel to the young person for meetings and that neither should give out their home telephone number.

Outcomes/learning points

Programme implementation
▶ It is advisable to use partners/agencies such as Rainer to find funding, help with administration, marketing and so on; a core team should be responsible for planning and scoping the scheme.

▶ It is essential to have a solid support structure in place and to ensure that any coordinator role is full-time if they are to keep on top of things and prevent relationships from fizzling out.

▶ The information pack provided to potential mentors was clear and informative and obviously aided their decision-making process.

▶ The open evening was regarded as useful and an important part of the process which helped people move on to the next stage.

▶ The training programme was regarded as very good, although more emphasis on the complex needs of young people would be a useful improvement.

▶ During the interview process for mentors it would be beneficial to have a young person on the panel.

▶ Following interviews, there should be a process for giving official feedback to attendees.

Mentors
▶ There was 100% retention of mentors over the 12 months' duration of the scheme and the majority of mentors expressed a wish to continue their involvement with mentoring.

▶ It does not matter how much training you give, mentors have a very steep learning curve and some may be disappointed.

▶ Mentors found their biggest challenge was when they did not get back an equal amount of response to the level of effort they were putting in. This resulted in demotivation.

▶ There was a level of frustration among some mentors that not everyone was able to commit to gaining a BTEC qualification – however, they were able to receive The Prince's Trust's own Certificate in Mentoring.

▶ Some of the mentors wanted to be involved in training the next group, so that they could share their experiences.

▶ Mentors enjoyed coming together in group sessions, as sharing experiences helped to broaden their outlook.

Mentees
Mentees valued having someone to talk to who was outside the care/social services system, particularly as the mentors were not paid and did this in their own time.

▶ In one instance, lack of the mentee's own availability brought an early end to the mentoring work.

▶ The positive nature of the programme was shown in an instance when a mentee moved out of the area, only to return later. Despite having had a formal ending with the mentor, this mentee sought the mentor out on their return and picked up the relationship – albeit in a more informal way.

▶ The process was seen as a positive experience and one that mentees would happily relay to others. 'It's like having another friend to talk to and get advice.'

Context for Action

In addition to the different methods of operating a mentoring scheme, there are, of course, many different reasons for introducing a scheme into an organisation. It can be aimed at developing specific groups of people or set up to support the overall strategic direction of the organisation in a wider sense. Ensuring that there is a clear context for the proposed scheme is all important: it refines the broadbrush definition and makes it real for the people who will be involved in it.

The following is an example of the context in which Smiths Group found themselves.

> Smiths Group was facing an issue which a number of organisations are facing in this competitive and fast-changing world: 'How do you recruit and retain your talent? How do you share the experience and learning with those coming up through the ranks to enable effective succession and career development?' One part of our approach to addressing this issue was to implement an internal mentoring scheme across the Group.

Amongst Focus Group members the most common reasons for operating mentoring schemes seemed to be to support graduate development, high-potential/fast-track programmes and for diversity. In some instances, organisations went outside to provide mentoring help to the local community.

There are many different applications of mentoring, as outlined in Figure 4.4.

Graduate	Leadership
Fast track/high potentials	Specific profession
Succession planning	New staff induction
Culture change	Teenagers
Equality/diversity/minorities	Head teachers
Knowledge management	Small businesses
Management development	Schools

Figure 4.4 **Different applications for mentoring**

Throughout this chapter there are examples of mentoring schemes which illustrate some of the organisational contexts which Focus Group members have looked at in order to learn more about the variety of ways in which mentoring can be used for strategic outcomes.

A BLACK AND ETHNIC MINORITY SCHEME

Dept for Work and Pensions

For the past few years, the Department for Work and Pensions (DWP) has been running a Realising Potential programme for black and ethnic minority staff. Its aim is for participants to be supported in their own development through a range of opportunities which increase their knowledge, skills and experience and result in increased competence and confidence. This would then enable them to compete on their own merit for opportunities that would help them fulfil their career aspirations. Operated within the terms of the Race Relations Act 1976, each programme runs for two years and permits the DWP to take positive action where particular groups are underrepresented in particular areas of work.

Whilst the DWP offers no guarantees (as this would be positive discrimination and, therefore, illegal), participation could result in a successful application for a new post, more job variety and enrichment, or even promotion. A number of participants have, in fact, been promoted and others have taken the opportunity to experience a completely different working environment.

Mentors are sought amongst managers with relevant skills and experience and from across all Business Units of the DWP. Typically they are more senior than the participant, although not in their direct line management. The mentors are expected to establish and maintain an open, honest and confidential relationship and make time available to support the participant and contribute to building their self-confidence. All participants choose or are allocated a mentor and, thus, gain access to an objective source of advice and support outside their normal management chain – someone who can offer a wider perspective, be a sounding board and provide a network of contacts.

A Mentoring Guide is given to participants and mentors following a one-day formal mentor training workshop. The Guide contains the following information: a definition of mentoring; benefits and roles of the three main groups of participants (mentors, mentees and line managers); strategies for mentors; the process – mentoring life cycle; guidelines for getting to know each other, for working and learning together and for ending the relationship. It also provides help for mentors to understand what skills are required, information about potential pitfalls and suggested areas for inclusion in a mentoring 'contract'.

The success of the programme has meant it is currently in its fourth cycle and has recently increased in size to accommodate a greater level of interest.

Another reason for using mentoring as a development tool is to support specific professional qualifications or develop specific skills, as outlined in the following case study.

MENTORING ENGINEERING PROJECT MANAGERS
RWE Thames Water

The following is taken from the *Mentoring Guidelines* which outline the process adopted by RWE Thames Water for mentoring new Project Managers (PMs) through a six-month induction and development plan.

Objectives and Benefits
It is important to provide a comprehensive induction to the role of the PM to ensure development to a competent level within six months of recruitment into their role. The Mentor is vital to

achieving this aim and has many bene-fits, some of which are listed below:

▶ More effective staff
▶ Demonstrates a commitment to training and development
▶ Ensures tangible and measurable gains if work tasks or projects are used as developmental tools
▶ Improved communication across the organisation
▶ Increased motivation
▶ Continued skill development of the Mentor

The Mentor

The Mentor will act as a guide to the PM. It is the responsibility of the Mentor to review the progress of the PM at regular intervals. It is important that the Mentor is as cooperative as possible in agreeing dates and adhering to them.

The Mentor is also responsible for offi-cially verifying that the PM has covered the key objectives using the compe-tency checklist. This will enable them to fulfil all the necessary objectives to complete a successful induction in their role.

The Mentoring Process

Allocation of Mentors to PMs
Senior Management will allocate Men-tors on the basis of project knowledge and skills matched to the PM.

Duration of Mentoring and Induction Period
The induction period will last for approx-imately six months from the PM's date of appointment.

Mentoring Meetings
It is important for the Mentor to arrange a first meeting to clarify roles and res-ponsibilities. It is suggested that regular meetings be arranged to monitor prog-ress throughout the induction process. The frequency of these meetings

should be reviewed as the develop-ment period proceeds.

Key Stages to Mentoring Project Managers

There are three key stages to the Men-toring process, which are:

▶ Evaluating
▶ Coaching
▶ Facilitating

Evaluating current knowledge and performance
It is essential to evaluate the PM's current skills, knowledge and performance level using the Roles and Responsibilities, and Competency Checklist (see over).

It is important to encourage self-analysis and offer helpful and constructive criti-cism. Listen actively and ask questions, encourage and provide enthusiasm.

Coaching
Provide guidance on how the PM will bridge gaps from the Checklist or develop new skills.

Facilitating and Monitoring
It is important that the PM's progress throughout induction is monitored by regular meetings. It is also important to support the PM when they are uncer-tain where to find information and knowledge.

Progress and Development

It is important to record the PM's prog-ress and development on a monthly basis. A copy of this form should be sent to Personnel and the Project Director.

Future Development of PMs

On completion of the induction process, it may be appropriate for the PM to continue to develop by means of the Project Management NVQ. Your support and guidance during this process may also be required.

The competency checklist consists of two parts:

Part One – Project Management Competency Checklist (yellow)
This checklist outlines generic core project management competencies (based on the NVQ standards) and the desired level to be achieved.

Part Two – Supporting – Key Skills for Development (white)
This checklist outlines specific Engineering skills and knowledge required and the designed level to be achieved. These support the achievement of the core competencies.

How to use the checklist
The checklists are discussion tools to assist the Mentor in developing the PM in the role of Project Manager over a six-month period. The desired level of knowledge is indicated by the shaded boxes on the yellow checklist. The white checklist is important to determine any gaps in knowledge of skills and comment on relevant action required.

The Mentoring Process Timetable

Preparation by PM	(i) Review Part One for discussion (ii) Pre-check Part Two
Start of Development Process (Major Review)	Explain core and supporting competency checklists Review current capability against **core and supporting** competencies Complete monthly progress form (indicate overall current level of knowledge)
During Month Two	Review current capability against **supporting** competencies Complete progress form
During Month Three	Review current capability against **core and supporting** competencies Complete progress form
During Month Four	Review **supporting** competencies Complete progress form
During Month Five	Review **supporting** competencies Complete progress form
During Month Six (Major Review)	Review core and supporting competencies Complete progress form and enter existing level of knowledge
Future development	Please discuss with Mentor and Line Manager, any development needs to be entered on development plan

Types of Mentoring Scheme

Many mentoring schemes begin from the assumption that the mentor must be in a senior position in an organisation to the mentee. This can cause problems in terms of ensuring an adequate supply of mentors the higher up in the organisation the scheme is positioned. If the reason for mentoring is analysed, it may well be possible to look at alternative ways of meeting the demand, through, for example, peer, cross-company or group mentoring.

PEER MENTORING

Peer mentoring, an activity which several of the Henley participating organisations had considered, is when a mentoring arrangement is set up between people of equal level or status in the organisation. This is not necessarily a reciprocal arrangement, but is something more than just a 'buddy' system. In terms of the Henley Focus Group Model of Mentoring, peer mentoring would usually fall on the informal side of the matrix and be either of the self-help type or, even more likely, the social. Nonetheless, as long as the objectives are clear and the terms of engagement established, this is a useful area to consider.

There is a variety of instances when peer mentoring could be used in preference to having a hierarchical scheme:

▶ Mentoring the mentors

▶ To reduce the feeling of isolation experienced by home workers/virtual team workers

▶ For specific skill sets, for example counselling

▶ To increase understanding across different divisions

▶ To facilitate change – peer mentoring is more easily available than hierarchical mentoring

▶ To smooth the path of mergers and acquisitions.

Potential benefits that could accrue from implementing a peer mentoring scheme include:

▶ Increasing the pool of potential mentors for other schemes

▶ Making mentoring available to a wider audience

▶ Increasing communication across the business – reducing the 'silo' effect

▶ Giving people the opportunity to find out about other areas of the organisation on a more formal basis

▶ Developing individuals' skills

▶ As equals, finding it easier to be more open and quickly build rapport

▶ Timescales are often shorter as it is for a specific purpose

▶ The 'rules' are the same as for other mentoring schemes.

The are also a number of possible drawbacks in doing peer mentoring, including:

▶ Without clear objectives and contracting, it could easily become an informal chat session

▶ It may take some 'selling' to convince people that someone at their own level can be useful to them – there is still a perception that a mentor should be someone more senior

▶ The programme may become too large to manage

▶ It could attract confidentiality and comfort issues amongst participants

▶ Where there is competition for promotion, it would not work

▶ It is not always useful in gaining a different strategic perspective – unless it is a cross-company scheme (see below).

In the same way as is necessary for any mentoring scheme, peer mentoring would need to show a real business benefit in order to gain organisational support. Working across boundaries and breaking down silos would usually be seen as legitimate reasons for considering it.

However, having clear objectives and process guidelines is important, just as with any other form of mentoring. This is what will differentiate it from more informal 'networking' and help people to understand what is going on. Training participants in the skills of mentoring and covering the basic principles needs to be done, in the same way as with a hierarchical scheme.

CROSS-COMPANY MENTORING

Another 'alternative' approach to mentoring that was discussed was cross-company mentoring. This usually involves a reciprocal arrangement whereby managers from one organisation set up mentoring relationships with managers in another, instead of mentors and mentees both being from the same organisation. Unlike peer mentoring, cross-company mentoring seems to require a significant level of formality to be taken seriously, but can be run either in an embedded way or on an ad hoc basis.

There was a great deal of interest within the Focus Group at the prospect of setting up a cross-company mentoring scheme. This ultimately proved unsuccessful, although is still discussed as a 'good idea'.

Some of the lessons learned from this process were:

▶ Choosing which company to pair with needs careful thought: if the culture and environment are too different, the participants may see no value. Pairing with an organisation from the same sector, but which is not an outright competitor, would be the ideal, for example a clothing and a food retailer. However, matching the latter with an engineering firm may require too big a leap of faith on the part of the participants to be successful. This was much more of an issue for would-be mentors and mentees than the scheme managers trying to set it up in the Focus Group anticipated.

▶ Geographical location is another key issue. It is sometimes hard enough to schedule meetings when both parties work for the same company. Being separated by distance exacerbates the problem and 'insufficient time' becomes an easy excuse for not meeting.

▶ Confidentiality presents an obvious concern, which can be addressed by both companies agreeing working guidelines. Some organisations may want the other person to sign a specific confidentiality agreement.

▶ Poaching of staff can present a concern and is another area for upfront discussion. This was the real reason for blocking the initiative for several line managers.

▶ Critical elements such as the approach to training, the process and evaluation/review – perhaps even a budget – need to be discussed and agreed.

▶ Both companies involved need to provide clear and visible support for the participants, in exactly the same way as for an in-house scheme. Making regular contact with the participants is essential – checking that they are meeting regularly, there are no issues, value is being gained and so on.

▶ Unforeseen events within one of the companies may cause the relationship to end. This type of scheme is vulnerable to the issues affecting two organisations, not just one, and thereby giving double the potential for interruptions.

▶ The term 'mentoring' didn't always encourage participation in a cross-company context, maybe being a step too far from known territory for some managers. 'External benchmarking' or 'external networking' were sometimes seen as more acceptable terms.

GROUP MENTORING

Another venture into alternative ways in which to set up a mentoring scheme is the idea of group mentoring. This can be useful where, as in the above two examples, the supply of mentors is a problem. Group mentoring can also be the 'scheme of choice', when there is an appropriate group of potential mentees who would benefit from the same kind of mentoring from the same

The concept of group mentoring was explored with Clutterbuck and Megginson at a Focus Group session.

Practitioners' Problem-solving

Questions and Answers with David Megginson and David Clutterbuck

What are the pros and cons of group mentoring?

I have been working with a bank on a group mentoring programme for the last couple of years. It has been the only intervention in their graduate scheme that has been of any significance. It has had an impact on the loss of graduates from 25 per cent a year to only 8 per cent a year. Positive feedback from the young graduate mentees is about the fact they have got somebody to go and talk to about their career moves and the frustrations that may make them leave. We managed to predict that not everybody would go on to create formal individual mentoring relationships after the first year of group mentoring, but on average two out of the ten graduates in each group actually did form a strong bond with their mentor and went on to have individual mentoring after the group mentoring had finished; most of those that started two years ago are still going. So group mentoring is a precursor to one-to-one mentoring and a lot of learning goes on within the group as well.

We do have a few cases of groups of people that come together to create peer mentoring networks of maybe seven or eight people. Some of them have gone on for years and years and have been very successful as people have moved through different stages of their careers.

One pitfall of group mentoring can be when people don't feel they can open up in front of their colleagues. **(DC)**

I have been working with a group of older chief executives from small companies in South Yorkshire and we worked the other way round. We started off with a skill development workshop, then one-to-one relationships and then every quarter we have a gathering where mentors and mentees come together. We find there is a tremendous amount of rich mutual support going on between mentor and mentor, mentor and mentee, and mentee and mentee. The idea of the gatherings is to widen your network of support. **(DM)**

mentor. This would be particularly likely with members of the same work team, for example, and where there was a specific objective as an outcome for the mentoring.

The case study below is from Henley member organisation EDS.

MENTORING A SMALL GROUP   EDS

EDS in the UK had a high-potential group that it felt would benefit considerably from greater access to the European managing director. Instead of asking the MD to mentor these managers individually, it was suggested he mentor them as a group – modelling their sessions on an existing business update forum held with European directors.

The group initially focused on key business areas such as what was going on in the organisation, strategy, the MD's current thinking on things, and a 'drains up' discussion of what was happening. However, instead of being simply a business update, the MD operated on a mentoring level as much as possible – given the different needs of the individuals. Each session was approximately half a day, with lunch. Training of the group consisted primarily of a briefing by the line manager on what mentoring was and why it was valuable; a *Guide to Mentoring* booklet and e-learning materials.

The beauty of the approach was that there were no real constraints. The MD set it up as an offline meeting, telling the managers they could go as far as they wanted to/felt comfortable to with him and could talk about anything. If it was inappropriate for him to comment or give information he would say so, but wherever possible he would be open.

With these limited ground rules in place, the meetings turned into extremely wide-ranging and beneficial sessions. As you would expect, they started off on a fairly high business level, skirting around issues. However, the MD was skilled at drawing people out – asking questions such as: 'What do you guys think?' 'How could it be done differently?' He asked for feedback on what the organisation looked like from their position and level in it. He was also good at challenging them by asking: 'If you were sitting here, what would you do about it? Give me a proposition and let's discuss as a group why that may or may not work.'

Gradually the discussions moved on to some really thorny issues as well as including things not normally covered in a business meeting. It became quite personal in a very positive sense, for example: 'How do you view development in this organisation? You are classified as high potential – what does that mean to you? Who's looking at you? Who's really interested in you? What other things could and should we be doing to develop you? What experiences have you had to get to where you are? What are the important things to focus on in the organisation?', and so on.

The effect was very powerful; the group met regularly and the format extended to other similar groups across Europe. Undoubtedly, the key success factor was the open and approachable style of the MD.

GLOBAL MENTORING SCHEMES

The concept of globalisation in terms of mentoring was explored in Chapter 2, with an example where an individual used mentoring to help get to grips with an assignment which was within the organisation, but to a different country and a different culture.

Many of the Henley Focus Group members are part of global organisations and, inevitably, mentoring across geographical boundaries and across cultures was the subject of discussion.

The challenges facing a global mentoring scheme are many: the first, but not always the most obvious, issue to consider is the difference in culture and business practice. The assistance that participants from different cultures will need when embarking on their relationship needs careful consideration.

There are also the difficulties of physical distance and the inability to meet face to face. Whilst some of these difficulties can be overcome by use of e-mentoring methods (see Chapter 21), participants often find that distance and time zone differences can make the formation of a successful relationship extremely challenging.

Careful forethought and planning will help to get a global mentoring scheme off to a good start. However, what plays a key role in its success is the ability of the scheme manager or local champions to keep in touch with the mentee and/or mentor, providing them with active support and encouragement. Regular communication from a support team also keeps them informed about progress and alerts them to potential issues.

The topic of global schemes and cultural differences was raised by the Henley Focus Group with Megginson and Clutterbuck.

Practitioners' Problem-solving

Questions and Answers with David Megginson and David Clutterbuck

What experience/advice can you give about global mentoring schemes and how do you accommodate cultural differences of company/country?

There are palpable differences in both country culture and in mentoring culture. I sometimes start a workshop by asking people to tell me about a good helping relationship they've experienced. In a particular instance, one person started talking about being plucked from obscurity and given a load of exposure and about being helped to get high-profile opportunities and build their career. While he was talking, I stood up and wrote one word on the board. When he had finished I asked him what company it was that he had worked for and he said Avon Cosmetics. The word I had written was 'American'. That sort of story is absolutely an American story; it's not about learning and development, it's not about absorbing company culture and not about challenging company culture.

The scheme at one international company raised some interesting questions: if you have a Dutch mentor and a French mentee working for an American company in England, where is the culture? In a lot of American companies in Europe it is the American culture that predominates over the national culture. However, strong cultural differences exist and these can be overcome if they are addressed and explored. You need to be conscious and aware of issues so you can talk about them and deal with them.

If you are familiar with Hofstede's work, power distance is probably a key variable: in France it is very high compared with the Netherlands where it is low. **(DM)**

A European airline deliberately matches people with somebody as different as possible, for example different nationality, different discipline, with the idea of getting as much of a spread as possible.

In another company we got the mentors to depict how they saw the emphasis of their behaviours in the relationship: very stretchy, very non-directive and not very much in the way of crying on shoulders and not very hands on – so not 'sponsoring'. They were flabbergasted that the expectations of the mentees were almost completely the opposite of this. At this point we said, look you've got to talk, haven't you, and find a compromise. So for a global programme, you may need to make adjustments and allow for people's needs for being supported and for some sponsorship element to come in there. The key is to be aware of the expectations of the various audiences. **(DC)**

It is possible that where there is a strong corporate culture, this will rise above differences in national culture; however, this is often not the case, as shown in the case study below.

AN EXPERIENCE OF IMPLEMENTING A GLOBAL MENTORING PROGRAMME IN SINGAPORE

Henley Management College has operated in Singapore for many years, and numerous other global organisations also operating in Singapore work with the college in a number of capacities.

There have been a few occasions when a mentoring scheme has been imported to the Singapore-based operation, from the head office of the organisation, and often a Western HR person has been responsible for trying to make it work. Typically, it has proved very difficult for any concept of mentoring other than the US sponsorship style of mentoring to be accepted. This has caused frustration, particularly where the mentoring process was envisaged as being part of the globalisation strategy. This would frequently mean that mentors would be selected from the parent company to mentor local employees as a way of developing a 'one culture' organisation.

Two major cultural behaviours in Singapore are found to block progress on this front. One is a reluctance to disclose anything which might be seen as a personal admission of weakness, especially to a superior; the other is a reluctance to share knowledge, as doing so diminishes the individual's personal power base. The Western style of mentoring does not fit easily into this kind of culture – and if managers are asked to engage with it, they find they are rapidly operating outside their comfort zone.

Simple examples like those given above make it clear that global mentoring is not quite as straightforward as it might appear on the surface. Consider all the potential difficulties carefully before blithely launching into a global scheme.

Summary

From the examples in this chapter, it is apparent that there are many ways of considering using mentoring as part of an organisation's strategic development or an individual's personal development. One of the objectives of this book, and the Focus Group itself, is to bring mentoring to the front of the minds of those in organisations making decisions about how to implement strategic change.

The more specific it is possible to be about the purpose of a mentoring scheme, the more straightforward it will be to set it up. Where all parties are clear as to the purpose, the chances of success are much higher.

It is certainly the experience at Henley that, used properly, mentoring can be the 'secret weapon' which really can speed up the change process and, at the same time, improve effectiveness, morale, productivity and much more. It is a really important intervention, available to all organisations, and should be considered as a mainstream, rather than a 'fringe', activity. To maximise the chances of success it is important always to take into account the context into which a mentoring scheme is being introduced.

5 The Differences Between Mentoring and Coaching

This chapter explores the differences between mentoring and coaching and helps to illustrate how to decide which intervention may be the most appropriate for a given situation.

In the Mentoring Focus Group, this subject came up for discussion on several occasions and it is a question that all scheme managers seem to have to answer whenever the subject of mentoring is raised for the first time. The need for clarification of the difference between mentoring and coaching has increased over recent times. It is noticeable that, in the early days of the Focus Group in 1998, 'executive coaching' was still a minority activity, with only a few individuals in an organisation receiving it for development purposes. Coaching was likely to be seen as a remedial activity, whereas mentoring was much more acceptable as a positive, developmental intervention. Coaching is now a great deal more aspirational, for a much wider range of managers. This means that the merging of coaching and mentoring in people's minds is actually more apparent now than it was previously. It is helpful, therefore, to have clear definitions for both activities and build this into any briefing activity.

In general terms, the Henley perspective is in line with the many textbook definitions of mentoring and coaching. Coaching is seen to be more skills-related, with specific, capabilities-linked outcomes. It would be perfectly acceptable, in many situations, for a line manager to coach a member of his or her staff and is often an expected role. Indeed, at Avaya, employees refer to their line manager as their 'coach'.

Mentoring is positioned much more around the whole person and the big picture and it is generally held that the line manager would not be appropriate as a subordinate's mentor. This is mainly because the line manager has a performance management responsibility, which could get in the way of genuine mentoring conversations.

The quick differentiation seems to be that the mentoring relationship is where a person would be encouraged to explore areas in which they feel they might need some coaching.

During a Focus Group meeting specifically devoted to discussing the difference between coaching and mentoring, it was felt that there was a clear disparity in perceptions of status between being able to say 'I am a coach' and 'I am a mentor' and that this was more marked amongst senior management.

The Group's discussions resulted in the list of differences shown in Table 5.1, which were based on the premise that coaching is about how to do things, whilst mentoring focuses more on the why and the bigger picture.

Table 5.1 **Differences between coaching and mentoring as seen by the Focus Group**

COACHING (the how)	vs MENTORING (the why)
Specific development/education	Holistic
Short term	Longer term
Development in attitude, behaviour, presentation	Larger – development in broader ways of thinking
Directive	Guidance
Help achieve a goal	'How things work around here'
Coach doesn't need to be an expert	Focus on retention and alignment; organisation development; business performance
Work on improving what already exists	
Training (new) → coaching	Training (improvement) → mentoring
Address specific issues	Larger
More frequent	Less frequent

Setting boundaries around the mentoring relationship is an area addressed in more detail in Part III, Setting Up and Running a Mentoring Scheme. Separating mentoring from coaching is one boundary which needs to be established early on. Another critical boundary is the one between mentoring and counselling: clear expectations need to be set in this area also, so that both parties in the relationship can be comfortable.

In terms of defining mentoring, Tables 5.2 and 5.3, produced by two of the Henley member companies for their schemes, are useful.

Table 5.2 **Defining expectations of a mentoring relationship at Zurich**

What Mentees should NOT expect	What Mentees can expect
To be managed	A sounding board, and/or
To be given answers/solutions	Encouragement, and/or
To be told what to do	A critical friend, and/or
To have an easy ride	Some emotional support, and/or
To receive favours	A confidant and/or a source of knowledge
To end the relationship too soon	
To gossip	
To whinge	
To get promotions, and so on	

Table 5.3 **Expectations of a mentoring relationship defined by a Focus Group organisation**

A mentoring relationship isn't …	A mentoring relationship is …
An opportunity to fix day-to-day performance issues	An active, learning one
An opportunity to bypass/usurp the authority of a line manager	A stretching, broadening experience for all parties
An opportunity to transform a career and ensure appointment to the next vacant role	Flexible enough to meet the needs of both parties
An opportunity to abdicate responsibility for ownership of personal development	Open, but confidential
Purely patronage or sponsorship	A positive and trusting relationship
Purely coaching	

A further clarification on the difference between mentoring and coaching was received from the two expert advisors in a question and answer session held at Henley. Clutterbuck and Megginson's responses summarise this issue well.

Practitioners' Problem-solving

Questions and Answers with David Megginson and David Clutterbuck

'Mentoring as a fashion accessory' is a witty phrase, but the one I see as a fashion accessory today is the executive coach, and I would be very interested to understand what you see as the difference between the two.

I think there's a lot of blurring at the edges between the two and very often people who are doing those roles confuse the two words as well. If you're going to be purist about it, 'executive coaching' is about performance and skills; 'mentoring' is about broadening out your horizons and enabling you to decide who you want to be and what you want to be. A mentor helps you decide what you need coaching on. **(DC)**

It is really important and useful to differentiate between the two processes and a good touchstone is: do you start from the learner's dream? If you do, it's probably mentoring. If you start from a list of corporate competencies or something like that, it is approaching coaching. The thing that is absolutely clear to me is that they are two different processes that are usefully distinguished. (Counselling and instructing need distinguishing as well.) I've worked in a number of organisations where what I call mentoring, they call coaching. There is a difference. But when I work in an organisation I'm not fussy about what they call it, so long as they are clear what process they are concerned with. **(DM)**

6 Taking the Decision to Introduce a Mentoring Scheme or Enter into a Mentoring Relationship

The whole book should, hopefully, be helping mentoring scheme managers and potential mentees and mentors with the decision as to whether or not introducing or participating in a mentoring scheme is the right thing to do in their given context. In this chapter, there are a few summary points to help this process along the way – a kind of quick reality check. A case study from YELL Ltd helps to illustrate how mentoring schemes can expand both within and outside an organisation and how different types of mentor and mentee can be available.

Objectives

Following closely behind understanding the context and purpose for the scheme, come the questions: 'What do you want to achieve? What outcomes are you looking for?' For scheme managers, defining a clear objective is essential to a scheme: it clearly lays out why it is being set up and what it hopes to achieve. A well-written objective provides future marketing materials with a strong focal point. In addition, it will enable the scheme manager to respond with clarity when asked for information about the purpose of the scheme.

> To develop high potential talent, enabling the organisation to prepare global managers for senior leadership roles within the organisation.
>
> Objectives defined by a Focus Group organisation

For potential mentors and mentees, objectives provide a focus for what needs to be achieved during the time available for the relationship. Being clear that mentoring is the right route to take (as against, for example, coaching) and knowing what changes are being sought helps both parties to establish a clear mandate for the relationship. It is also appropriate to consider whether the objectives will best be achieved through a mentoring relationship within the organisation, or whether it is better to look outside, that is, for an independent or cross-company person.

Scope and Approach

Once objectives have been clarified, there are two areas to consider before deciding to take up mentoring: scope and approach. The scope of a scheme refers to the size and extent of it: who it will be for and how many people will be involved. The approach being taken to mentoring covers elements such as the proposed mentoring model (formal or informal) and the level of support offered to those involved.

MENTORS AND MENTEES

For participants, knowing the intended scope or reach of a proposed scheme (if, indeed, there is a specific scheme available to you) helps in the decision-making process by indicating what level of support will be available. It is also helpful to understand the model of mentoring that will be in place (see Chapter 4) and whether it will be an informal scheme where participants need to be self-sufficient and self-regulating, or whether the relationship will be established within the bounds of a formal, centrally managed scheme where a higher level of support is available.

A more formal scheme can provide opportunities for mentors and mentees to share experiences with other people who are in a mentoring relationship within the same overall context. This can be immensely helpful in establishing and keeping the relationship on track, particularly if things are not going quite as intended: it can be very helpful to have other people with whom understanding can be checked. Formal schemes usually provide some form of face-to-face training which allows participants to have common expectations and understand the boundaries of the scheme. Guidance is available throughout the lifecycle of the mentoring relationship, including how and when to review the effectiveness of the relationship.

Within an informal structure, participants are more likely to have free choice over the person with whom they pair; indeed, it is possible they may need to seek out their own mentor or mentee. In these instances, being clear about objectives and the type of help being sought is essential. Training in the form of face-to-face sessions is less likely and individuals could have to learn about mentoring and how it works from written information, either in the form of a book or guide or an internet or intranet website. Another part of the decision-making here is how much support will be needed along the way. This could be help with matching and disengaging if it does not work, having guidance on how to review progress and evaluate outcomes and so on.

For some, it may be that an informal approach will best suit the achievement of their objectives, especially as there are no 'rules' imposed on the relationship. Others may feel more comfortable having a structure and framework of support. Alternatively, it is possible that having more than one mentor or mentee will be the best solution and a combination of formal and informal scheme may be ideal.

From the mentor and mentee's perspective, the most important issues affecting the decision-making process are usually linked to, firstly, understanding the overall context, the big picture, of mentoring in their organisation. Secondly, a clear understanding of the 'terms of engagement' are important to help individuals to decide whether entering into such a relationship is something with which they are personally comfortable. If someone enters into a mentoring relationship with some concerns at the personal level, the chances of the relationship succeeding are adversely affected. Mentoring is, in the end, a personal affair and for the true benefit to be achieved from this activity, a high degree of trust and security is necessary. Being taken out of a comfort zone by thoughtful, provocative questioning is a useful learning experience but for many people it is necessary to be sure of the nature of the relationship before this is completely possible.

SCHEME MANAGERS

For scheme managers a key question is how widely available a mentoring scheme is intended to be. Will the scope of the scheme be for anyone, or will it target specific groups locally, nationally or globally? Several of the Henley organisations 'went global' with their mentoring programmes, which brought into play additional considerations – not least of which was geography. E-mentoring became the most practical way of overcoming distance and this is covered in more detail in Chapter 21.

If the proposed model for the scheme is a formal one, it is worth considering what size of scheme is manageable in the first instance. In the Focus Group organisations, it was often the case that the first scheme was seen as a pilot before extending it more generally throughout the organisation. In these situations, thought will need to be given in advance to the level of resource available to support the bigger scheme. If a scheme is designed as an informal 'self-service' one then, beyond providing e-learning materials, general information, a database and so on via an intranet site, the day-to-day interventions will be potentially few. If there is a more formal structure involving training programmes, specific matching, facilitation of first meetings and so on, scheme managers need to be ready to provide a high level of support. The risks of not doing so could be that willing participants are trained but not matched, expectations are not met, apathy sets in and the programme loses credibility.

A universal comment from all members of the Henley Group was that running a successful mentoring scheme demands an appropriate level of resources.

The more successful a scheme, the more likely that demand will increase from other areas of the organisation. It does not work if there is no one in the organisation with enough time to manage the process in a hands-on fashion.

It will be useful to have a strategy to manage this situation, whether it is one of containment or expansion. The important thing is that there is one.

Mentoring can also go well beyond the bounds of the initiating organisation. Cross-company mentoring has already been looked at in Chapter 4. Some commercial organisations have schemes which go beyond the bounds of their organisation and involve their managers in mentoring processes with community, rather than organisational, benefits. There are obviously developmental benefits for the mentors in such a process, but the issue for the scheme manager is that once mentoring becomes an established part of a company's management culture, the potential applications are almost limitless. It is helpful to have an active policy of managing the introduction of mentoring schemes so that they have the best chance of success and, in turn, continue to give mentoring a good name.

An Example of Different Approaches to Mentoring

As an example of where mentoring can go, once it has become embedded in an organisation's culture, the following case study illustrates how mentoring expanded within YELL Ltd. The examples of mentoring in the wider community may offer potential mentors and mentees additional perspectives.

COMMUNITY AND COMPANY MENTORING SCHEMES — YELL Ltd

Within the UK, YELL has introduced a number of different mentoring schemes externally in the community, through both face-to-face meetings and via e-mentoring. By using its company intranet, YELL employees can access a policy guide and register online to instigate schemes internally; as a result, mentoring is growing throughout the company. Brief outlines of the various schemes on offer are set out below.

YELL HR Community Initiative
In January 2000, YELL decided to increase its contribution to the community by working with the Education Business Partnership (EBP), Business in the Community (BITC) and the local Slough Education Action Zone (EAZ). Examples of schemes supported by YELL are set out below:

▶ Small Business Mentoring – This scheme assists senior managers, in businesses of up to 50 employees, in any area of management and business. It is facilitated by BITC, which is a government-sponsored national organisation.

One head teacher received assistance implementing a three-year school development plan. He received advice on staffing, personnel, finance, strategy, vision, premises, PR, information management and curriculum development.

Another had issues with staff resisting change – the YELL change management department advised the best way to move her people forward, preparing them to accept as well as implement change.

▶ Head Teacher Mentoring – This scheme supports newly appointed head teachers in the running of their schools. Senior managers from YELL mentor head teachers for periods of up to a year. Meetings are held throughout the year, with topics ranging from support with health and safety risk assessment to full budgetary management. The head teachers find it particularly useful to talk to someone who is neutral and non-judgmental.

▶ Teenage Mentoring – This scheme helps students, particularly those with specific problems, achieve 5 GCSEs (grades C and above). Not without its challenges, the scheme enables students to focus on their studies while receiving support and encouragement throughout.

Overall, face-to-face and e-mentoring via the EBP has proved very successful; the students' commitment to develop underlies its success.

Setting up a Scheme – an example
Education Business Partnership (EBP)/Teenage Scheme*
After familiarisation meetings with the organiser, YELL coordinators ask managers for team volunteers. Once committed to the scheme, volunteers are vetted by the EBP (*the EBP/Teenage Scheme includes police checks for child protection reasons) and successful volunteers are trained in mentoring and matched to students.

The EBP takes into account a variety of areas when selecting mentors, such as communication skills, attitude, perceptions and position. Matching is achieved by matching common mentor/student interests, for example shared hobbies, sports and business interests. Sometimes a student's personal circumstances are taken into consideration; the current EBP same sex mentoring policy operating in the UK has proved very successful.

Teachers are given the opportunity to act as coordinators between students and mentors and are encouraged to hold informal meetings to monitor feedback. At the end of an exam period, a scheme's success can often be measured via a student's exam results.

In future, students will make the final decision on their choice of mentor, having discussed two predetermined topics at an informal meeting.

YELL Internal Mentoring Schemes

▶ Individuals – these operate for a variety of reasons, for example self-development, achieving qualifications and so on. Feedback confirms that success is dependent on matching the 'right' mentor and student, having clarified expectations from the outset.

▶ HR/Senior Management Development – this is part of an executive development programme for senior managers. Individual training needs are addressed and behaviour patterns explored via the introduction of competencies for superior performance. Internal and external consultants are employed and its success is dependent on the quality of the mentoring relationship. HR facilitates matching and structure, for example clear objectives, start/end date, feedback and so on, and outcomes are agreed by mentor/manager. This approach encompasses two elements:

▶ Executive Coaching – short-term initiative addressing specific issues.

▶ Mentoring – longer term initiative covering a broader range of issues. Previously explored areas have included self-confidence, promotion, broader support elements, development, behaviours, mentor observation and feedback, personal impact, board member interaction, understanding the political element, leadership and delegation, widening business, strategic and commercial skills.

▶ Graduate Trainees all have at least one mentor during their 18-month traineeship.

Summary

Making the decision about whether or not to become involved in mentoring requires careful forethought. Understanding what is meant by the term 'mentoring' is a good start; following that, it is important to understand why involvement in mentoring will help and what will be achieved.

The most important message coming from the Henley organisations is that it is essential to be clear about the objectives and purpose of a proposed mentoring scheme and then everything else stems from this. Mentoring as a 'good thing' is not a strong enough message to make a programme successful.

Once a mentoring scheme has run successfully in an organisation, and a number of managers have been involved either as mentors, mentees, line managers or other stakeholders (see Part III), then it is likely that interest in using mentoring for a wide range of purposes will grow. Mentoring can be embedded into the culture of an organisation so that it becomes a normal expectation of a management role to mentor and be mentored and for a variety of purposes.

In this section, there have been examples of some of the wider applications of mentoring which many organisations are now trying out. For mentors and mentees who have participated in an organisational scheme, it may be appealing to become involved in a local community mentoring scheme, supporting schools, young people or local businesses.

Gathering as much information as possible about the proposed scheme and/or the roles of mentor and mentee allows for better informed decisions about whether to become involved. Parts III and IV of this book give further information about setting up and running a scheme and also about taking part in a mentoring relationship.

PART III

Setting Up and Running a Mentoring Scheme

7 Introduction

Setting up and running a mentoring scheme involves behind the scene tasks upon which not only the success of the particular initiative depends, but also probably the reputation of mentoring within the organisation for the foreseeable future. Mentoring is often still one of those 'fringe' organisational activities which depends upon good feedback from all stakeholders in order to survive and thrive, and the programme manager is a critical part of this equation. If the infrastructure of a mentoring programme is solid, then it can take a few mismatched relationships or frustrations.

This section looks at the tasks involved in setting up and running a scheme, including getting the buy-in from the business to support it. It is important not to underestimate the amount of time it can take, initially and once the scheme is up and running. A further point is that if the first mentoring programme is a success, it is likely that word will get out and other parts of the organisation will also want to do it. This is a great outcome, as long as there is an infrastructure to support it. The clearer the setup for the first scheme, the better the chances of mentoring spreading through the organisation to become part of the culture. It is important to make it as easy as possible for other people to replicate the original process for setting up and running a mentoring scheme. The critical stages to this, which are covered in this section, are:

▶ Influencing key stakeholders

▶ Marketing the scheme

▶ Defining the mentoring process and planning

▶ The matching process

▶ Training the participants

▶ Maintaining, concluding and developing a scheme

▶ Evaluation and review of the scheme

▶ A summary of scheme manager activities.

Much of the literature around learning shows that the most cost-effective and powerful learning interventions are often mentoring, coaching and action learning. This and the large number of company case studies available should help you put a business case together. Useful references to support your case include Hamel et al. (1996), Wilson & Elman (1990) and Pearn et al. (1995).

8 Identifying and Influencing Key Stakeholders

Introduction

This chapter looks at the different people who can be interested in, or affected by, a mentoring scheme. This usually involves a much wider range of people than simply the direct participants and the scheme organiser. Once the stakeholders have been identified, gaining commitment to the scheme is discussed. A number of areas to consider when building the business case are offered, together with examples of potential success criteria and suggested benefits and risks to the participants and organisation.

Identifying the Stakeholders

The term 'stakeholder' is very appropriate. It implies a person with a vested interest in the operation, and it is important to consider that the various different stakeholders will have quite different angles of interest. The motivation of the mentee in a relationship will be different from that of the mentor, in terms of what they hope to get out of the relationship. The motivation of senior management or line managers to support a mentoring scheme will be different again. The same core messages may need to be communicated in a variety of different ways to these different stakeholders, in order to influence them appropriately.

The informed support of the key stakeholders for a mentoring scheme has been raised again and again at Focus Group meetings as vital to the viability of the scheme. Successful mentoring depends greatly on the context and climate within which it is couched and the key stakeholders can play a significant part in getting this right.

These individuals and groups of people can hold the key to the success of the initiative, and identifying who the key stakeholders are, and how best to influence them and obtain their support, is critical. The first step is, of course, to identify who the key stakeholders for a mentoring scheme might be.

Some thoughts from the Henley Focus Group include:

▶ *The target group of mentees*

▶ *Line managers of the target group of mentees*

▶ *The target group of mentors*

▶ *Senior management – often line managers of the mentors, or mentors themselves*

▶ *HR and personnel staff who might be involved*

▶ *Section heads of divisions supplying mentors for cross-divisional mentoring*

▶ *The whole organisation from a public relations point of view – via a newsletter or other appropriate communication*

▶ *The MD or CEO, in order to give top-level endorsement*

From this list it is already possible to see that the range of individuals who can be included as stakeholders is wide. A strong message from this is that mentoring is seen as a cultural statement within an organisation, and it is important not to underestimate the impact that can be made when introducing a scheme into an organisation for the first time.

> *I believe that having a mentor speaks volumes about the company's commitment to my future development. As a relative newcomer, the mentoring scheme provides me with a fast track route to understanding who's who in Smiths Group and also a valuable source of impartial career advice.*
>
> Smiths Group mentee

One organisation working with Henley to implement a mentoring scheme concurrently with a management development programme, both for the first time, found out the hard way that it is not possible to do this 'quietly'. No formal announcement was made to explain the rationale behind the decision to set up a mentoring scheme, and the grapevine went into overdrive very quickly. Interestingly, some of the loudest sources of discontent were senior managers who had not been asked to become mentors

> *I would be very happy to be involved with this initiative as I agree that developing and energising our people is the key to success. I strongly believe that this process will help develop me as well as the mentee.*
>
> Zurich mentor

for the first intake of delegates. 'Why wasn't I asked' was a question the scheme manager had to address from a number of senior people in the organisation, whom it had been assumed would have been too busy to be interested.

Gaining Organisational Commitment

Once the key stakeholders have been identified, and appropriate communication strategies planned, it is then important to consider the organisational side of the stakeholder groups. This might include any or all of the following issues – it will be useful to be able to answer questions around each of these areas:

▶ *Organisational support* – what level of organisational sponsorship is necessary? If it is high level, is a senior manager/director supporting the proposal and ready to back it with his/her colleagues? What level of line involvement will there be; will the line own the programme or will it be HR?

▶ *Business results* – does the current state of the business allow time to focus on mentoring? Is mentoring in line with organisational objectives? How can it be positioned to underpin the achievement of business outcomes?

▶ *Business case* – why should an investment be made in such a programme at this time? What benchmarking has been done?

▶ *Pace of change* – is the organisation undergoing radical change, for example downsizing, such that launching mentoring might be seen as inappropriate or, conversely, as a positive move?

▶ *Attitude to employee development* – is development seen as 'nice to have' or essential? What should we be doing within our 'corporate governance' responsibilities?

▶ *Stakeholders* – does the objective have something in it that all the involved parties (mentors, mentees, line managers, the organisation) can relate to?

▶ *Success criteria/measures* – how will success be defined/measured?

> *Mentors as well as mentees can find it an invaluable development tool – it increases our understanding of both people and the organisation.*
>
> Yorkshire Water mentor

It might be a useful idea to produce a paper with answers to each of the above points clearly defined. This could then act as the core positioning statement about the mentoring scheme and its value to the business.

In addition, when working towards gaining commitment from the organisation to a mentoring programme, it helps to be clear on the following points before actually approaching potential sponsors and stakeholders:

▶ *Definition* – understand what is meant by the term 'mentoring' within the context of the organisation.

▶ *Scope of the proposed scheme* – who it is being targeted at; what it includes and does not include.

▶ *What needs to be done to get the right level of organisational support and commitment* – know the risks and benefits of what is being proposed, not forgetting the line managers' involvement.

▶ *Evaluate comprehensively and then justify what resources might be needed.* Consider whether it would be prudent to ask for support from the line – perhaps in the form of a local champion.

'Getting buy-in' has always been an important topic for debate amongst the members of the Focus Group. Having good answers to the above lists of issues is a good place to start – the lists themselves have been compiled by members of the Group who have had to do exactly this as part of getting buy-in from their organisations to their own schemes.

An excellent way of gaining top management support is to invite a senior executive from another organisation, who has experienced good mentoring programmes or is the product of mentoring him/herself, to talk to senior managers for the programme now being proposed and/or meet the MD of the company. This form of peer 'pressure' can be very powerful. At Avaya high-level support is clearly visible as the divisional VPs act as mentor to their own divisional mentors. B&Q senior management demonstrate commitment to the scheme by participating in the mentoring training days.

The 'expert panel' was asked the following question, which is of relevance here, and this is the answer they gave.

Practitioners' Problem-solving

Questions and Answers with David Megginson and David Clutterbuck

Why invest in mentoring?

I would simply ask what the company's purpose is in offering the scheme. If you can't show some kind of significant link to a business problem that the organisation has, then you probably shouldn't be doing it – you should just allow it to happen. But you can find data that shows the impact of what happens when people in companies do have mentoring schemes and when they don't. A major pharmaceutical company analysed staff turnover figures amongst its IT and finance people: turnover amongst those who had a mentor was 2%; amongst those who didn't, it was 27%. So if you want to link mentoring to retention, then there is your evidence. If you define the purpose of the scheme, you can then put some value on it.   (DC)

Lex's HR Director said they had not made elaborate measures of how successful the scheme was because these people were so driven and so busy, that if they were taking the time for mentoring, it was obviously something sensible and which they should be doing.   (DM)

Objectives and Success Criteria

Defining a clear objective is essential to a scheme: it clearly lays out the purpose of the scheme and what will be achieved. Also, being able to be explicit about the success criteria used for a mentoring scheme is extremely helpful.

Examples of criteria used in some of the Focus Group schemes are shown below.

▶ Number of promotions or cross-functional changes

▶ Engagement in training and other developmental activities (participation and delivery)

▶ Results attained during advanced learning programmes

▶ Participation in projects, key business initiatives and so on

RWE Thames Water

Key Success Factor:

Succession planning: 70% of role vacancies will be filled by internal candidates.

B&Q

The objective of implementing a mentoring process is to ensure that employees gain as much insight into an organisation as possible, but is also an alternative means of career development.

Avaya

Risks and Benefits

Having a clear idea of the potential gains and possible pitfalls is another important part of gaining organisational commitment. Ensuring that these have been considered and are ready to share with the various stakeholders at appropriate times will certainly help to smooth the path from the planning stage to implementation. Tables 8.1 and 8.2 show a selection of potential benefits and risks devised in a Focus Group session, from the perspective of mentees, mentors and the organisation.

POTENTIAL BENEFITS

Table 8.1 **Potential benefits of implementing a mentoring scheme**

MENTEES

▶ Improved confidence and self-esteem

▶ Confidential coaching

▶ Safe learning environment to test out ideas

▶ Continuity of support in a changing environment

▶ Access to different perspectives and experience

▶ Development of transferable skills including: management, leadership, behavioural, professional

▶ Sense of value within the organisation

▶ Opportunity to broaden networks

▶ Help in developing long-term career and development goals and plans

▶ Develop a wider view of the organisation – being helped to understand and resolve organisational and political issues

MENTORS

▶ Improved job satisfaction/revitalised interest in work – be challenged, tested and stimulated

▶ An opportunity to influence the way things are done – passing on their own experience, knowledge and skills

▶ Increased peer recognition – seen as a role model

▶ New perspectives – challenging own assumptions

▶ An opportunity to question their own views and values

▶ Opportunity to influence the next generation of managers and demonstrate their own commitment to the future of the company

▶ Self-development – using and improving skills, particularly behavioural ones

▶ Get/keep in touch with the grass roots and manage their own team better as a result

cont'd

Table 8.1 **cont'd**

BENEFITS TO THE ORGANISATION

▶ Increased motivation/retention of employees by investing in their development

▶ Helps stabilise and reinforce the company's values and culture

▶ Professional standards are maintained

▶ Improved communications – both laterally and vertically, and particularly across cultures

▶ Productivity gains – mentees working smarter and developing two for the price of one

▶ Knowledge management, that is, sharing and retention

▶ Enhances the practice and culture of continuous learning

▶ Improved succession planning – more information is available

▶ Increased speed of change

▶ Strengthening of business relationships

Figure 8.1 shows the organisational benefits that the European division of a global company foresaw in implementing a mentoring scheme for high potentials.

Figure 8.1 **Benefits of mentoring foreseen in a high-potential scheme**

POTENTIAL RISKS

Table 8.2 illustrates the potential risks to viability of the scheme itself, as well as those which may affect the participants and the organisation.

Table 8.2 **Potential risks to implementing mentoring successfully**

PARTICIPANTS

▶ Seen as special by other, uninvolved groups

▶ Behaviours are not conducive to fostering a good mentoring relationship

▶ Line managers feel exposed, not knowing what's going on

▶ Relationships don't 'gel'

▶ Lack of commitment (perhaps generated by 'I've been told to do this')

▶ Overcommitment to mentoring actions which infringes on primary job responsibilities or work–life balance

SCHEME

▶ Insufficient investment

▶ Lack of a dedicated scheme manager, leading to insufficient time available to support participants

▶ Tactical cost controls prevent travelling to meetings (particularly relevant in global schemes)

▶ The internal climate is not supportive

▶ No senior management sponsorship resulting in little take-up

ORGANISATION

▶ Economic conditions bring a business downturn

▶ Implementation of radical change diverts the attention of the organisation

▶ Inflexible work processes that don't allow time for mentoring as a natural part of business

▶ Mentoring being seen as a 'quick fix'

A fear expressed by one potential mentor was that mentoring would get confused with sponsorship and that cliques would form. This illustrates the importance of setting the context for the scheme and ensuring that participants (and others) are properly informed.

Less frequently promoted areas of benefit are those that will accrue for line managers. In the Focus Group we felt that, as a result of their employees being mentored, line managers would see:

▶ increased motivation and improved performance, helped by an increasing ability to identify and resolve issues early on

► a better relationship between themselves and the employee, who in turn might get on better with the rest of the team

► retention of valuable staff – in an increasingly efficient team.

> *They are all getting better ideas about what they want to do; they're better at identifying areas for developing.*
>
> Avaya line manager speaking about direct reports who are mentees

In addition, where a line manager is also a mentor, they would be encouraged to use their mentoring skills and approaches in the daily line management role.

It had become apparent from discussions amongst scheme managers working with Henley that if line managers were brought on board and engaged in the scheme early on, there was a much stronger chance of a mentoring scheme running successfully.

Summary

Gaining commitment from the organisation to the idea of implementing mentoring is critical to its success. The first step is to identify and engage all the potential stakeholders, from the direct participants (mentors and mentees) to their line managers and organisational sponsors.

Creating the business case involves understanding the organisational context in which the scheme will operate; clarifying the meaning of the term 'mentoring' within the organisation; and determining the scope of the scheme and the resources required to implement it. To gain the necessary commitment for a scheme, it is also essential to be able to discuss the potential risks and benefits to all stakeholders and propose clear objectives and success criteria.

Once the foundation for the scheme is solid and the organisational climate and stakeholders judged to be supportive, it is then time to look at how to market it.

9 Marketing the Scheme

Introduction

Once the ground covered in the previous chapter has been addressed and organisational buy-in has been secured, marketing a mentoring scheme should be a relatively straightforward task. This chapter looks at a variety of marketing methods and tools that can be employed to attract interest and promote the scheme. In addition, the option of using mentoring champions to market and support the scheme is explored.

Marketing the Scheme

Considering how to market mentoring is an important first step in gaining interest in the scheme and finding volunteers to take part.

The culture into which the mentoring scheme is being introduced plays an important part in determining the most appropriate way of marketing the idea. In an ideal world, a 'learning culture' would already exist in the organisation and mentoring would be a natural fit.

The following advice from our two expert practitioners is useful for situations where there is still some work to be done.

Practitioners' Problem-solving

Questions and Answers with David Megginson and David Clutterbuck

How do you create a learning culture where learning is a weakness?

If you have a learning culture, you would expect there to be learning taking place on all three levels of the company: the organisation, the teams and the individuals are all learning and you might also say there will be an integration between those three levels. (A development climate survey – questions that pinpoint behaviours/characteristics of the organisation – can be used to test the waters and see where they are.)

If you have a highly hostile developmental climate, it is more likely that mentoring will tend to flourish, as it is the only way that people can get development. If you have a highly positive climate, then formal structures

perhaps work less well, as informal structures are more supportive – people find mentors from their peers and those around them. It's when you have a neutral climate that formal structures have the most impact.

If you want to create a learning culture, it is one of those things that has to start at the top and one of the first things I ask within an organisation is: what kind of role model is top management? How much of their time do they spend on learning? How much of their time do they spend on helping other people to learn? How much time do they spend talking about learning? Do they come along to training courses and emphasise how important it is and how it fits in with what the organisation is doing? **(DC)**

MARKETING AND SUPPORT TOOLS

Cultural norms will drive the marketing approaches through one or several of the methods outlined below, which have been used effectively by Focus Group organisations:

▶ **Booklets** for mentors and mentees covering the objectives, benefits, overall process, roles/responsibilities, help and support available.

▶ **Policy or process document** – Avaya have a Mentoring Process document, which is available on the intranet and contains the following sections:

  ▷ *Overview*
  ▷ *Eligibility*
  ▷ *Process*
  ▷ *Guidelines for assigning mentors*
  ▷ *Frequency of meetings*
  ▷ *Content of meeting.*

▶ **Mentoring websites** have been set up on a number of company intranets, including general information about the process and how it works, reading lists, links to other sites, useful models, process documents, Q&A and so on. Besides giving information, these may also be useful as a gateway for applying to become a mentee or mentor.

▶ **Champions** – use people who have experienced mentoring programmes or, even better, been the product of them, to act as champions for the programme. (This concept is explored later in the chapter.)

▶ **Information workshops** – short, lunch-time sessions to inform employees about the scheme.

▶ **E-mail and voice mail** – useful mechanisms for letting the entire organisation know about the scheme or, say, an information workshop or intranet site launch.

If some form of mentoring already exists in the company, albeit on an informal basis, it may be helpful in the marketing process to promote the fact that there is an existing foundation upon which this new initiative is being built.

Again, depending on the culture, it can be useful to prepare a number of pro forma documents for use in the process and make them available via a web page. This allows potential participants to gain a fuller picture of what might be involved in mentoring.

Such documents could include:

▶ Mentee application form or résumé

▶ Mentor volunteer form or résumé

▶ Draft agenda for the first meeting

▶ Mentoring contract

▶ Mentor/mentee preparation document

▶ Mentee/mentor diary or log

▶ Mid-point review document

▶ Final review and evaluation.

It is worth considering that in some organisations participants will feel stifled by the 'bureaucracy' that the documents represent and never complete or use them. Many of the mentors/mentees we spoke to said that while they discussed ground rules and boundaries, they never actually signed a formal contract document.

In *Mentoring Executives and Directors* (Clutterbuck & Megginson 1999) Nick Holley of Lex is quoted as saying:

> Paperwork may have a role in some organisations but not in ours. Paperwork would kill it, so there isn't any. Indeed, if need drives it and ownership is everything, why do you need paperwork? (p. 75)

Attracting Mentors

Marketing also plays a role in recruiting participants to the programme. Methods for finding internal mentors that have been used include:

▶ Making a specific approach to an individual – this can be very flattering and allows the targeting of people it is believed will be good mentors.

► Identifying mentors through performance management reviews or succession planning/talent management processes. There are often managers who will not progress further themselves, but are excellent at developing others – invite their involvement.

► Gaining interest via indirect 'publicity' methods:
  ▷ Include mentors' names in reports on the mentees' progress
  ▷ Ensure mentors receive personal 'thank you' letters from top management
  ▷ Invite mentors to present at future training sessions
  ▷ Include success stories in company newsletters.

► Using team meetings to float the idea to potential mentors – building an image about 'being a mentor' and what it would be like.

► Advertising on the intranet/internet or via e-mail.

► Providing recognition for mentors – EDS found that this had positive results for it: it did this by including mentoring as one of its specific objectives and allowing mentors to include time spent mentoring on their time sheets.

► Existing stakeholders: mentees who have gained benefit from their own relationship may well wish to go on to develop their skills by becoming a mentor. Equally, line managers may see the value in taking on this role.

In addition, organisations are increasingly using diagnostic and assessment tools with their managers, which means that added information could be available to the scheme manager in identifying potentially suitable mentors.

A point worth considering when starting up a traditional, hierarchical mentoring scheme is that mentors can quickly become scarce commodities. Figure 9.1 quickly shows (a) how difficult it can be to allocate all potential mentees a mentor from the hierarchical level above them and (b) why the chief executive usually has a mentor from outside the organisation.

However, a positive, likely outcome is that once the first group of mentees has completed the lifecycle, there is the potential to add them to the pool of available mentors.

As the practice of mentoring becomes more commonplace, many mentees are seeing the developmental advantages of becoming a mentor themselves. Indeed, it is now often the case that, along with 'line manager as coach', taking on a mentoring role within the organisation is recognised in the mainstream performance appraisal system and rewarded accordingly.

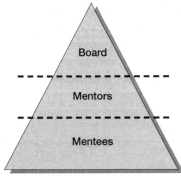

Figure 9.1 **The mentoring pyramid**

Using Mentoring Champions

In recent years, the concept of using 'champions' to support many different types of initiative has increased dramatically in organisations. The Focus Group discussions led to the belief that mentoring champions could play a valuable part in ensuring the success of a scheme. They not only provided an additional level of support, but could also be instrumental in gaining acceptance of the mentoring scheme by the line.

The role of a mentoring champion could be seen as being any or all of the following:

▶ An information source for participants and potential participants.

▶ Part of the scheme design and ongoing improvement team.

▶ A member of the team, and knowledge source, during the matching process.

▶ A local training resource.

▶ A PR person – promoting the scheme within the local community and encouraging more people to become mentors.

▶ A guardian of the scheme, ensuring that the scheme's principles work and are upheld locally.

▶ A first stop for participants to go to.

▶ The 'ears on the ground', good at checking with individuals and feeding back what they hear on the grapevine, so that potential issues can be nipped in the bud.

> *Our mentoring champion is the barometer at the sharp end. He's down there every day and if someone's having a problem, he is going to know about it before I do.*
>
> B&Q scheme manager

Not everyone will be suited to such a role. Useful attributes to look for in a mentoring champion can include:

▶ Respected by other employees; has 'street cred'

▶ Able to maintain confidentiality

▶ Known to act with integrity

▶ Good at the 'day job'

▶ People-focused

▶ Generally supportive of development

▶ Enthusiastic about mentoring

▶ In the location and/or function

▶ Knowledgeable about the culture and local issues.

Summary

In this chapter, the whole area of the sphere of influence of a mentoring scheme has been explored and, as has been seen, the agendas of the various stakeholders need considering carefully. Mentoring lives or dies by its reputation, and so winning over some key champions for the cause is a very useful thing to do, early on in the process. Good communication between all stakeholders is the other essential part of the marketing process, which will ensure that things run as smoothly as possible once the mentoring scheme begins to roll out.

10 Defining the Process and Planning Phase

Introduction

This chapter deals with the process and planning phase of a mentoring scheme, starting from the point where the go-ahead has been given and the key stakeholders are engaged. The important issues then become the mechanics of recruiting participants for the programme, that is, the mentors and the mentees, and the support processes which need to be in place to enable the scheme to run smoothly.

The chapter gives examples of principles that might be used in defining a scheme. It also addresses the need for clearly defining the role and responsibilities of the various participants, together with points of contact for participants and stakeholders in the scheme, should there be any queries or problems which need addressing along the way. Approaches for finding mentors and mentees are explored, including the qualities that might be looked for in either person. The chapter concludes with a series of questions that a scheme manager might find useful to ask when at this stage of implementing a mentoring programme.

The Mentoring Lifecycle

Mentoring is not a static operation. It is not intended that, once a scheme is set up, those relationships should continue for ever and, indeed, this would be a significant failure of most schemes, should it happen. Elsewhere in the book, there are sections dedicated to how to stop mentoring, as well as start it.

An effective mentoring relationship, one in which the outcomes and objectives of the participants are achieved, will follow a lifecycle. At the end of this, there is a natural time for evaluation and, if it is felt useful and appropriate to both parties, then a new phase of a mentoring relationship could be entered into between the same partners. This may well involve going round the mentoring lifecycle again, rather than being seen as a continuation of the original activity.

Figure 10.1 summarises the mentoring lifecycle, as seen by Focus Group members.

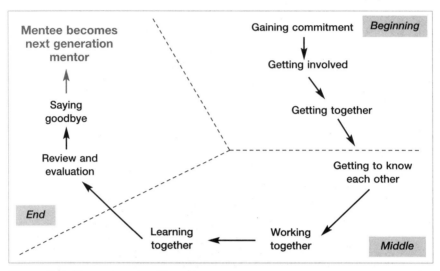

Figure 10.1 **The mentoring lifecycle**

This is a simple model of the process, which covers all the stages in a typical mentoring scheme. It is important that there is a clear understanding amongst everyone involved of how the process is designed to work, what will happen when and how to go about it.

Besides the basic model laid out in Figure 10.1, it may be necessary to include stages which link the scheme with business objectives and other organisational processes such as performance management and development. For example, in one organisation where the scheme was part of a leadership development programme, the lifecycle was 'topped and tailed' with discussions at the annual senior management Development Committee (a succession planning/development forum).

Design Principles

The Focus Group organisations identified a number of key principles when they began designing their schemes. These incorporated organisational values, defined who the scheme was aimed at and from where mentors would be drawn, as well as giving more detailed guidance on how the scheme would operate. A common thread within these principles was the mention, in some way, of the confidentiality of the relationship.

An alternative to doing it 'in-house' is, of course, to engage consultants to design the scheme and, perhaps, help to deliver the training programme, as well as assist at the review/evaluation stage.

Examples of principles incorporated in various companies' designs are given in Figure 10.2.

A Graduate Mentoring Scheme

▶ Voluntary (for both mentees and mentors)

▶ Confidential relationship between mentors and mentees

▶ Mentors to be an offline manager, up to 3 grades above the graduates

▶ Managed programme

▶ Formal duration of 18 months (ongoing informal relationships beyond that time)

▶ Meetings should take place at least every 4–6 weeks

▶ Option always available to change mentor without blame or fault, if the relationship is not working

▶ Expectation that the graduates will progressively manage their mentor, and that the mentor will facilitate this

▶ A voluntary mid-point review meeting with mentee and mentor groups to share experiences and receive further mentoring skills development (outputs can also form part of the programme evaluation process)

A Pan-European High Potential Scheme

▶ Formal scheme, centrally managed

▶ Integral part of existing Leadership Programme

▶ Voluntary participation – mentors to be drawn from top European Directors

▶ Maximum of 40 mentees (max 2:1 ratio)

▶ 12-month contract

▶ Cross-unit, cross-culture pairings

▶ E-mentoring an integral part

Yorkshire Water Graduate Scheme

▶ Voluntary for mentors

▶ Mandatory for graduates

▶ Mandatory training for both parties

▶ Lifespan of 2 years

▶ Evaluation at 6-month intervals: questionnaires and group meetings

▶ Confidential relationship

▶ Emphasis of independence from usual line management processes

▶ Mentors to be offline; emphasis on experience rather than level

▶ Social events arranged by mentees

RWE Thames Water, High Potential Scheme

▶ Lifespan of 12–15 months

▶ Evaluation at 6-month intervals

▶ Mentors from senior executives and directors

▶ Linked in to succession planning

▶ Mentees involved in 360° feedback near programme end to define an ongoing development plan

A Graduate Scheme

▶ Compulsory element of the 2-year development scheme

▶ Confidential relationship

▶ Mentors to be at Senior Manager level or above; voluntary participation

▶ Meetings every 2 months, but to be flexible depending on mentee's needs

▶ Graduate is to 'own' the relationship and their own development

Figure 10.2 **Examples of the principles incorporated in various organisations' designs**

Planning

Everyone has different ways of going about planning and implementing a programme, but steps that might be considered once organisational commitment has been gained include these followed at B&Q:

> *Be careful to get things in the right order and to give yourself enough time to complete one stage before you try and start another. Also make sure you allow enough time to be able to get dates into people's diaries.*
>
> B&Q scheme manager

▶ Identification of mentors

▶ Potential mentees identified (via Management Development Review meeting)

▶ Invitation to Mentor Training Day

▶ Invitation to mentees to participate in an information session about the scheme

▶ Mentor Training Day

▶ Launch meeting for mentees

▶ Matching

▶ Mentee training and first meeting between pairs

▶ Three-month review.

Once the scheme is defined and an overall approach outlined, it is time to start thinking about what practical things may be needed to help to support the process itself and market the scheme. These may include:

▶ The roles and responsibilities of key stakeholders

▶ Resourcing levels necessary to support the proposed size of scheme

▶ Use of technology to promote and administer the scheme

▶ How to find volunteer participants and ensure their commitment

▶ Qualities to look for in mentors and mentees

▶ Guidelines on meeting frequency, length and location

▶ Suggestions for the first meeting and ongoing discussion topics

▶ How matching will be done; what will happen if relationships do not work

▶ What training will be required.

The Henley organisations found that it was necessary to provide guidance as to how often mentoring meetings should occur, how long they would typically last for and the best type of location for them. Sharing potential discussion topics with participants (generally during training) also helped to focus their minds on possible outcomes.

As part of managing the process and planning stage, it can be very useful to generate pro-formas to assist with the information-gathering process.

The example in Figure 10.3, from one of the Henley organisations, helps volunteers to structure their application and, at the same time, enhances commitment during the completion process.

Mentor Programme Volunteer Form   AVAYA

| Last Name: | | First Name: | | Location | |
| Job Title: | | Organisation: | | Phone No: | |

I can be a mentor: Immediately ☐   In 2-4 months ☐   In 6 months. – 1 year ☐

I have been a mentor previously: Yes ☐   No ☐

Number of mentees you are prepared to help [Ideal and Maximum 3] ☐

Please indicate with a ✓ the areas of expertise which you could provide in the mentoring relationship:

	Areas of Expertise	Comments
Client knowledge/focus		
Customer Services		
Knowledge of the business		
Adaptability/flexibility		
Collaboration		
Influence		
Courage		
Global focus/cultural sensitivity		
Change management		
Industry knowledge		
Sales/marketing		
Team building		
Leading teams		
Communication Skills		
Developing/analyzing policies		
Finance/accounting		
Personal interactions		
Project management		
Dealing with conflict		
Strategic planning		
Risk taking		
Career planning/development		
Other – please list:		

Please describe your current job responsibilities: _____
_____

Other comments you'd like to share: _____
_____

Return form to:

Figure 10.3 **Mentor programme volunteer form**

Roles and Responsibilities

Having defined how the process will work, it is useful to consider what role the participants will play and what their individual responsibilities will be. This means that when conversations begin with potential mentees/mentors, a clear picture can be painted for them as to what they will be expected to do. Roles to consider include the key players:

▶ Mentees

▶ Mentors

▶ Line managers

▶ Scheme manager.

Tables 10.1 and 10.2 and Figure 10.4 show how several organisations have specified the roles and responsibilities of the various stakeholders in the process.

Table 10.1 **RWE Thames Water's high-potential scheme**

Mentors will	Mentors will NOT
▶ Meet with mentees for confidential discussions ▶ Prompt mentees to draw up their own development plans ▶ Prompt mentees to make contact with others who might be able to provide useful information or advice ▶ Prompt mentees to approach their line managers to seek specific support for developmental activities	▶ Take action on behalf of mentees ▶ Intervene on behalf of mentees ▶ Expect to act as role models except in terms of applying the corporate values in all they do ▶ Take part in any succession planning discussions that relate to their own mentee ▶ Discuss the mentee with the line manager

Mentees will	Mentees will NOT
▶ Meet with mentors for confidential discussions ▶ Access other sources of information and advice as may seem appropriate ▶ Share information about their strengths, weaknesses, ambitions and so on openly with their mentor ▶ Take responsibility for drawing up their own development plans ▶ Take responsibility for appropriate contact with their line managers about development issues ▶ Initiate their own development	▶ Expect their mentor to take any direction on their behalf ▶ Attempt to force their line manager into account by quoting their mentor

Line Managers

▶ Will allow mentees time to attend mentoring sessions
▶ Will provide whatever support is feasible to the development of the mentee
▶ Will not attempt to talk to the mentor about the mentee

Table 10.2 **Roles and responsibilities defined in a Focus Group organisation's high-potential scheme**

MENTEE	MENTOR
Role: Learner and developer and driver of the relationship	**Role:** One of guidance and teaching, focusing on the mentee's future performance in more demanding, more senior roles
Responsibilities: ▶ Defining expectations and objectives for the relationship: having a planned outcome is critical to the success of the relationship ▶ Agreeing and managing the 'working process' (mentoring contract) ▶ Commitment to completing agreed development tasks without neglecting other responsibilities ▶ Being open and honest	**Responsibilities:** ▶ To encourage and motivate the mentee ▶ To agree and keep to a mentoring contract ▶ To manage normal work objectives and the mentoring relationships – especially time commitments ▶ To improve the mentee's breadth of knowledge and skills by providing a broader perspective of the organisation, its culture and strategies ▶ To help employees realise their career plans through development and experiential learning ▶ To ensure the key skills of counselling, coaching, facilitation and networking are up to date ▶ To ensure confidentiality of the relationship ▶ To agree with the employee a debrief for the local and organisational Development Committees
LINE MANAGER	

Responsibilities:
▶ Setting out and reviewing day-to-day performance objectives. This includes the identification and support of development activities – for example, coaching to rectify performance gaps

SCHEME MANAGER

Role:
To ensure the smooth running of the scheme

Responsibilities:
▶ To ensure top management – the organisation's – commitment
▶ To identify, match and brief potential participants
▶ To ensure confidentiality of the scheme
▶ To provide a 'ready ear' to all participants – giving guidance to ensure the relationships are productive
▶ To hold periodic reviews to ensure the effectiveness of the programme

---

Role of the Line Manager

The primary focus of a line manager is the performance of individual members of staff in their current post and their long-term career development. It is for this reason that line managers should recognise the benefits to a member of staff having a mentor outside the line management structure as this will enhance the individual's contribution to the team. It is important that there is as much openness and honesty as possible between the line manager, mentor and mentee without breaching the confidential nature of the mentoring relationship.

Figure 10.4 **Department for Work and Pensions: the role of the line manager in a mentoring scheme**

In addition, it may be useful to think about what role the organisation will play and whether champions can be used to help to promote and support the scheme. In some of our companies mentoring champions were used, mainly as an information source and local contact (see Chapter 9 for further information on using champions).

A key role of the organisation is to provide visible support and recognition that the scheme is an important part of employees' development. An example of this might be the attendance of the key organisational sponsor at a final, closing event for the programme – particularly if he or she is able to speak briefly about its value and outcomes.

Support Levels

Over the lifetime of the Henley Focus Group, several members reiterated the importance of not underestimating the level of support required by formal mentoring schemes – particularly in the first 12–24 months as the concept and process become embedded into the company.

The amount of time needed by the scheme manager will be less if he or she is able to involve the line in both the design and implementation of the mentoring scheme. Having line support has many advantages in that they understand better what will or will not work in their area or culture and can be the scheme manager's eyes and ears on a local basis. B&Q found that seeking line involvement resulted in a programme which was accepted and owned by that function, rather than it being seen as 'yet another HR programme' – a view which can often cause issues in launching new development initiatives.

An added dimension is that, in schemes supporting high-potential development, the mentees tend to be moved around the organisation frequently in order to give them new experiences and challenges. In large, multifaceted or global organisations, merely keeping up with such changes can take a tremendous amount of time – particularly where the mentee moves to a different continent and prefers to have a more local mentor. One scheme manager described it as being 'difficult to keep your finger on the pulse', which could probably be considered an understatement! In these situations, having locally based champions is invaluable.

Participants as Volunteers

In many of the Henley schemes the mentees are from an identified group such as graduates or high-potential/fast-track people; the mentors also come from a defined group such as the directorate or a divisional senior management team. In others, the scheme is open to all-comers. Whatever the scope, it has become abundantly apparent that any involvement should be on a completely voluntary basis, otherwise commitment will not be there and success is unlikely.

> *I am happy to do my bit. However, I am very conscious of the conflict between (a) the demands on my time and (b) the need to make this a success and formally establish it as part of how our business works.*
>
> Comment from a potential mentor

When looking at the process of finding volunteers, it is useful to have some marketing tools available, in whatever form has been selected to represent the scheme. As seen in the previous chapter, these may be a brochure, directions to a website or contact details for key sponsors or champions. Whatever the material, it needs to be readily available and consistent for everyone.

FINDING MENTORS

Questions that were commonly asked when scheme managers were talking to potential mentors include:

> *It is equally important that mentors are asked if they have a mentor and mentees are asked if they're mentoring anyone. Think of it as creating a mentoring chain (like house buying). People are always looking upwards for a mentor, but rarely think: 'Who can I mentor?'*
>
> Scheme manager – Zurich

▶ Deliverables: what are the outcomes and expectations?

▶ Relationships: who? Where do they fit?

▶ How would we be matched?

▶ What would you tell the mentee about me (confidentiality concerns)?

▶ What happens if we don't get on?

▶ How can I refuse/do I have a choice (this was linked to having confidence in the process)?

▶ Do I have the knowledge or experience?

▶ How much time will it take?

> *If you don't give the senior team a choice about being a mentor, I'd be very surprised if any of them felt they could say: 'Actually I don't feel I'm skilled enough to be a mentor, I'm not the right person'; of course they're going to agree.*
>
> Quote from a scheme manager

EXTERNAL VS INTERNAL MENTORS

Generally speaking, the scheme managers in the Henley Focus Group sourced mentors from within their organisations. However, situations could be envisaged where the need for going outside the company could be foreseen, and these included:

▶ The seniority of the mentee (for example, the person who mentors the MD)

▶ For specific professional help

▶ Where a mentee cannot find a mentor internally – perhaps they are seen as a 'problem employee'

▶ To support equality and diversity programmes

▶ To uncover best practice in other organisations/sectors through peer mentoring.

FINDING MENTEES

Any of the methods described earlier can be used.

Questions that potential mentees might ask and which need thinking through before approaching them include:

▶ Who would be my mentor?

▶ How would we be matched?

▶ How long would it last?

▶ What's in it for me?

▶ What would we talk about? How confidential would it be?

▶ Will they help with my career moves?

▶ What if we don't get on?

At B&Q, potential participants were invited by a personal letter from their functional director to attend an information session about the planned scheme (Figure 10.5).

Dear ...

For some time now we have been considering how we can better support the development of our highly talented team within the Division. As our challenges and targets get ever more stretching, this development needs to be sustained for the benefit of both the individual and the business.

With this in mind, I would like to take this opportunity to invite you to participate in a new scheme we are launching. Beginning in May, we intend to offer, to an initial group of people, the opportunity of having a Mentor. The Mentors will come from within the Division's management team.

In order to explain more about our plans and to answer any questions you may have about the scheme, we are holding an initial meeting on .... at ....

The scheme breaks new ground for us and we are all committed to making it a success and, hopefully, rolling it out further.

Figure 10.5 **Director's letter to potential mentees at B&Q**

The most novel approach in the group was at Avaya, where mentors advertised for mentees (Figure 10.6).

MENTOR SEEKS MENTEE!

Looking for close match or total opposite for two-way productive relationship!

On my side I can offer GSOH but I'm not a lightweight; I have some ideas that might be described as non-establishment but others might call innovative; I'm a pretty good listener and can empathise – but I try hard to be impartial.

[Box 12345]

ARE YOU TAKING CARE OF YOURSELF AT WORK?

Weary of the daily grind? Concerned about your future? Unsure of your career direction?

Why not take the opportunity to work with someone who would like to help?

As a mentor, I am here to devote some time to you.

Our conversations will be confidential and impartial, and are focused on helping you succeed.

I am an experienced and successful person and will aim to provide energy and creativity in helping you. I believe that the relationship will be most successful when based on mutual trust, honesty and integrity.

Over an agreed period of time we'll work towards your objectives, focusing and clarifying your direction to enable you to achieve your desired success.

Contact: ....

MENTOR
Available for personal coaching

What other mentees have said about me:

■ 'Has really helped me to see the way that I can develop my career.'
■ 'Has helped me to avoid falling into the same traps many times over.'

Do you experience these difficulties?

■ Don't know where your next career move is?
■ Have problems with people not delivering what whey should?
■ Are relationships with others holding you back from promotion?
■ Need to introduce internal change?

This mentor will help you to help yourself through:

■ Integrity
■ Confidentiality
■ Results orientation

Helping YOU to achieve YOUR goals!

Figure 10.6 **Advertising for mentees at Avaya**

Testing Commitment

Volunteers could easily be swept up in the 'I should/could do this' feeling and then back out later on. It is recommended that some way is found to test commitment after the initial 'yes, I'll do it', so that there is not a sudden with-drawal of mentor nominations at short notice before the planned launch of the programme. The latter was the experience of several scheme managers, where schemes were marketed internally in a high-profile way and there was pressure exerted to volunteer. Suggestions for dealing with this include:

▶ *Profiles, résumés and questionnaires*

Ask prospective mentors/mentees to write their own profile, specifically including a section on why they are volunteering and what they believe they can offer or are looking for. This will not only test commitment, but will help to ensure that the right people are recruited, as well as providing detailed information for use in matching.

▶ *Self-assessments*

Alternatively, ask mentors to complete a skills and attributes self-assessment questionnaire in order to provide a profile against which mentees can select (for an example, see Chapter 3 in *The Manager as Coach and Mentor* by Eric Parsloe, 1999).

▶ *Workshops*

The following three-step process is used by a Focus Group organisation to test the commitment of potential mentors:

1   Issue a general invitation to managers via an e-mail that includes criteria for mentors, attributes and brief details about the programme.

2   Write to the resulting volunteers, giving more detail of expectations, mentor characteristics and the process, and request confirmation of their willingness to participate.

3   Mandate attendance at a mentoring workshop prior to their being considered for final selection (an excellent way of testing commitment).

Mentor Qualities

Once volunteers have been found and commitment has been tested, it is then also essential to make sure that the basic skill requirements are in place – particularly for mentors. In any group, it will be quite likely that there will be one or two individuals (or more) who are not suited to the role of mentor without some significant coaching themselves on behavioural skills.

Criteria generated by the Focus Group give an indication of the basic skills and qualities deemed necessary in a mentor. A mentor is someone who:

▶ Listens

▶ Is an opposite

▶ Uses non-judgmental questioning

▶ Offers different perspectives

▶ Has specific knowledge

▶ Cares; is warm; wants to help

▶ Can relate to your issues

▶ Sees patterns

▶ Has experience

▶ Is trustworthy/ensures confidentiality.

Figures 10.7 and 10.8 are examples of criteria used for identifying potential mentors that have been developed by two Focus Group organisations.

MENTORS HAVE:

▶ Relevant job-related experience/skills

▶ Well-developed interpersonal skills

▶ An ability to relate well with people who want to learn

▶ A desire to help and develop mentees

▶ An open mind, flexible attitudes and recognition of own need for support

▶ Time and willingness to develop relationships with mentees

▶ Experience of facing difficulties, new challenges, being helped themselves, working with others, contributing, achievement/success/failure, being responsible for self/learning/trauma/setback, dealing with stress

THE MENTOR CAN HELP THE MENTEE TO:

▶ Understand appropriate behaviours in social situations

▶ Understand the workings of the organisation

▶ Acquire an open, flexible attitude to learning

▶ Understand different/conflicting ideas

▶ Be aware of organisational politics

▶ Overcome setbacks and obstacles   ▶ Acquire technical expertise

▶ Gain knowledge/skills   ▶ Develop personally

▶ Adjust to change   ▶ Develop values

Figure 10.7 **Extract from *The Mentoring Guide* (Zurich)**

What distinguishes the really effective mentor?   *Abbey*

▶ *Genuine care for the development of people*

▶ *Commitment to the work and success of the organisation and its goals*

▶ *Readiness to spend time and thought on the mentoring activity*

▶ *Knowledge of the organisation, its history, politics and culture*

▶ *Knowledge of how things really happen*

▶ *A desire to create and work in a relationship of trust and confidentiality on both sides*

Figure 10.8 **Identifying potential mentors at Abbey**

Participants at the EMC/SBS mentoring research conference [held in 1994] were asked to draw their own images of mentoring. From the range they drew, strong messages came about mentoring being about:

■ big ears, small mouth

■ finding the tune that the learner wants to play

■ harmonising the various contributors

■ being in the delivery room, supporting new growth

■ an upward, widening spiral

■ seeing life as a tree, with roots as deep as the branches are high

■ a 'Nellie', sitting alongside

■ a laser beam

■ a hand, a book and a boot

■ a pebble in a still pool sending out ripples that extend in space and time

Figure 10.9 **Extract from *Mentoring in Action* (Megginson & Clutterbuck, 1995)**

Mentee Qualities

It is also worthwhile thinking through the qualities that are desirable in a mentee: this information is a useful part of the training process as it helps mentees to understand a part of what is expected of them. Suggested mentee qualities, again generated during a Focus Group meeting, are shown below, followed by an example from a Focus Group organisation (Figure 10.10):

▶ Motivated

▶ Articulates expectations and own objectives

▶ Meets commitments

▶ Accepts feedback and acts on it

▶ Listens

▶ Self-aware

▶ Open

▶ Trustworthy

▶ Understands programme objectives/process.

What a mentor might look for in a mentee		
Skills	**Attributes**	**Knowledge**
Communication	Motivated	Preferred learning style
Influencing	Open	Expected outcomes
Time management	Committed	Roles within mentoring
Planning/organising	Trusting	Stages of the relationship
Objective setting	Empathetic	Cognisance of own strengths and weaknesses

Figure 10.10 **Mentee qualities defined by a Focus Group organisation**

Questions about finding the right participants were raised with the expert panel at a Henley meeting.

Practitioners' Problem-solving

Questions and Answers with David Megginson and David Clutterbuck

How important is it for mentors to be volunteers?

Very. A large retail organisation sent a memo round to all store managers saying that as of now you are a mentor, here is a one and a half page sheet telling you how to be a mentor. Of course it was a complete waste of time and it was almost impossible to get mentoring going in that company for a very long time afterwards. (DC)

How do you tell someone that they should not be a mentor?

So, when you put out the call a senior person in an organisation volunteers to be a mentor and you're the person whose career is on the line: what do you say if it is someone that you don't feel will be suitable? Invite everyone along to a mentor training session and once you have your pool of mentors you can say to them, well sorry, but actually we never found anyone that suits your particular talents.

If you are courageous enough you can allow them to come on the training session: they may learn something from it and then you counsel them. Indeed, the facilitator has a duty to counsel them and be upfront about their limitations. Most of the time people can tell that they wouldn't be suitable and it's often a relief to them; they may even find out they want to be a mentee. (DC)

Finally, whilst planning a mentoring scheme, it is worth considering what obstacles and issues may arise and have contingency plans and actions in place. One of the objectives of this book is to share the experiences of a number of existing mentoring scheme managers with prospective or new scheme managers, on the 'forewarned, forearmed' hypothesis. Given below are some of the practical steps for scheme managers to take and questions to ask when defining and implementing a mentoring scheme:

1   Define your process – how will people become involved? What stages will there be? How will you review it?

2   Identify roles and responsibilities – what will participants be expected to do?

3   Qualities – what should you be looking for in mentors and mentees?

4 What might occur that will disrupt relationships? What plans or strategies should be in place to deal with these?

5 How important will it be to have quality and consistency of mentors? How can we do this? Would they be interested in gaining some form of external certification?

6 Will technology and systems help to support the programme – if so what and how?

7 Marketing – how will you publicise the scheme and provide information to participants and others? How will you find volunteer mentors and mentees and ensure their commitment?

8 Support documents – what might people find useful to help them to get started? Will you provide pro formas – for example, of contracts?

9 Matching – what criteria for matching people will be best suited to your scheme and your organisation? Do you need a matching process? Will you need help in completing the matching – particularly if your scheme crosses boundaries?

10 Training/briefing – how will you inform participants about the process and give them the necessary skills? When will this best be done?

11 Guidelines – will it be helpful to provide a guide to meeting frequency, duration, location and discussion topics?

The majority of the points raised above have been discussed during this chapter; matching and training participants are covered in the following chapters.

Summary

When speaking at Henley about his leadership model, John Adair would emphasise a quote from his time with the armed forces at Sandhurst:

Time spent in reconnaissance is seldom wasted.

For a mentoring scheme to run effectively, and meet the expectations of the various stakeholders, it is essential, firstly, to define the process clearly and then to plan. Once a scheme is up and running – maybe a whole pilot scheme has worked through its entire lifecycle – then it is possible to become more relaxed and adopt other informal schemes, as identified in the original Henley Focus Group Model of Mentoring (see Chapter 4). For the first run of a scheme, tight definitions and thorough planning will pay off. This was a clear message from all the scheme managers involved in the Henley Group.

11 Matching

For many schemes, and scheme managers, the process of matching mentees with mentors is potentially one of the most problematic. There are many issues to consider around how the matching should be done, what criteria should be used, what happens if it does not work and how transparent the process should be. The topic of matching also appears in Part IV of this book, where it is considered from the perspective of the participants.

Matching Criteria

Possible criteria for the initial selection of pairs are given below; it may be necessary to use a combination of these or, alternatively, use self-selection. If, for example, the scheme is designed to support better cross-organisational communication, then 'cross-functional' and 'knowledge wanted vs knowledge offered' may be key criteria.

▶ Cross-cultural, that is, from different nationalities

▶ Cross-functional

▶ Gender alike or cross-gender pairings

▶ Similar or different experience/background

▶ Similar or different characters

▶ Knowledge wanted vs knowledge offered

▶ General 'wants' and 'offers' approach

▶ Profiling, for example MBTI®, emotional intelligence

▶ Learning styles

▶ Location, geography

▶ Tenure – long vs short

▶ Common interests (for example sports, hobbies).

> **Yorkshire Water's Criteria:**
>
> 1 Learning styles – using different styles
>
> 2 Cross-functional – for greater business awareness and networking
>
> 3 Business experience

When working with schools or young people, YELL found that other considerations came in to play:

▶ Police checks – for child protection reasons

▶ Personal circumstances, for example an absent parent

▶ Gender – while a woman may be matched with a boy, a man would never be matched with a girl.

> *My mentor was very good at questioning my thought process and working out why I had dealt with situations in the way I had. My mentor was more reflective than myself and we found that this was very complementary.*
>
> Yorkshire Water mentee

The Focus Group discussed various methods of matching and whether it was important to have similar or different styles and experiences. Having similar styles/experiences would lead to a 'comfortable' relationship, whereas having different styles/experiences would provide greater possibilities for learning and, perhaps, the biggest risk. Whatever the mix, provided the scheme's manager has a good reason for making the match, it should be valid to try it. (There was also a speculative discussion as to whether the results of tools such as an emotional intelligence questionnaire could provide an 'in' to having discussions with potential mentors who had poor interpersonal skills – a perennial problem.)

Matching using profiling/diagnostic tools, such as the Myers–Briggs Type Indicator® (MBTI), formed the basis of several group discussions at various times. The obvious thoughts were that matching like with like would make for easy, but not necessarily useful, relationships. Opposite matchings might prove difficult, unless the individuals were made aware that the differences were something that brought extra development opportunities to the whole mentoring relationship. The most agreed use of such instruments in the matching process was for something like the MBTI® (and this was by far the most popular instrument used). It was also used to open up dialogue around interpersonal issues which might otherwise be more difficult. To achieve this, several organisations included a session on the instrument used in a mentoring training day, run for both mentors and mentees, so that there was sufficient understanding of how to make use of the information available, in a mentoring situation. This was felt to be well worthwhile.

> **RWE Thames Water Matching Criteria:**
>
> 1 Location
>
> 2 Business experience
>
> 3 Compatibility (not 'chumminess') – established through MBTI® and EI tools.

Where schemes cross boundaries of some kind, for example in cross-functional, regional, European or global schemes, it will be unlikely that the person doing the matching has personal knowledge of every participant. Where this was experienced, for example in a pan-European scheme, local knowledge was used to help do the matching, that is, local HR and training/development staff from different geographical locations pooled knowledge and worked together to complete the matching.

Matching Process

The process for doing the matching also needs consideration, this means:

▶ Will mentees have a choice of mentors or will the pairs be assigned?

▶ If there is a choice, how will the choosing process work – self-selection, preferred option, direct match?

▶ Will matching requests be invited (such as for specific experience)?

Some of the Henley organisations took the route of offering an element of choice wherever possible (Zurich, Avaya, RWE Thames Water), while others worked with pairs matched by the programme manager (Smiths Group, YELL, B&Q). All participants were reported as wanting to know how the matching was done, so it is important to be clear about the method used. Including this detail as part of the scheme's training/guidelines/process/general information is recommended.

Methods used for the matching process amongst Focus Group members included the following:

▶ *Blind dating*

If the situation allows, it can be possible to offer mentees a choice of mentors. This was the case in one of our Focus Group organisations, where the process used was one of 'blind date' matching. To avoid the temptation to reject mentors because of reputation or simply knowing nothing about them, mentees were shown mentors' résumés, from which all identifying sections had been removed. The ability to make a choice from two 'blind' profiles was received very positively and, in 90 per cent of cases, the scheme manager's preferred choice of mentor was accepted by the mentee. In other organisations, this approach did not work.

> *It's an ideal match, I can see a lot of value.*
> Mentee in a global organisation

▶ *Exploratory meetings*

At Avaya, the programme coordinator linked a mentee with two potential mentors; all parties were then advised of the possible matching. It was then the responsibility of the mentee to contact the two potential mentors for a short initial meeting, the objective of which was to find the best fit for both parties. Ideally this would be completed within four weeks of notification and the programme coordinator advised of the result.

> *I just went for the first [mentor] on the list. It helped to know that I didn't have to stay with that person – but as it turns out they are fine.*
>
> Avaya mentee

▶ *Database*

Mentees are able to select from a database made available on the internet.

Other approaches were often more individualistic, with personal approaches being made to individuals, and relationships being 'brokered' on a one-to-one basis. This can work well, but only in a small scheme, and it can be subjective, time-consuming and very frustrating.

Figures 11.1, 11.2 and 11.3 show some examples of company forms used at this stage of the process.

ZURICH SENIOR MENTORING PROGRAMME
MENTOR/MENTEE PROFILE
STRICTLY CONFIDENTIAL

Please complete this form if you are volunteering to act as a mentor, or looking to be mentored, or both.
Section 1 should be completed in all cases – Section 2 is for mentors only.

SECTION 1 - to be completed in all cases

NAME:
AGE:
CURRENT ROLE & TIME IN POSITION:
LOCATION:

EDUCATION & QUALIFICATIONS:
(Including particular skills such as fluency in foreign languages)

WORK EXPERIENCE:
(Including details of any training, other jobs/roles, other areas/departments worked in, other organisations)

LIFE INFORMATION:
(Including interests, achievements, goals, ambitions)

ASSESSMENT OF STRENGTHS:
(Technical, interpersonal/leadership, functional/organisational, start-up, turnaround, operational, specialist)

SECTION 2 - to be completed if you are volunteering to act as a mentor

PARTICULAR STRENGTHS YOU BELIEVE YOU COULD OFFER A MENTEE:
(e.g. ability to listen, encourage, challenge, debate, empathise, provide knowledge and expertise, support, coach)

ISSUES YOU WOULD PARTICULARLY WANT TO FOCUS ON INITIALLY WITH A MENTEE:

DOWN TO WHAT LEVEL (IF ANY) WOULD YOU BE PREPARED TO MENTOR COLLEAGUES? (Eg A5 and above):
Would you be prepared to mentor one of our graduates?

ANY OTHER INFORMATION OF RELEVANCE:

Figure 11.1 **Pro forma used at Zurich**

MENTORING RÉSUMÉ ~ MENTOR DETAILS	
Name	
Organisation	
Role	
Contact Details (Address, telephone, fax, e-mail)	
Do you personally use a PC on a daily basis?	Yes/No
MBTI® (Myers-Briggs) type, if known	
Summary of Functional areas worked in (eg Marketing, Sales)	
Areas of Key Experience (roles)	
Activities or experiences which have proved most beneficial to your personal development/ career progression	
Describe what strengths you will bring to a mentoring relationship	

Figure 11.2 **Pro forma used in a pan-European scheme**

Mentee Personal Profile

Name: ....

Who I am : Something about my background ...

5 words which I feel describe me are ...

The things I would like as a Mentee ...

The things I don't want as a mentee ...

Other things about me: (Hobbies, Interests, Experiences etc.) ...

Figure 11.3 **Pro forma used at B&Q**

And if it Doesn't Work …

One of the first things many mentors and mentees say to their scheme managers when the matching process begins is, 'what happens if it doesn't work?' There is a natural reluctance on the part of participants to 'reject' someone with whom they have been paired and yet, at the same time, the chance to have a mentoring relationship is often seen as very precious and it must be 'right'.

The experience of the Henley Group members is that the anticipated problems are often much worse than the actuality once the relationship is under way. As can be seen from some of the quotes in this chapter, many people who feared that they would not get on with the individual with whom they had been paired went on to have a fruitful relationship.

The way in which the expectations are set is one area where the scheme manager can exercise some control over this situation. If concerns are acknowledged, and the matching process is framed within the context of learning from people different from yourself, this can make the recipients more flexible.

However, it is important there is a very clear message that if either party in a mentoring relationship is not comfortable with the way it is going, for whatever reason, they can talk to someone about this and something can be done. All the schemes run by members of the Focus Group had this facility in place. The interventions that were made tended to be one of two kinds: either facilitation of a mentoring meeting occurred, to enable the two participants to work through any difficulties and then continue with the existing pairing; or, where this was not appropriate, then the 'no blame' divorce process was invoked by the scheme manager. This relieved either participant of the potentially embarrassing prospect of having to terminate a relationship personally. Appropriate debriefing was always given to both parties, where a relationship was terminated, to ensure that the individual concerned understood why it had not worked on this occasion, but that on other occasions yet to come, they could be a very effective mentor (or mentee). This was seen as an important part of managing the whole image of mentoring in an organisation – so that it is positioned as a developmental experience, whatever happens, not something at which it is possible to 'fail'.

We have made it very clear that people can come back to us if they feel the relationship isn't working – the door is wide open.

B&Q mentoring champion

If the mentoring scheme is backed up with clear 'process', and this is introduced at the outset, then this takes a lot of the anxiety out of the matching stage, for both mentor and mentee. There needs to be a formal stage where the two parties who have been matched together agree that it is useful and state that they want to proceed. It should not be assumed that everything will go ahead unless someone makes a fuss – many people will not want to 'make a fuss', but if there is a problem that is not surfaced and dealt with at the start, then it can undermine the whole process later on. The key part to this is to allow each party to run through a checklist with a third party (often the scheme manager), to ensure that the person with whom they have been paired meets their personal criteria. Frequently this may not always happen, but the important part is that in the introduction to mentoring, the idea of having personal criteria to be satisfied, through the mentoring process, needs to be made clear to the participants. This will then enable individuals to explain why they do not want to work with the person with whom they have been matched, without the need to become too personal in their rejection of them.

Summary

There are obviously many different ways of matching people, but the useful message from the Henley Group is that if there is a formal structure, with supporting documentation in place, it makes the whole process a lot more straightforward. It also makes the process seem more objective and takes away some of the personal concerns about whether people will 'like' each other, which can appear to form the basis of decision-making unless something objective is put in place.

12 Training Participants

There is a lot of anecdotal evidence that formal training of mentors and mentees has been an important part of many successful mentoring schemes. As well as specific skills development opportunities, training sessions have also provided the forum for commonly held concerns and questions to be acknowledged and dealt with. The formal bringing together of all participants of a new mentoring scheme (whether mentors and mentees are trained together or separately is another decision to be made) allows the overall context of the scheme to be set, and for general messages from the organisation to be made.

Whether or not to run formal training sessions for mentors, mentees, and sometimes other stakeholders, such as line managers, was an issue upon which the practice of the Henley companies varied considerably.

Where mentors were senior managers/executives, use of words such as 'training' and 'soft skills' was found to be counterproductive and not at all recommended. A more fruitful approach was to engage them in dialogue, perhaps in small groups of three or four, posing questions such as: 'How do you get your knowledge and experience across in a way that's really going to help someone else?'

Most senior managers were very interested and keen to take part in such activities, seeing them as a key part of the new venture in which they were involved.

Where there are actual skills-related training needs, such as in some of the interpersonal behaviours, then these issues were definitely reported as best handled early on, as part of the mentor selection process itself. Once someone is on board as a mentor, it can be very difficult, and sometimes quite negative, to start suggesting, for example, that the person might need to polish up on his or her listening skills before starting.

Research has shown that relationships are three times more likely to succeed if both mentee and mentor are trained. The way in which this is done needs to fit in with the situation at the time. In the previous chapter, we talked about how using a diagnostic such as the Myers–Briggs Type Indicator® for mentors and mentees has proved useful for some organisations. This is obviously not possible, or even desirable, for all organisations, but such an activity can be usefully built in to a mentoring training day, in appropriate situations. Alternatively, a training day can be a purely pragmatic information-giving session and a formal statement about the start of the mentoring programme, for example. Topics that could be included are shown in Figure 12.1. A point worth stressing here is that, during training

Topics to consider including during training or briefing sessions include:

▶ The scheme itself: purpose, objectives and process (including matching)
▶ Mentor/mentee roles and responsibilities
▶ Equality of the relationship
▶ Contracting
▶ Support available
▶ Disengaging
▶ Essential values and beliefs for mentoring
▶ Coaching and facilitation skills
▶ Interpersonal skills: giving and receiving feedback; building rapport; questioning techniques; listening skills
▶ Learning styles
▶ Business skills, for example problem-solving
▶ Roles plays – 'what if' scenarios
▶ Q&A
▶ Models and tools for mentors
▶ Diagnostic tools – Myers–Briggs Type Indicator®, emotional intelligence, 360^0 feedback, career anchors inventory, and so on

Figure 12.1 **Topics to include during training/briefing sessions**

sessions, there was usually a request to know how matching of the pairs would be or had been carried out – so it is an aspect that should be included.

At B&Q, there were initially no plans to train the mentees. However, during the mentor training, a strong feeling emerged that this should be done and, as a result, a mentee training day was included.

Some scheme managers used individual or group briefings, together with written booklets, as a means of ensuring that participants understood the process and what was expected of them. Generally speaking, the mentees were more willing to undergo classroom training than mentors, particularly where the latter were senior managers or executives.

Examples of training programme agendas used in some of the Henley organisations are given towards the end of the chapter.

Training Line Managers and Others

A further thought in the Focus Group was: 'What about including the line managers in the training?' This would give them a much fuller understanding of the process and, as a result, they would feel less threatened and better able to support the scheme. If this was not possible, then some other means of educating the line managers about what to expect was agreed upon as a good course of action – particularly if mentoring was to be included within the normal performance management process administered by the line manager.

In one organisation, the mentors came from the executive board and received individual briefings about the scheme prior to starting out.

However, as the pairs progressed, it became evident that it would have been extremely helpful to have briefed the mentors' assistants about the scheme and the planned relationship between the executive and the mentee, as difficulties over meetings and keeping in contact would have been alleviated.

Training Process

If the training route is taken, then training both mentors and mentees may be part of the plan and the idea of training them together is one to consider. Joint training might sound rather awkward, but a number of organisations have found that this has been a successful approach. The scheme manager either ran the day, or was available to take questions about the process, and line

> *A big win we had was on the mentee training day during which the matched pairs met for the first time. Some mentors came in from their holidays, determined not to let their potential mentee have no-one there for them. So, every mentee had their mentor there; that was incredibly powerful.*
>
> B&Q scheme manager

managers or senior managers also made time available, on some occasions, to show support and reinforce the importance of mentoring to the business.

If the participants are distributed over a wide geographical area and face-to-face training is not a viable option, then it might be possible to run appropriate training via e-learning. This could either be via a website with chat room facilities, interactively and live, using a package such as PlaceWare, or by using a self-study package delivered by CD or over the network. The latter may be a useful option where, for example, several different languages are involved; for third parties such as line managers; or for mentors to refresh their skills.

One important tip mentioned by several scheme managers is not to leave too long a gap between training and completing the matching, so that the first meeting can take place fairly quickly after the training. The longer the gap, the more distant the training becomes and support may be needed to facilitate the first meeting.

Comments from participants following a mentoring training day:

▶ Include a session from a current mentor to share experiences

▶ Particularly liked the idea of the contract/first meeting agenda; it will provide me with the necessary groundwork to keep me and my mentee on track!

▶ The 'summary of the process the mentees go through' was very useful

▶ Include feedback from previous mentees

▶ I appreciated the additional information provided during breaks and syndicate exercises, for example background to the initiative and progress to date

Department for Work and Pensions

Figures 12.2–12.5 are examples of training agendas used by the Focus Group members.

MENTOR WORKSHOP Prepared by Clutterbuck Associates	
DAY 1	**DAY 2**
Purpose of the programme What is mentoring? Mentoring in the organisation Stages in Mentoring How to get the most from each stage How Mentors help others How do Adults learn? How do people learn in business? What makes a good mentor	Review Mentor Skills – advanced techniques Working through practical situations (goal setting, action planning, reviewing/progressing action plans, difficult situations) Matching Next steps Summary & close

Figure 12.2 **Training agenda used in a privatised utility**

MENTOR BRIEFING

1.	Introduction Establish previous experience of formal/facilitated programmes
2.	Summary of key points in briefing booklet (sent for reading prior to meeting) – purpose; objectives; benefits; target community; success criteria

3.	Key points made to mentees:
	– what mentoring isn't/is; not answers or direct sponsorship; confidentiality
	Key words:
	   mutual trust/respect; confidentiality; sounding board; pull & stretch;
	   commitment

4.	Benefits to Mentor
5.	Matching process – mentee needs/objectives vs mentor experience Timings
6.	Support and help available: 'ready ear'; disengagement; website; skill refreshers Link back to leadership programme/high potential development context

Figure 12.3 **Topics covered when briefing senior executives in a pan-European scheme**

Programme outline for the Avaya Mentoring Programme

(prepared by Henley Management College)

Day One: Objectives:

▶ To establish a clear understanding of the Avaya Mentoring Programme, processes and critical success factors
▶ To build an active network of Avaya mentors
▶ To review 'best practice' and introduce effective tools and techniques
▶ To begin developing interpersonal skills to increase mentors' scope for handling different mentoring requirements

This day will begin with a review of mentoring in Avaya, and an up-date on issues relevant to the mentors in their current stage of mentoring. Time will be spent looking at mentoring 'contracts', and the success factors for the programme. The second part of the day will involve practical exercises designed to give mentors more tools and techniques to use in their mentoring relationships. The day will end with the completion of a personality questionnaire, which will provide information for use in Day Two.

Day Two: Objectives:

▶ To raise participants' awareness of their interpersonal style and impact, using personality questionnaire data (Myers–Briggs Type Indicator®)
▶ To increase the range of behavioural flexibility in participants, to widen the range of possible mentoring relationships
▶ To develop skills to help with understanding the responses you get from other people
▶ To introduce the topic of Emotional Intelligence, and give participants the opportunity to get feedback from others on their behaviours in this context

The second day will largely focus on personal skills development and self-awareness, with the aim of making it easier for participants to deal with a wide range of different people and situations in mentoring relationships. This will include techniques for managing difficult situations, or conflict.

Day Three: Objectives:

▶ To use the Emotional Intelligence feedback data to identify areas for personal development to improve mentoring skills
▶ To investigate the role of mentoring in building the company culture
▶ To broaden understanding of mentoring including executive coaching and peer mentoring
▶ To review the success criteria for mentoring in Avaya, to make it measurable and core to the business

The final day of the programme will further develop the personal skills and self-awareness theme. The day will then broaden out the topic of mentoring, and look at other ways in which participants may consider using their skills. This will link into the company-related issues of culture and using mentoring at the core of the business to strengthen business success. A structure to continue the networking and support amongst mentors will be set up at the end of the day, to ensure the process continues.

Figure 12.4 **Avaya mentoring programme**

Overview of B&Q's Training Programme

(prepared by Creativedge Training and Development)

Session 1: Introduction	Welcome and Introductions Aims and Objectives Setting the Scene for Today
Session 2: What is Mentoring?	Your perceptions of mentoring Mentoring definitions What it takes to be a great mentor Building mentor credibility
Session 3: Mentoring Benefits	Benefits of mentoring 12 habits of the ineffective mentor
Session 4: Mentoring Perspectives	Mentoring v coaching? Key roles of a mentor Line manager v mentor?
Session 5: The Mentoring Process	Objectives of the B&Q Mentoring Programme – key dates/phases and so on How mentees have been selected How mentors and mentees will be matched Clarity: a Mentoring Charter The 5C Model of Mentoring – overview The mentor's road map
Session 6: Key Mentor Skills	What it takes to be an effective mentor – knowledge, skills and attitudes Core mentoring skills explored (communication, questioning, listening, building rapport, perception)
Session 7: Mentoring in Action	Practising Individual review of mentor strengths/ development needs Group review and discussion of outcomes
Session 8: Mentor Profiles	Develop 1 page self-profile
Session 9: Mentor Troubleshooting	Identify potential problems/issues in mentoring relationships and develop strategies to overcome 9 scenarios to use
Session 10: Summary and Next Steps	Review of workshop content Key learning points Clarification of next steps, responsibilities and timescales Evaluation and Close

Figure 12.5 **B&Q's training programme**

These examples are illustrations of the kind of ground that different organisations have thought important to cover with their participants before commencing mentoring activities.

There is rarely enough time on any of these training sessions to go into detail about skills development which might have been identified as necessary for certain individuals before they will make good mentors. This type of intervention would need to be addressed on an individual basis; alternatively, if it was felt that some basic refresher training on active listening, rapport building, questioning techniques for mentoring and so on would be useful for the whole mentor group, then a separate workshop could be arranged. The content of the types of training programme outlined above, however, is focused around ensuring a shared understanding of the reasons for the mentoring scheme, a thorough understanding of expectations and the 'contractual' details between mentor and mentee, and the success criteria for the scheme.

Summary

The actual details about a particular mentoring scheme are variable, company to company, context to context. The most important thing scheme managers can do, once they have the stakeholders' wishes incorporated into a workable model, is to ensure that the expectations of the key parties – usually the mentors, the mentees and the line managers – are all aligned. The chances of success of any scheme are greatly enhanced if care has been taken over this point, whether during a training programme or individual briefings.

The Focus Group members all believed that training was essential for both mentors and mentees and that including the line managers in some way was almost as important. How the training was done varied considerably – from half-day to two-day programmes or by an hour's personal briefing. The critical thing was that all parties had a common understanding of the scheme, its process and the roles of the various participants – including that of the scheme manager.

13 Maintaining, Concluding and Developing the Scheme

Introduction

This chapter offers a chance to look at the various hurdles which may need to be cleared when a mentoring scheme is up and running. It also covers the later part of a scheme's lifecycle and proffers ideas for how schemes can be drawn to a formal conclusion, whilst addressing demand for the next one. Finally, it examines how a scheme can develop and grow, as mentoring becomes part of an organisation's culture.

Each of these stages benefits from formal planning and, maybe also, contingency planning. This can be particularly important, as it is not easy at the beginning of a scheme to know if mentoring is going to take off in an organisation in the anticipated way. Experience shows that the results can often be surprising – mentoring can take off in an organisation where it was expected that it would be an uphill climb, or it can fall flat when least expected, due to lack of stakeholder support. It is as well, therefore, to have plans for a range of possible ongoing scenarios. This means that it should be possible to respond, in an appropriate way, to whatever the demand for mentoring is, rather than having a 'one size fits all' approach, which tends not to work.

A common finding amongst members of the Henley Group was that a mentoring scheme developed organically over its lifetime and, by the end of the formal time span, it bore little resemblance to its original conception. The way in which news of a successful scheme can spread throughout a company, and generate requests to set up additional schemes on a 'me too' basis, was also something which had caught practitioners off guard. The final section of the chapter covers this important area of growing and developing a mentoring scheme.

Maintaining the Scheme

The main activities required from the scheme manager at this stage are those of supporting the mentees, mentors and line managers. Setting up formal

(reviews) or informal (e-mails, phone calls and so on) communication mechanisms for getting regular feedback makes it possible to keep in touch with
how things are going and find out quickly when an intervention might be
needed. Asking for volunteers to write short articles for the website or
newsletter is one way of gaining information.

Ways in which the scheme manager might be required to intervene could
include:

▶ helping pairs through possible or actual disengagement

▶ assisting mentors when discussions move beyond their confidence level

▶ encouraging progress reviews

▶ arranging skills training where needed.

This is a time when visible and active support will reap dividends.

What can cause a scheme to collapse? Probably the most commonly
quoted reason would be that scheme managers took their eye off the ball. If
running the scheme is not their only responsibility, then it is worth setting
specific time aside daily, weekly and monthly to dedicate to the mentoring
scheme, rather than expect to fit it in whenever the opportunity arises.

Examples of events encountered by the Focus Group which can interrupt
the smooth running of a mentoring scheme include:

▶ Budget restrictions midway through the programme. This occurred in
one organisation shortly after the programme began; however, an inbuilt
e-mentoring strategy meant it was not as significant an issue as it might
have been. One pair successfully established a relationship via video-
conferencing, e-mail and so on, following an initial face-to-face meeting.

▶ Organisational restructuring or ordinary job moves may cause difficulties
where participants move to different locations and it becomes difficult to
meet.

▶ Mentors who may be getting out of their depth, for example moving into
what is really a professional counselling situation.

It is also useful to be constantly on the look out for new mentors: this may
include suggesting to responsive mentees that it is a role they could progress
on to.

DISENGAGING

A concern present in the minds of many mentoring scheme managers is:
'What if the members of the pair are unable to get on?' To cater for this
eventuality, the scheme's design should include the ability to dissolve the

relationship through mutual agreement and it helps to relieve participants' anxieties if this is made clear to all those involved from the outset.

If, for any reason, the relationship is not achieving its objectives and is not being productive, then the opportunity should be there to disengage without prejudice. Although the scheme manager will be available to provide support in any such instance, the first step should be for the parties involved to have an open and frank discussion about the causes, to see if they can be resolved.

In one high-potential scheme, pairs are asked to try and make the relationship work for six months on the basis that the mentees will need to be able to manage all types of relationships during the course of their career. If there is no progress at the end of that time, they are asked to give specific reasons and examples as to why not.

Alternatively, a relationship may have run its natural course and disengagement is the accepted next stage. Depending on the context of the scheme and their individual objectives, the scheme manager may need to find a mentee a number of different mentors during the defined term of the scheme, for example where they are working towards a professional qualification.

A rematching may also need to occur if either party changes roles, moves locations or leaves the organisation and continuing the existing relationship becomes impracticable.

During the middle section of the mentoring lifecycle, these are potential activity areas for scheme managers:

1 *Discussion topics* – do mentees have a clear idea of what they want/what their goals are or will suggestions be helpful?

2 *Questioning skills* – do mentors need help with these?

3 *Training* – do participants need more formalised help – particularly where an initial training programme was not possible? Are there skills they could do with having refreshers on?

4 *Practical meeting management* – how can the pairs be helped to make best use of their time? What practical tools could they have?

5 *'I'm out of my depth'* – is there access to specialist skills?

6 *E-mentoring* – would it help to encourage more frequent contact via methods other than face-to-face meetings?

7 *'It's not working'* – what strategies are in place for these circumstances? Is there a 'pool' of mentors to draw from?

8 *Reviewing* – how will you find out how everything is going – what formal and/or informal communication lines need to be set up?

9 *Line managers* – how are they reacting to the programme?

The best way of keeping a scheme running on track is to seek regular feedback, not only from the participants, but also from other stakeholders such as the line managers and the sponsor(s). Evaluation is covered in more detail in Chapters 14 and 22, but it cannot be separated out from the successful maintenance of the programme in hand.

ISSUES AND CONCERNS

This section contains the output from a number of group sessions, with contributions from scheme managers from a wide range of organisations. This is really 'core content' from the coalface: the issues which can arise and which a mentoring scheme manager has to deal with are almost limitless in number, but the main areas of common concern are covered here.

Regular meetings

How do to scheme managers keep track of whether meetings are actually taking place, especially if the mentoring pairs are based remotely from them?

It is essential for the scheme manager to keep in regular contact with participants. Doing this informally enables any problems to be picked up before they become a serious impediment to progress, but it is a time-consuming part of the job. Formal checks at three- or six-monthly intervals will give you more factual information – this can be by questionnaire or short workshops with mentors and mentees.

In a global scheme, technology can provide a useful medium to help with this issue – setting up a web-based 'chat room' for participants, organising a teleconference for mentors or mentees and setting up e-mail distribution lists will all provide a quick and easy means of getting in touch. Locally based champions may also prove invaluable in keeping up to speed with developments and we cover this role in more detail later in the chapter.

Keeping on track

Are the discussions still focused on meeting the defined objectives of both the mentee and the organisation, or have they strayed onto more social topics?

Setting clear expectations and gaining buy-in at the outset are important factors in ensuring that participants understand what the scheme is there to do and see a value in participating.

Whilst there is a social/rapport-building element to any session, it is

> *I ask my mentees to come with objectives to each meeting and at the end we score how well we've achieved each objective out of 1–5. If the overall scores drop to an average of 3 or under, then we've probably reached the end of the relationship as I've stopped being of use.*
>
> Avaya mentor

rarely the intention of the organisation that subjects such as improving golf handicaps should be the focus of a meeting! Discussion of objectives is an important issue for the first or second meeting, and these should be reviewed on a regular basis.

Discussion of work–life balance will frequently arise – it is one of the critical issues that has emerged for organisations over the last 10 years. Mentors are often invaluable in helping mentees to think through the consequences of their work–lifestyle and so help to lessen the stress. A payoff here is that such discussions may also cause mentors to examine and adjust their own working practices.

Line managers

How are they reacting to the scheme? Do they understand properly how it works and how it could benefit them? Do they want to become a mentor themselves?

There has been a constant theme in this book about the importance of involving line managers, right from the start. This can be done in many ways: from the stage of planning and gaining commitment to the scheme; during training; by including mentoring in the performance management process; asking them to give feedback on changes in performance; and by sharing overall outcomes with them and involving them at the end of the cycle. Line managers who see positive results in their employees may be encouraged to become mentors themselves. It would be worth extending an invitation to them each time new mentors are needed.

Achievements

What success stories can be shared with the participants and organisation as the scheme progresses?

If a formal and informal review process has been put in place, it should be possible to track whether or not the scheme is on course, in an ongoing way. As part of this, it will also be possible to uncover other benefits ensuing from the mentoring process, such as improved cross-boundary relationships, better cultural interaction, or an increase in the pace of change. This is not only good PR for the mentoring scheme, it is good for the business. It would be beneficial to summarise the benefits from the scheme on a regular basis and feed them into appropriate management reports, company newsletters and so on. This again helps to embed mentoring into an organisation's culture and encourages other areas of the business to consider it worth the investment.

Supporting the scheme

Is the scheme still manageable with current resource levels? Are offshoot schemes starting up with no real structure and support behind them?

When mentoring schemes work well and there are visible results, other employees may want to be included or other departments/functions may see the value of such a scheme. This is the stage at which careful thought needs to be paid as to how to manage an expansion. This topic will be addressed in more detail later in this chapter. The important point to make here is that the more clearly the process has been mapped out and thought through for the first scheme, and the more 'champions' that have been created as a result of an effective scheme, the easier it will be to control and support mentoring as it takes off in the organisation.

Flexibility

Equally, is the relationship flexible enough to change objectives if circumstances warrant it?

Opportunities or crises may arise for the mentees at any time and it requires flexibility on both sides to recognise this and adjust the focus so that mentors can help their mentees through major decision points. Covering this possibility during the training or briefing helps to manage the actuality. The mentoring relationship is there primarily to help the mentee – if the mentee's priorities or focus changes, the mentoring relationship should be a valuable part of the support mechanism for the mentee. This can only be the case if the mentor understands, and is willing, to be flexible and adjust objectives and agenda to suit the circumstances.

Mentors moving roles or taking on added responsibilities

Can a mentoring relationship survive the changes?

Where mentors are within six months of starting a new role, major project, assignment or significant added responsibilities, it is recommended that they do not take on a mentoring role. They almost certainly will not have the time to devote to it, however committed and however good their intentions.

This is an eventuality that can occur at any time within an established mentoring relationship and is best handled by a proactive discussion between mentor and mentee. The main options to discuss would be whether it would be more appropriate to help the mentee to find a new mentor or, alternatively, how best to handle the new challenges the mentor faces while maintaining the relationship.

Quality and consistency of mentors

How do you measure this? How do you set the standards and raise awareness and skill levels?

Training is a key factor in ensuring that mentors know how the scheme works and what is expected of them. It enables the scheme to begin with a fairly level playing field. Where training has not occurred, the effectiveness of the scheme will have been compromised.

Seeking feedback, formal and informal, as often as is practical allows a picture to be built up of how relationships are progressing and where mentors may need guidance or skill refreshment. Sharing experiences and best practice during group sessions with mentors can be a valuable way of improving their effectiveness.

The option of measuring mentors in some way is also available; for example, the success of the relationship and achievement of the business-related objectives could be criteria which were quantified and reviewed with the participants. This, in turn, may result in mentors looking for some form of recognition for this activity – monetary or otherwise.

Over recent years qualifications have been developed for mentors and this may be a route some wish to pursue. In 2002, the UK's Chartered Institute of Personnel and Development (CIPD) launched a Certificate in Coaching and Mentoring. Completed over seven months, the flexible structure of the programme includes a personal coach-mentor, learning sets, peer mentoring and feedback, skills coaching and knowledge-based materials.

Other UK-based qualifications in mentoring include an MA in Coaching and Mentoring Practice at Oxford Brookes University; an MSc in Mentoring and Coaching from Sheffield Hallam University; and the Oxford School of Coaching and Mentoring offers Diplomas in Professional Coaching and Mentoring and in Senior Executive Coaching and Mentoring.

Figure 13.1 provides further information about the Certificate and is taken directly from the internet; further information can be obtained from the CIPD website – see Chapter 25 for details.

Today more than ever, coaching and mentoring is the preferred method for implementing development programmes. For individuals and organisations alike it is effective in accelerating learning and raising performance levels.

The Certificate in Coaching and Mentoring has been developed by the CIPD, in association with the Oxford School of Coaching and Mentoring (OSC&M), to enable organisations and individuals alike to harness the potential that effective coaching and mentoring offers.

The programme provides students with a thorough understanding of the theory and practice of coaching and mentoring using a blended mixture of face-to-face, distance and online learning methods. The rigorous qualification process incorporates the techniques, tools, standards and ethics essential for effective, high quality professional coaching and mentoring.

The Certificate complies with the national occupational standards issued by the Employment National Training Organisation (EMPNTO) and the professional code of ethics and standards developed by the European Mentoring and Coaching Council (EMCC).

A key benefit of the Certificate programme is the highly practical focus on 'learning by doing'. Students work with 'learners' for the duration of the programme to develop their own coaching and mentoring expertise. They also undertake regular coach-mentoring sessions with their own personal coach-mentor. The students on both programmes also attend seminar days and work online to exchange and explore ideas and issues with peers, based on their own coaching and mentoring experience.

There is also the benefit of being very flexible – students are guided through a structured programme yet are able to undertake both study and practice at a time and pace that suits them.

Figure 13.1 **Overview of the CIPD Certificate in Coaching and Mentoring**

Dealing with difficult personal situations

Personal crises such as bereavement, divorce, maternity/paternity leave

Ensuring that mentors and mentees understand the boundaries of the role is essential. In addition, an uninvolved third party, for example the scheme manager or a professional counsellor, should provide a 'ready ear' and support the mentor in handling a given situation in the best way. This is often an area of key concern for mentors and potential mentors who do not feel qualified, or comfortable, dealing with difficult personal matters in a mentoring relationship. It should be made explicit in the initial training or briefing of both mentors and mentees that counselling is a specialist skill, and provision can be made separately for this should the need arise. It is not appropriate for a mentor either to offer, or feel pressured into providing, this type of intervention. Sympathy and friendly support should be the limit of the mentor's role in this area.

Maternity leave is an issue that arose for a mentor in one of our organisations: however, it was not seen as a major issue and the pair proactively discussed the mentor's forthcoming absence. They agreed a development and action plan for the mentee to work on during the absence and the mentor was open to the mentee contacting them at home.

Mentors not wanting to be outshone by their mentees

Where the mentor starts to feel threatened by the success of their mentee, and the temptation to give advice

In some, thankfully rare, instances a mentor may feel unsettled by the apparent success of the mentee as a result of their relationship. For example, in a scheme focusing on fast-track/high-potential candidates, it is possible that the mentee could become a peer of the mentor or even leapfrog them and so, feeling threatened, they start holding back and missing meetings.

Often, the mere fact of mentees being labelled 'high potential' implies an expectation of empowerment, innovation, creativity, forward thinking and so on. However, unless the (internal) mentors are open to the prospect of such change and encourage it, ideas may get stifled and motivation lost: 'That's not how we do things around here'. In these situations, we would recommend looking for external mentors.

We have also experienced the situation where a mentor in a hierarchical scheme has not properly embraced the mentoring philosophy and continually uses their 'stripes' – essentially saying: 'I'm more senior/more experienced than you, this is what I want you to do'. This is another example where keeping in touch with the participants will help to identify a problem earlier rather than later, and measures can be taken to help both parties re-establish productive roles for themselves in the relationship.

Apathy

Fatal to mentoring schemes and relationships!

This may set in on either side and is often illustrated by a low response rate to a feedback questionnaire. Although in many firms, 'survey fatigue' can be a problem, a low response may well indicate some underlying issues. This could be due to poor or unrealistic expectations set by the organisation and/or the pair themselves at the outset; so resetting the expectations and objectives of the relationship may be useful. Alternatively the matching may not have worked, with both parties reluctant to admit it: regular checks with participants can help to identify this issue early on.

Where more junior levels of staff are being mentored, it may be that line managers are not releasing them to attend the mentoring sessions or that the mentees themselves are reluctant to ask for the time. This again illustrates the importance of educating and involving line managers at the outset, so that they have their own set of expectations about what will happen. A scheme process which clearly sets out guidelines for meeting frequency, duration and so on can help, although this may be overly prescriptive for some cultures or individuals.

Apathy is, perhaps, more often encountered where there is no defined limit to the relationship. Whether the 'limit' is the achievement of specific objectives, or a defined period of time, it will serve to focus the minds of the participants. In one organisation, a sense of focus (and perhaps urgency!) was created by scheduling a meeting with the chief executive at the end of the defined timescale. A flourishing and productive relationship can always be extended for another term, as appropriate, but placing a framework around the initial activity was seen as a useful thing to do.

Mentees with a short-term attention span – wanting quick hits

The 'quick wins' which aid motivation and generational differences in expectations

The 21st century is the era of the sound bite and instant gratification. Younger employees are technologically wise, having grown up with the high-speed, hi-tech revolution, and are used to accessing information 'on tap' via the internet and the plethora of media available. They are good at multi-tasking and easily distracted, looking to get a quick result and then move on. Having a mentee from a younger generation can help managers to understand these new generations better and learn more about how to recognise and handle their needs – in a sense, an informal upwards mentoring process.

Many mentors will not come prepared with bite-sized chunks, however, and the process in which the mentor and mentee are engaged is one which is designed to encourage reflection and an understanding of the bigger picture. It is for this reason that mentoring is extremely useful amongst the population described above. Some of these points can be usefully made in the initial briefing sessions and expectations should be managed at this stage. Thinking in terms of some 'quick wins' is always good for motivation and the pair should discuss this when setting their objectives early on in the relationship. This is not usually the overall purpose of the mentoring process, however, and needs to be explicit from the outset.

Who mentors the mentors?

Another level of support to ensure the success of a mentoring programme

In previous chapters we've commented on the level of support needed to ensure the success of a mentoring programme. An essential aspect of this is providing help for the mentors, particularly when a scheme is being introduced for the first time and they are learning and developing new skills. Ways in which mentors in the Henley Group's schemes have been supported include:

▶ Training – in a number of cases attendance has been mandatory.

▶ Information/process guides.

MENTORS' DEVELOPMENT CLUB   Avaya

A significant outcome of mentoring in Avaya has been the emergence of a strong development forum for the mentors. The mentoring scheme has been running for 3 years and now has over 40 mentors involved. Mentors were originally specifically targeted, but word of mouth about the scheme has spread and managers are actively asking to join what has, in effect, become a 'Mentors' Club'.

New mentors have a mandatory one-day training programme covering basics about the process. Following that, the Mentor group undergoes 3 or 4 formal training sessions during the course of a year. Development has focused primarily on interpersonal skills including, for example, a Myers–Briggs Type Indicator® session. During this session the importance of understanding difference was pressed home in a 30-minute role play, during which opposites in a dimension were deliberately put together.

The learning focus of the 'Club' is now poised to move out into other development areas: managers do not see this as conventional training (and, therefore, not a priority) and are keen to be involved.

Figure 13.2 **An example approach for mentor development at Avaya**

▶ Providing a ready ear/help line contact – usually the scheme manager.

▶ Providing facilitators to help pairs to get started or work through a problem patch.

▶ Having an experienced mentor as their own mentor.

▶ Creating opportunities to share experiences and best practices with other mentors, such as in the example at Avaya outlined in Figure 13.2.

The emergence in recent years of more and more independent (external) coaches and mentors has led to concerns over levels of competence and effectiveness. In addition to the route of formal qualification outlined previously, a number of other initiatives are materialising. For example, in 2003 the European Mentoring and Coaching Council (EMCC) introduced Ethical Standards for all its members; the concept of mentor supervision is now being more widely considered; and organisations commissioning external mentors are requesting evidence of ability. In *The International Journal of Mentoring and Coaching*, Merrick & Stokes (2003) examine the question of mentor supervision and offer a conceptual framework of mentor development based on their experience in scheme design and mentor development. They recognise that there is a clear need for structured research into the whole area of mentor development and supervision.

Concluding the Mentoring Lifecycle

As a mentoring lifecycle draws to a close, the scheme manager will need to pay attention to a number of areas:

▶ How the programme is to be reviewed and evaluated and who will be involved.

▶ How mentors will be advised to respond if their mentee does not wish to end the relationship.

▶ What the most appropriate kind of formal ending to the scheme will be and whether it will be appropriate to give recognition for achievements.

▶ What outcomes there are for the organisation and other stakeholders and what key messages will be taken forward to improve subsequent schemes.

It is worth paying specific attention to the end of a mentoring relationship and encouraging the pairs to have some kind of formal conclusion rather than just letting it fizzle out. Completing a review/evaluation process will start this and give mentees a sense of continuance, as an ongoing development plan can be agreed for the mentee to work on during the months ahead.

> *Mentoring is not for life – there is a finite period when you can be of use to an individual; then they need to move on to someone else.*
>
> Avaya mentor

Some mentees may find it difficult to be, in a sense, cast adrift without their mental/emotional crutch and so it might be appropriate for the relationship to continue on a more informal basis, outside the bounds of the structured scheme. Mentors, also, may feel the 'loss' of their protégé and be willing to continue the association. However, much of this type of response can be contained by setting expectations for the duration of the relationship at the outset.

> **Endings:**
>
> *Sometimes it helps if the scheme manager plays a formal role at this conclusion and holds a three-way meeting, covering topics such as: 'What worked, what didn't, what's changed as a result, what contributions have been made to the organisation' and so on. This is a very popular approach with senior managers.*
>
> Scheme manager – Zurich

RECOGNISING ACHIEVEMENTS

The need to say goodbye presents a wonderful opportunity for the scheme manager to help participants to celebrate what has been achieved from the perspectives of all the stakeholders.

It may be appropriate for the scheme manager to produce a report or hold a closing social event with all the participants/stakeholders. This is an opportunity to give feedback on the overall outcomes and success stories of the scheme – perhaps inviting willing participants to talk about their experiences. It is also a good idea to invite the scheme's main sponsor to be present to recognise formally the contributions made and progress achieved.

The end of the event would then represent the point at which the relationships are officially dissolved.

Extending and Developing the Scheme

Once the initial scheme has proved its worth by achieving the anticipated objectives, it may well be the case that there is interest in the organisation in extending the process further. This may be driven either by other employees seeing the success their colleagues have enjoyed with the original scheme, or by the organisation realising the benefits that can occur as a result of this kind of employee development.

Some of the implications and options around this area are shown in Figure 13.3.

Many of the areas outlined for consideration in the diagram have been covered previously. We will focus here on three specific elements: resources, technology and administration.

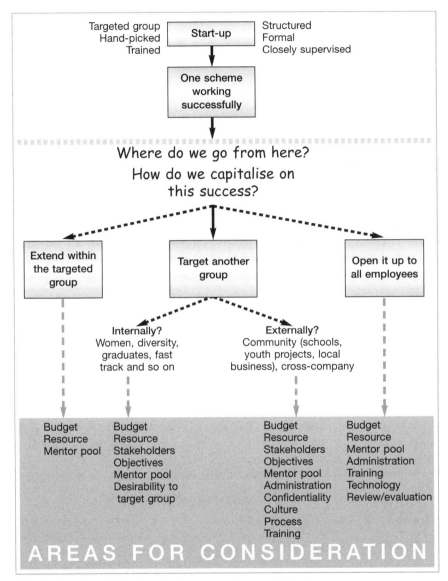

Figure 13.3 **Considerations when extending and developing a mentoring scheme**

RESOURCES

This refers to the people available to support the scheme. Throughout this book we have stressed the importance of ensuring that you have sufficient resource in place to support the achievement of the scheme's objectives. Besides designing and launching it, this involves constantly keeping a finger on the pulse and checking with participants and other stakeholders that everything is running smoothly.

Extending the scheme will clearly put pressure on the resources you already have – in many cases this is the scheme manager alone. Possible ways of dealing with this are to use technology to a greater degree or to put in place local mentoring champions.

TECHNOLOGY AND ADMINISTRATION

Many of the schemes referred to here began with relatively small numbers – in the order of 12–20 pairs. Even a small scheme like this takes a surprising amount of time to support and administer and so, wherever possible, technology can be used to ease the load. A number of suggestions are outlined below:

1 **Using the web:** a website could be set up on an intranet/extranet to provide:

   ▶ general information on mentoring and what it is

   ▶ internal guidelines on how the process works and who is involved

   ▶ a gateway for applications to become a mentor or mentee

   ▶ access to a database of mentors for self-selection by mentees

   ▶ pro forma documents for use in the process

   ▶ examples of models and frameworks for use by mentors

   ▶ links to mentoring websites

   ▶ a list of references and reading material

   ▶ a chat room for mentors and for mentees

   ▶ distance learning materials about mentoring (alternatively, use CDs)

   ▶ a directory of local champions

   ▶ a direct mail link to the scheme manager/administrator

   ▶ facilities for sending in general comments and feedback

   ▶ a means of administering the review process.

2 **Using telephone systems to facilitate meetings:** where geographical distance separates the pairs or, indeed, the scheme administrators, technology can be used in a number of ways to ensure that this does not become an insurmountable problem:

   ▶ video-conferencing for the mentoring pairs when they cannot meet face to face

   ▶ conference calls to have group reviews with mentors and with mentees

   ▶ conference calls to keep up to date with other administrators/ champions.

3 **Using software for matching and administering the scheme:**

   ▶ Setting up a database, or using special software, can be invaluable in the matching process.

   ▶ A database provides a tool which mentees can use to self-select a mentor; this can be particularly useful where the scheme is designed to support achievement of a professional qualification.

   ▶ It will also help you to administer the scheme as it is an easy means of logging process steps, such as who has been trained, whether every pair has had their first meeting, who has completed the six-month review and so on.

   ▶ A database also provides an easy way of recording comments made in 'corridor chats', although, in this instance, you may need to consider who has access to the database, so that confidentiality is not compromised.

4 **Using e-mail/voice mail to facilitate communications:**

   ▶ e-mail for receiving feedback, comments, completed questionnaires and so on from participants and other stakeholders.

   ▶ Regular e-mail contact with participants – setting up automatic distribution lists takes the pain out of this approach and provides a simple method of keeping mentoring in people's minds.

   ▶ Using voice mail as a marketing tool – you might wish to advertise a mentoring information workshop locally, or announce the official launch of a scheme.

The following box outlines how a successful graduate scheme, begun at Yorkshire Water in 1999, blossomed into other schemes supporting apprentices/technical trainees, functional mentoring and management development.

Yorkshire Water's (YW) mentoring scheme for graduates has proved extremely successful. It commenced in 1999 with the annual graduate intake and the scheme has continued to run in the ensuing years.

YW have also introduced mentoring for other new recruits in the business for example for apprentices and for technical trainees. The same principles are used for the scheme that is, it is a developmental relationship, matching mentors with mentees using learning styles; having 'offline' relationships. The main difference with the schemes for apprentices and trainees is that YW consider location; they also allow mentors and mentees who work in the same function to be matched, as their development needs are often of a more practical nature than graduates. Many of the Graduates who have completed their two-year development programme with a mentor, now successfully mentor apprentices.

The scheme has also been adapted for people who attend YW's management development programmes in conjunction with Leeds University. All participants of the two-year Diploma in Management are given a mentor based on the usual YW mentoring principles: matched using learning styles, cross-functional and based on management experience as well as seniority.

YW under-estimated the amount of other people that might want mentors – once graduate, apprentices, trainees and people participating in management development programmes started mentoring relationships, other people began to want a mentor. This included senior managers who felt that, after being a mentor, they would benefit from having one too.

To manage this, a mentoring database is being established to enable people to find out more about mentoring and to allow them to approach mentors themselves. With over 130 trained mentors actively mentoring, the scheme is progressing much faster than ever anticipated: never under-estimate the success of the scheme!

Another way of extending or growing a scheme is to consider whether peer mentoring would be appropriate. Some organisations have found that peer mentoring has evolved naturally amongst their pool of mentors, particularly where group mentor meetings for sharing experiences and best practice have occurred (see Chapter 4 for more information on this).

Summary

The maintenance of a programme is never a static thing – new issues are always going to emerge and the programme or the organisation itself can change direction as part of the normal path of business life. There is no reason, however, why a good mentoring scheme cannot bend with the organisation and accommodate any changes along the way – in times of change, mentoring can be one of the most useful ways of keeping up morale. In this chapter some of the more common issues which can arise have been discussed, with suggestions as to what to do about them. There is never a perfect answer, but there is usually a way in which the scheme manager can get things back on track. This is why the role of the scheme manager is so important and should not be underestimated. If there is one lesson which all the Henley Group participants would wish to make, it is that once the setup of a mentoring scheme has been sorted out, the real work has only just begun. It is not an activity which can be handed over to the participants with the expectation that it will run itself. Setting up appropriate resources to maintain and manage the programme from the outset is an important feature in a successful mentoring programme.

This chapter has also looked at ways in which a mentoring scheme can be drawn to a formal conclusion and why this is a 'good thing'. As with many issues here, the important messages – those which ensure the smooth running of a scheme – are best given out at the beginning, so that they form part of the setup and context for mentoring in the organisation. This should include a timescale for the relationships and preferably some indication as to what options are available for development after it has finished. One of these options can be for ex-mentees to think about becoming the next generation of mentors.

There are many ways in which a mentoring scheme, or the idea of mentoring, can be taken forward in an organisation, once the basic model has been seen to work. The organisational needs, and the perspectives of all the stakeholders involved, should be sought with each new initiative. What has worked effectively in one context may fall completely flat if transplanted in its entirety without question. This, in turn, would run the risk of destroying the carefully built up good name of mentoring in that organisation.

Once mentoring is begun, in a planned and appropriate way, then it will be able to grow organically, as ex-mentees become the next generation of mentors and champions, and the number of individuals who can help with any or all parts of the process grows. As the scheme manager's job is so critical in underpinning the success of any programme, the more experienced and informed people there are available in the organisation to help, the more the chance exists to embed mentoring culturally in the organisation.

14 Evaluation and Review of the Scheme

Introduction

In this chapter, the subject of evaluation of mentoring schemes is covered, both in the light of how the evaluation and review of a scheme needs to feed back to the stakeholders for the sake of the future of mentoring in the organisation, and also from the perspective of various Focus Group members who were able to share their actual approaches with the Group. The overall message is strongly that it is not only necessary to have a formal review and evaluation structure in place for when the scheme is at an end, but also that an ongoing review process, as part of the programme maintenance, can play an important part in the overall evaluation.

First, we look at the subject in a more general sense. Evaluation of training and development is a requirement of most initiatives in organisations, and some of the thinking around evaluation can be applied just as well to mentoring programmes as to other forms of development. However, with mentoring, it will be seen that there are a few additional issues which complicate matters and there are some ways around these that practitioners have found helpful.

The chapter then moves on to give some practitioners' examples and suggestions for evaluation of mentoring. These range from Focus Group discussions in general, to specific member organisation's approaches and include the thoughts of some of the key mentoring experts quoted throughout the book.

By the end of the chapter, it is hoped that every scheme manager will be able to draw up an evaluation process and plan as part of their scheme management project plan, and make it an integral part of the programme.

An Overview of the Evaluation Process

For the mentoring scheme manager, there may be a number of reasons why evaluation of the scheme is important. These are likely to include:

▶ To identify issues and barriers that need to be overcome for the programme as a whole and to enable continuous improvement.

▶ To ensure that the needs of all the stakeholders identified in the early stages are being met, and to motivate key sponsors to continue supporting the mentoring scheme, with justification for continued funding or resources.

▶ To motivate existing participants and encourage new mentors and mentees to join the scheme.

▶ To identify 'problem' relationships and facilitate appropriate resolution.

▶ To assess whether the programme has met its original objectives and perhaps had other beneficial consequences.

Evaluating mentoring programmes is perhaps even more challenging than evaluating other types of developmental activity. In addition to the difficulties of isolating the effect of mentoring from other activities, the evaluation of mentoring will need to take account of the confidentiality, privacy, informality and interactivity of the relationships.

In general, an evaluation strategy should try to use multiple methods and obtain both quantitative (numerical or 'hard') data and qualitative (non-numerical or 'soft') data. In addition, it is vital to obtain 'base' data against which any changes can be measured. Possible measures will depend upon the purposes of mentoring, but may include:

▶ Recruitment levels and vacancies

▶ Promotion rates

▶ Readiness for higher level responsibilities

▶ Employee skills and competencies

▶ Attitudes and motivation of both mentees and mentors

▶ Costs of training and development

▶ Public opinion about the organisation.

In evaluating a mentoring programme against its original objectives, it is important not to miss unintended consequences – whether positive or negative – and an approach that is in part 'goal free' may be helpful in identifying other potential benefits or problems that can be experienced.

A useful approach to the question of what to evaluate is provided by Kirkpatrick (1967), who identified four levels of evaluation:

Level 1: *Reaction* – initial thoughts and feelings

Level 2: *Learning* – the acquisition of knowledge, understanding and skills

Level 3: *Behaviour* – the transfer of this learning to on-the-job behaviour

Level 4: *Organisation performance* – the impact of this behaviour change on the 'bottom line'.

Figure 14.1 is an example of how one organisation used this model to identify the success criteria, against which its scheme would be evaluated.

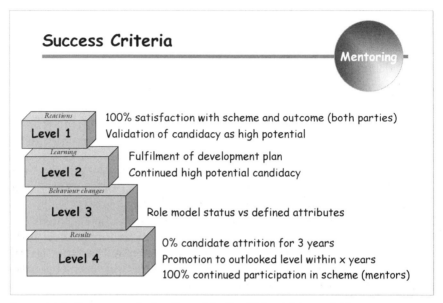

Figure 14.1 **Success criteria aligned to the Kirkpatrick model in a high-potential scheme**

In turn, the focus of these levels of evaluation needs to take account of three aspects:

1 Individual mentee and mentor development

2 Mentoring relationships

3 The mentoring scheme.

1 *Individual mentee and mentor development*

It is likely that the most effective means of establishing the development of mentors and mentees is through the ongoing performance management process within the organisation. In addition, other measures could include promotion and retention figures and attitude questionnaires.

2 *Mentoring relationships*

This aspect of mentoring may be difficult to evaluate, given the issues of confidentiality. Nevertheless, it may be possible to obtain measures on the number and frequency of mentoring meetings, the average length of mentoring relationships, the number of requests for new mentors and the number and proportion of relationships with agreed mentoring contracts. In addition it may be possible to obtain non-attributable feedback on the perceived satisfaction or value of the mentoring relationships in the scheme – a confidential third-party evaluation approach may be useful here.

3   *The mentoring scheme*

If mentoring is to go into another cycle, feedback needs to be obtained on the overall design and implementation of the scheme; for example: how the process itself worked; the value of the training provided; the level of on-going support available to participants; the effectiveness of communication channels and so on.

Megginson & Clutterbuck (1995) report on research undertaken by the European Mentoring Centre with a number of organisations, which suggested that the basic elements for measuring mentoring are as shown in Figure 14.2: programme level, relationship level, process and outputs. The model depicted has been developed further to add examples of what might be evaluated in each area. Megginson & Clutterbuck's view was that few schemes are systematically evaluated, although this is a critical part of maintaining the scheme's credibility and relating it back to the organisational benefits.

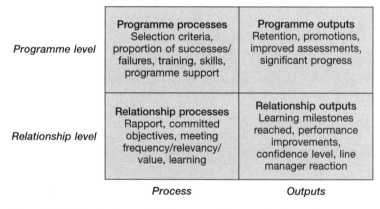

Figure 14.2 **Basic elements for measuring mentoring schemes**
Source: Based on Megginson & Clutterbuck (1995).

The following checklist may be useful to scheme managers in evaluating the effectiveness of the mentoring scheme:

▶ Were there clearly articulated and measurable objectives and expected outcomes, aligned to the culture and strategy of the organisation and integrated with other development initiatives and processes?

▶ What level of commitment existed from key stakeholders, especially top management?

▶ Were the roles and responsibilities of all stakeholders clear, understood and adhered to?

▶ Were the levels of support sufficient from the perspective of the participants and the administrators themselves?

▶ How did the selection, briefing, matching and introducing of mentors/mentees work, and how involved were they in these processes?

▶ Were the mentor and mentee free to define their relationship and expectations in the context of overall programme objectives?

▶ Where relationships needed terminating, how did the process work?

▶ Was there ongoing evaluation at both programme and relationship levels, which considered both process and outputs and used multiple approaches, hard and soft data and allowed sufficient time for consequences to emerge?

▶ What level of continuous development of the programme has occurred as a result of learning from the evaluation process to ensure that it meets the evolving needs and expectations of the organisation and the participants?

Evaluation of a mentoring programme will involve a number of people:

▶ The mentor and mentee themselves

▶ Line managers and other stakeholders

▶ The mentoring scheme administrators, working for the scheme manager

▶ An objective third party, such as personnel or the HR department.

Whether a mentoring relationship ends because 'time is up', it is not working, the professional/vocational qualification has been achieved or the overall objective has been met, it is helpful for all parties involved to have feedback of some kind. It is worth repeating here that the evaluation aspects from the perspective of the mentee and mentor and the scheme manager need to include the subjective side in any review of success. These may include:

▶ the way in which the mentoring was done (skills/behaviours/feelings/processes)

▶ whether the mentor and mentee achieved their personal objectives

▶ how well the process met the needs of those involved

▶ the line managers' views of the scheme

▶ the return the organisation has got on its investment, that is, have the immediate success criteria been met? How has mentoring contributed to the overall development process and, therefore, to the organisation as a whole?

▶ what improvements can be made

▶ whether the existing mentors can be retained and mentees encouraged to take on the role.

Key methods of evaluation can include questionnaires, interviews, focus groups, review meetings, review of progress against personal development plans, learning logs and diaries and statistical analysis of key measures against the 'base data' referred to earlier. Each of these approaches has its advantages and disadvantages, but some combination of these techniques, as appropriate for the individual context, will give a useful, formal evaluation of a mentoring scheme.

Questionnaires can also be used to gather information for planning the next scheme, that is, whether mentors wish to continue in the role, what further development they might need, what improvements participants would like to see and so on.

Once information from the reviews has been collated, evaluation of the scheme can take place and outcomes versus the original objectives and success criteria can be established and made available. This information is obviously invaluable in making improvements to the next scheme.

Practitioners' Approaches to Evaluation of Mentoring

One Focus Group discussion looked at this subject and came up with the following thoughts (this is repeated from the participants' perspective in Part IV: Taking Part in a Mentoring Relationship, as it is relevant to scheme managers, as well as participants, in a mentoring scheme).

WHAT

▶ Programme elements (both qualitative and quantitative information), for example training; relationships; process; success of the matching approach
▶ Logistical elements, that is, frequency of meetings; achievement of objectives
▶ Soft skills, that is, interpersonal skills
▶ The perceptions of mentors, mentees, line managers, scheme manager

WHEN

▶ Periodically during the lifecycle and at least quarterly
▶ Every six months
▶ At the conclusion of the lifecycle

HOW

▶ Formally
   – questionnaires using both open and closed questions
   – round table meetings
▶ Informally, during review meetings, corridor chats and so on

During one of the Focus Group meetings, Eric Parsloe expressed the view that frequency and completed plans were the two most useful measures. Whatever the programme measures, the mentor and mentee should review between themselves whether their own measures of individual actions have been achieved. They may also spend time agreeing a review document for the line manager (or any other parties appropriate to the context), which outlines in more general terms the degree of progress, learning and change achieved.

An interesting approach suggested in the Group's discussion was to gather perceptions about the programme from the participants' line managers – a group of people often forgotten in reviewing and evaluating schemes. A way in which this could be formalised would be to include mentoring in the official performance management process. Where mentoring is specified as an individual (either as a mentee or mentor) objective or development action, then it can be reviewed at an appropriate time. This gives line managers an opportunity to reflect on what benefits they have realised out of the scheme, as well as reviewing what it has done for the individual.

Examples of evaluation methods can be seen on the following pages (Figures 14.3–14.7).

YORKSHIRE WATER: REVIEW PROCESS

Regular scheme reviews should ideally include both evaluations of individuals and pairs, plus review meetings for mentors and mentees. Separate review meetings for mentors and mentees can make a key contribution in maintaining and growing a healthy scheme.

At YW a review meeting is held attended by all mentors and another is held for all mentees. These meetings form a valuable part of the process by:

► Sharing best practice.

► Re-energising the process.

► Identifying potential refresher training needs.

► Giving early warning of potential disengagements – the separation can then be managed to maximise the chances of future relationships being successful.

Prior to the review questionnaires are sent to all mentors and all mentees; the results are collated confidentially and then this feedback is used as a basis for discussion at the Review meetings. Again this is another indicator of possible disengagements – the Scheme manager can then discuss confidentially any issues with mentors or mentees if required.

On a more informal basis, but proving almost as important, can be social events attended by both mentors and mentees. Mentees and mentors can share experiences in a way which, given the right company culture, does not endanger mentee-mentor confidentiality. More importantly it creates additional contact opportunities between mentor and mentee in a very informal, non-work environment. At Yorkshire Water these social events have evolved and initially were driven by graduates – they have been considered extremely successful.

Figure 14.3 **Evaluation methods used by Yorkshire Water**

SEMISTRUCTURED INTERVIEW QUESTIONS USED WHEN INTERVIEWING PARTICIPANTS

Meeting Arrangements

- How do the meetings get arranged?
- Who sets the agenda for the meeting?
- When the two of you meet, how does what you end up talking about get chosen/decided?
- What preparations, if any, do you make prior to the meeting?

Activities at Meetings

- What happens at your meetings?
- What did you discuss at the first meeting?
- How did you feel after the first meeting?
- How do you feel after meetings now?
- How could the meetings with your mentor/mentee be improved?
- How do you keep track of what advice/suggestions you have provided during the meetings? (mentor only question)
- How formal/informal are the meetings?
- How often do you feel challenged by your mentor/mentee?

The Relationship

- How would you characterise the relationship you have with your mentor/mentee?
- How well would you say it worked?
- What was the first meeting like?
- What has gone well since the relationship started?
- What has not gone so well?
- Describe an episode or incident that stands out to you
- What has been the most valuable part of the mentoring relationship to date?
- How well matched are you to your mentor/mentee?
- How open do you feel you can be with your mentor/mentee?

Mentor Skills (questions put to mentees only)

- How useful do you find the input of your mentor?
- How often do you act upon advice/suggestions of your mentor?
- Describe something that has been offered by your mentor that has been helpful
- From your experience of help, what would you say were the most important aspects of it?
- How would you rate the skills of your mentor?
- What would you say were the most important qualities in a mentor?

General

- How well has the training prepared you for the mentoring process?
- How do you assess whether the mentee has taken your suggestions on board? (mentor only question)
- How well have your expectations of mentoring been met?

Figure 14.4 **An example of semistructured interview questions used in a privatised utility**

RWE THAMES WATER
Form used for monthly progress reports in a project manager mentoring scheme

NAME OF PM _____
NAME OF MENTOR _____
SENIOR MANAGER _____
INDUCTION START DATE _____
PROPOSED FINISH DATE _____

Please agree and record brief details of progress attained by the PM throughout the induction process on at least a monthly basis using the appropriate headings below. It is important at the first meeting for the Mentor to assess gaps and prioritise action required.

Current and attained level of competence
In order to identify development progress please indicate the PMs' level of competence at the start and end of the mentoring process.

Experienced
TW Project
Manager

```
|----+----+----+----+----+----+----+----+----+----|
0    1    2    3    4    5    6    7    8    9    10
```

MEETING NO.	DATE
General comments on progress	
Issues or Concerns	
Agreed action for next meeting	

SIGNED (PM)_____ SIGNED (MENTOR) _____

DATE _____

CC: Personnel Group

Figure 14.5 **Monthly progress report from RWE Thames Water**

MENTEE EVALUATION

AVAYA

GENERAL INFORMATION

Your Name		Today's Date	
Who is your mentor [name]?			
What date did you first meet ?		Date	
When did you last meet?		Date	
How many times have you met since the first meeting?		Number of times	

MENTORING PROCESS

You were originally given a choice of 2 potential mentors. Why did you choose this one?			
Comments please.			

Do you have specific objectives for your meetings		YES		NO	

What stage in the mentoring process in your opinion do you believe you are at ?						
Rapport		Direction Setting		Progression		Maturation

Do you have a 'contract' or agreement in place with your mentor?	YES		NO	
Do you review your meetings for effectiveness?	YES		NO	
If yes how have they improved.				

CAREER PLANNING

Do you have a personal development plan or career plan in place now?			YES		NO
Did you have one before the mentoring relationship?			YES		NO
If there was one in place, have significant changes been made?			YES		NO
How useful is the current personal development plan you have now?	1 Not at all	2 Limited	3 Somewhat	4 Very	5 Extremely

MENTORING RELATIONSHIP

Evaluate the overall effectiveness of each relationship in terms of how beneficial in your opinion it has been to your personal learning and development using the scale below.

1	No significant learning or development came from/is coming from the relationship
2	Of limited benefit in terms of personal learning and development
3	Some useful personal learning and development has taken/is taking place
4	Considerable learning and development has taken/is taking place
5	One of the most powerful learning and development experiences I have taken part in.

What subject areas are you working on in general terms [only comment if you wish to]

Career Planning		Feedback on experiences	
Performance Management		Conflict resolution	
Work based support		Networking	
Personal Support		Personality profiles	

Use 1-5 scale where 1 is low and 5 is high	1 Low	2	3	4	5 High
How well do you feel the mentor listens to your point of view?					
How much does your mentor stretch and challenge you?					
How much has your confidence improved?					
How much are you prepared to invest in making the relationship work?					
How much do you enjoy your meetings?					

OVERALL	1 Not at all	2 Limited	3 Somewhat	4 Very	5 Extremely
How would you rate the benefit to **YOU** of the mentoring programme					
How would you rate the benefit to **Avaya UK and Ireland** of the mentoring programme					

Please respond on the email on any general comments you would like to make, all feedback welcomed

Are you still happy with this mentor?	YES		NO	
If No would you like the programme co-ordinator to contact you to find a new mentor?	YES		NO	

Figure 14.6 **Mentee evaluation form from Avaya**

RWE THAMES WATER
High Potential Programme – 6 month evaluation

MENTOR QUESTIONS	Strongly Agree	Agree	Disagree	Strongly Disagree
My mentee demonstrates and shows: 1) A good understanding of their own strengths and weaknesses 2) An ability to explain their career aspirations 3) An open, honest direct and personal attitude towards me 4) A planned approach to their career ambitions 5) They network at all levels in order to get things done 6) Confidence in aiming for what he/she wants 7) A responsibility for their own development 8) A good knowledge of business priorities and needs 9) A good understanding of people issues 10) A good understanding of political/regulatory issues 11) A willingness to constructively challenge and improve operational/people issues 12) Rational decision-making techniques 13) Initiative and drive 14) An ability to articulate their key concerns 15) Flexibility				

MENTEE QUESTIONS	Strongly Agree	Agree	Disagree	Strongly Disagree
1) Our meetings were well organised in advance. 2) On average, each meeting lasted 3) My mentor is approachable before and after our meeting 4) I am able to share information about my strengths, weaknesses and ambitions openly with my mentor. 5) I felt our discussions were in confidence. 6) Since the programme's start 6 months ago, I have met with my mentor on x occasions 7) I have found the meetings worthwhile and beneficial. 8) We focussed on short-term issues primarily (0-6 months) 9) We focussed on long-term goals primarily (24-48 months) 10) We used a number of techniques for problem solving such as mind mapping, SCOD analysis, force-field analysis, levels of discounting, objective setting trees or other less formal processes (please state which below). 11) My Mentor demonstrates appropriate listening skills. 12) My Mentor demonstrates appropriate questioning skills. **What were the results of your discussions?** 13) Future direction within Thames Water. 14) Information about development opportunities 15) Feeling 'good' (reassured & valued) 16) Greater discussion with other key staff (spot mentors) 17) Greater political awareness about internal processes 18) Improved career skills 19) Improved contacts with suppliers and/or strategic/alliance partners.	½, 1, 1½, 2 hrs, other 0, 1-2, 3-4, 5-6 occasions, more			

Figure 14.7 Six-month evaluation form from RWE Thames Water

Summary

Evaluation and review of mentoring schemes is an ongoing process and one about which it is not easy to be empirical. Many of the established approaches and models of evaluation of development may be used – the scheme manager has the job of presenting the findings back to the stakeholders in such a way that the context and background to the scheme is also represented appropriately.

Mentoring is, ultimately, a private thing, between the mentor and the mentee. If it is being done within the context of an organisational scheme, then the organisation may expect to benefit, although the tacit understanding may be that the benefits could be rather more indirect than those from some other, more skills-based forms of development. It is essential, therefore, that expectations, not only about the mentoring scheme itself, but also about the evaluation process and findings, are managed. If this is thought out in advance, and included as part of the upfront communication and training for the mentoring scheme, then things should run smoothly.

Trying to evaluate the effectiveness of a mentoring scheme retrospectively can quickly result in a collection of anecdotal evidence and comments from individuals about their subjective experiences, and little else. This is unlikely to be enough to help advocates of mentoring to put together a convincing business plan to win resources to support a further scheme. In order to position mentoring as part of the mainstream of organisational development, a rigorous evaluation process is a key tool, which needs to be in place at the outset of the scheme. Stakeholders need to be involved in the setting of success criteria, which can be built into the evaluation process from the beginning. This will, in turn, meet the expectations of all those involved.

15 A Summary of Scheme Manager Activities

This chapter is intended to give mentoring scheme managers a quick reference guide to things they may need to consider during the various stages of the mentoring lifecycle. Whilst not all points will be appropriate in every context, the following pages illustrate key areas that can usefully be discussed and thought about when: shaping initial thoughts; gaining organisational commitment; planning and launching the scheme; ensuring it progresses smoothly; evaluating and then continuing the scheme by developing it further.

Shaping Initial Thoughts

These are some of the questions and points it was felt useful to consider when you begin thinking about mentoring and need to put some shape to the initial ideas:

▶ *Definition* – what is meant by the term 'mentoring' within the context of your own organisation? Does it differ from 'coaching', if so, how?

▶ *Recipients* – who will the scheme be aimed at: everyone, or a specific target group such as graduates or executive directors?

▶ *Type of scheme* – think about what type and model of scheme you want:
  ▷ A formal, structured one or a more informal, 'help-yourself' scheme
  ▷ Will a centralised or decentralised model suit you best?
  ▷ Would peer mentoring provide an advantage over hierarchical mentoring in any areas of the organisation?
  ▷ Do you need to bring fresh perspectives into the company – by setting up a cross-company mentoring scheme, for example?

▶ *Keeping on track* – how helpful would it be to have some standards for the scheme – either creating them yourselves or looking for externally written standards?

▶ *Identify objectives with clear outcomes* – know what you want to achieve from an organisational perspective and for the key stakeholders.

▶ *Consider the scope of the programme* – what will it include and not include?

How many pairs will you be able to support effectively? How long will it run for?

Gaining Organisational Commitment

▶ Weigh up the cultural climate and whether circumstances are right for launching a scheme at this time.

▶ Carefully consider what you need to do to get the right level of organisational support and commitment – know the risks and benefits of what you are proposing, not forgetting the line managers' involvement.

▶ Evaluate comprehensively and then justify what resources you might need:
  ▷ How much support will the projected numbers need – particularly from the scheme manager?
  ▷ Will technology and systems help to support the programme – if so, what and how?
  ▷ Will you be looking for support from the line – perhaps in the form of locally based mentoring champions?
  ▷ What is the proposed budget?

▶ In terms of measuring progress and achievements, would it be helpful to include mentoring activity in the performance management process? If so, how will you engage line managers?

▶ Will you be officially recognising or rewarding the mentors in any way?

Planning and Launching the Scheme

At this stage a great deal more needs to be done in terms of defining the detail of the scheme and how it will best work in your organisation:

▶ *Map out your overall process* – how will people become involved? What stages will there be? How will you review it?

▶ *Identify roles and responsibilities* – what will participants (including the scheme manager) be expected to do or not do?

▶ *Qualities:*
  ▷ What should you be looking for in mentors and mentees?
  ▷ How important will it be to have quality and consistency of mentors? How can you do this?
  ▷ Would they be interested in gaining some form of external certification?

▶ What might occur that will disrupt relationships? What plans or strategies should be put in place to deal with these?

▶ *Marketing*
  ▷ How will you publicise the scheme and provide information to participants and others?
  ▷ Volunteers – how will you find mentors and mentees? What mechanisms will you use?
  ▷ How will you ensure all the volunteers really are committed to mentoring?

▶ *Support documents* – what might people find useful to help them get started? Will you provide pro formas?

▶ *Matching*
  ▷ What criteria for matching people will be best suited to your scheme and your organisation?
  ▷ What will be the most suitable matching process?
  ▷ Will you need help in completing the matching – particularly if your scheme crosses boundaries of any kind (for example functional, geographical or organisational)?

▶ *Training/briefing* – how will you inform participants (including line managers) about the process and give them the necessary skills? When will this best be done?

▶ *The first meeting* – how and where will they first meet? What will you do to facilitate this – or what recommendations will you make?

▶ *Meeting frequency and length* – what guidelines will you give to the participants? How will you make line managers aware of this?

▶ *Discussion topics* – would it help to provide a suggested agenda or other means of helping them to get started?

▶ *Contracting* – if this is a part of your scheme, do you have example contract and 'ground rule' documents to help start them off?

▶ *Building rapport* – apart from training, what practical ideas can you give to help the pairs begin to feel comfortable with one another? What help can you offer in terms of facilitation?

▶ What should you be doing once the scheme is actually launched?
  ▷ checking that the first meetings are happening
  ▷ providing support where necessary
  ▷ watching for any negative emotions which may emerge
  ▷ keeping in touch with participants

Ensuring a Smooth Progression

During the middle section of the mentoring lifecycle, Focus Group members found it important to keep in touch with what is going on. These are potential activity areas for the scheme manager:

▶ *Forming goals* – do the mentees have a clear idea of what they want and what their goals are for the relationship?

▶ *'It's not working!'* – what will you do in these circumstances?
  ▷ Will it be helpful to facilitate a meeting?
  ▷ Are there fundamental differences which diagnostic tools may help draw out?
  ▷ Do you have a 'pool' of mentors from which to draw if rematching is necessary?

▶ *Training and development*
  ▷ Do your participants need more formalised help – particularly where an initial training programme was not possible?
  ▷ Are there skills they could do with having refreshers on, such as questioning and listening?
  ▷ What support can be provided in terms of facilitating the sharing of experiences and best practice?

▶ *'I'm out of my depth'* – when mentors feel that they do not have the necessary skill or matters have gone beyond the boundaries of mentoring, what access do you have to specialists, such as professional counsellors and help lines?

▶ *Practical meeting management* – how can you help the pairs to make best use of their time? Where pairs are having difficulty finding time, what practical tools or help could you give them?

▶ *E-mentoring* – would it help to encourage more frequent contact via methods other than face-to-face meetings? These might include: e-mail, video-conference and telephone.

▶ *Reviewing* – how will you keep a finger on the pulse?
  ▷ What formal and/or informal communication lines have you set up?
  ▷ How often are the pairs reviewing their own progress?
  ▷ If there is a defined timescale, will you have a mid-point review?
  ▷ How are the line managers reacting to the scheme?
  ▷ Will you be keeping the organisation and stakeholders informed of progress, if so, how?

Ending and Evaluating the Scheme

As the mentoring lifecycle draws to a conclusion, there are a number of activity areas for a scheme manager to consider:

▶ What will be the best way for the pairs to say 'goodbye'?

▶ Will you arrange a formal ending to the scheme? How will you involve all the stakeholders?

▶ How will you advise mentors to respond if their mentees do not wish to end the relationship?

▶ Will it be appropriate to give recognition for achievements? How will this be done?

▶ How will the programme be reviewed and evaluated? Who will be involved?

▶ What outcomes are there for the organisation and other stakeholders?
  ▷ Have the original scheme objectives and success criteria been met?
  ▷ What outcomes are there for the mentoring pairs and the line managers?
  ▷ How effective were the mentoring champions (if used)?
  ▷ How well did the overall process work?
  ▷ Do the outcomes justify continuing with mentoring?

▶ What key messages can be taken forward to improve subsequent schemes?

▶ How can the pool of mentors be retained and increased?

Growing and Developing the Scheme

Once you have been through a successful mentoring cycle, how can you maintain momentum and/or grow your scheme further? These are some points for consideration:

▶ What happens next?
  ▷ Will you extend the scheme within the same target group?
  ▷ Do you want to increase the number of pairs? If so, how will you resource this?
  ▷ Do you want to target another group, either internally or externally via community or cross-company mentoring?
  ▷ Is it appropriate to open up mentoring to all employees?

▶ What do you need to be thinking about and doing differently as a result of the outcomes from the previous scheme?

▶ How many of the original mentors wish to continue in the role?

▶ Have any of the mentees expressed a wish to become a mentor?

PART IV

Taking Part in a Mentoring Relationship

16 Introduction

This part of the book has primarily been written to help those taking part in a mentoring relationship to learn from the experience of others. It will, however, be equally applicable for those setting up and running schemes or those wanting to train mentors and mentees in how to derive maximum benefit from the mentoring relationship.

The mentoring lifecycle shown in Figure 16.1 identifies the various stages in the mentoring relationship. Part III explored the mentoring lifecycle from the perspective of the scheme manager. Part IV has been specifically written for the mentor and mentee. The chapters that follow will take the readers through the key stages of the lifecycle.

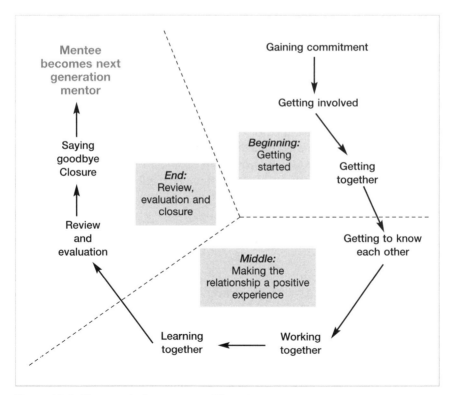

Figure 16.1 **The mentoring process lifecycle**

Beginning – Getting Started

Chapter 17 will look at benefits and risks as part of the gaining commitment stage. Mentors as well as mentees have reported gaining benefits from the mentoring process, but there can also be risks associated with the relationship. The effect of risks can be reduced if care is taken at the outset to build a positive mentoring relationship and the expectations of key stakeholders are appropriately managed.

Having explored the benefits and risks, the next stage is to find a mentor or mentee. The mentee needs to consider whether he or she wants a senior manager or a peer and whether the mentor should be within the organisation or be external. Advice will be given and the key skills, knowledge and attributes to look for in a mentor and mentee and the ways of matching explained in Chapter 18. This is not easy and the mentoring pair needs to focus on the objectives of the mentee to ensure the best match possible.

Those embarking on a mentoring relationship for the first time frequently express concerns about how to get started. Chapter 19 provides a clear structure for the first meeting. An understanding of the roles of not only the mentors and mentees, but also line managers, can help to overcome these uncertainties and provide a good platform on which to build a longer term relationship.

Middle – Making the Relationship a Positive Experience

Building rapport between the mentor and mentee and drawing on appropriate skills is an essential part of the relationship. This is a well-researched area and following recommended guidelines will help both parties to develop a useful relationship. For many experienced managers the skill set needed to be an effective mentor or mentee once rapport has been built is very similar to the skills used on a day-to-day basis. Taking part in a mentoring relationship does, however, provide an excellent opportunity to enhance the skills. Chapter 20 gives guidance on strategy, tactics and the skills needed to build a positive relationship.

End – Review, Evaluation and Closure

In taking part in a mentoring relationship, both mentors and mentees need to take account of and value differences and consider the context within which the mentoring relationship is taking place. Many schemes have been set up to encourage a range of diverse relationships and specifically encourage diversity. Looking more broadly, the context of the mentoring relationship does need to be taken into account. The context will be fundamental to what actually happens in a mentoring relationship. The nature of mentoring in the United States, for example, is very different from the European approach to mentoring. Thus, a mentor in America will view the person he or she is mentoring as a protégé, who in turn would expect his or her mentor to influence career progression. In Europe, learning is the main purpose of a mentoring relationship.

Throughout the mentoring relationship, both mentor and mentee need to consider how to evaluate the relationship. This can be done during the meetings as an ongoing review, enabling adjustments to be made immediately. Evaluation by both mentor and mentee can then take place after the meeting to help the planning process for the next one. The final review and evaluation is particularly important and helps to capture learning and benefits from the process. It also helps to close the relationship. This is important if the mentoring pair want to avoid the relationship fading away at the end without proper closure. Chapter 21 summarises the key issues impacting on mentors and mentees. Chapter 22 gives guidance on how to review and evaluate the relationship.

17 The Mentoring Experience from the Perspective of a Mentor and Mentee

Introduction

Before entering a mentoring relationship, both mentor and mentee need to be clear about their expectations of the relationship: what are the benefits to help sustain motivation but what are some of the potential risks? There are benefits for mentors as well as mentees. Mentors are sometimes surprised at the learning they gain from a mentoring relationship. Mentees are likely to gain in the short and longer term. However, entering a mentoring relationship is not without certain risks. Some of the contents of this chapter have already appeared in Chapter 8, but are repeated here as mentors and mentees need to be quite clear what they can realistically expect from the relationship and be mindful of the risks.

Benefits and Risks

Having a clear idea of what you will gain and potential pitfalls is part of effective preparation to enter a mentoring relationship. A variety of benefit and risk elements are given in Tables 17.1 and 17.2 – they may or may not be appropriate, depending on the context of the mentoring relationship.

POTENTIAL BENEFITS FOR MENTORS

When managers act as a mentor for the first time, they often express surprise at the extent that they benefit from the relationship. As Table 17.1 shows, the benefits range from personal learning, particularly being able to develop behavioural skills, to gaining a greater understanding of a different part of the business. Clutterbuck (2001) said that all

> *I think that I would probably gain as much from it as the person that I'm mentoring.*
>
> Mentor in a high-potential scheme

surveys and reviews highlighted four powerful benefits for mentors:

1 The learning they take from the experience, both in having to explain intuitive reasoning and in listening to a different perspective (for example, the problems that mentees have with their bosses often cause mentors to reflect on similar issues their direct reports may have with them).

2 The mentoring meeting provides an opportunity to take reflective space in a hectic daily schedule.

3 The satisfaction of knowing that they have made a difference to someone else.

> *I've found that the mentor gets enormous benefits as well. The mentor gets to step completely outside his or her normal world and really think about what is important in terms of process and approach to real problems. ... Helping mentees think through their issues is just like going back to school for the mentor – it teaches us to stop, and think, and analyse, and assist with finding the RIGHT approach – not the politically or practically expedient one.*
>
> Smiths Group mentor

4 The intellectual challenge provided when required to work on issues that are not the mentors' personal responsibility and may take them into unfamiliar territory.

Table 17.1 **Potential benefits of the mentoring relationship for mentors**

MENTORS

Vehicle for learning/stimulation

▶ Self-development: using/improving skills, particularly behavioural ones

▶ Improved job satisfaction/revitalised interest in work – be challenged, tested and stimulated

▶ Safer environment for developing new skills

▶ Learning from helping the mentee address problems with their boss

▶ The opportunity to take time out and be reflective

Increased influence and recognition

▶ An opportunity to influence the way things are done – passing on their own experience, knowledge and skills

▶ Increased peer recognition – seen as a role model

▶ Opportunity to influence the next generation of managers and demonstrate their own commitment to the future of the company

Broader perspectives

▶ New perspectives – challenging own assumptions

▶ An opportunity to question their own views and values

▶ Get/keep in touch with the grass roots and manage their own team better as a result

▶ Increased knowledge of a different part of the business

POTENTIAL BENEFITS FOR MENTEES

The mentoring relationship can be equally fruitful for the mentee, provided he or she is prepared to take responsibility for his or her learning. A discussion in the Focus Group concluded that learning for the mentee goes beyond being a

> *The meetings have been extremely useful in understanding where my management 'holes' are perceived to be, as well as methods for bridging the gaps. An extremely useful exercise which I would like to continue into the future.*
>
> RWE Thames Water mentee

> *We discussed what I should be doing next and I realised I could really make a difference and add value to this business.*
>
> YELL mentee

vehicle for learning. The mentor can provide support for mentees during change, particularly when they are managing difficult transitions, for example mentees on a

Table 17.2 Potential benefits of the mentoring relationship for mentees

MENTEES

Vehicle for learning

- ▶ Improved confidence and self-esteem
- ▶ Development of transferable skills including management, leadership, behavioural, professional
- ▶ Creativity and problem-solving
- ▶ Become more self-aware

Support

- ▶ Confidential coaching
- ▶ Safe learning environment to test out ideas
- ▶ Continuity of support in a changing environment
- ▶ Support whilst undergoing a major transition
- ▶ Sense of value within the organisation

Broader perspective

- ▶ Access to different perspectives and experience
- ▶ Exposure to a senior manager who can be a role model as a leader and manager
- ▶ Develop a wider view of the organisation – being helped to understand and resolve organisational and political issues
- ▶ Opportunity to broaden networks

Career development

- ▶ Help in developing long-term career and development goals and plans graduate programme who often have a mentor. Like the mentor, the mentee can also expect to gain a broader perspective from learning more about the organisation to building an increased network of people. The process can also help the mentee to clarify long-term career goals and plans.

Guest (2001) highlighted the following benefits for mentees:

▶ Having a sounding board

▶ Having someone who listens objectively

▶ Getting help on working out the best course of action

▶ Reflecting on the outcome

▶ Someone to challenge assumptions

▶ Having help with raising the performance bar and realising potential.

POTENTIAL RISKS FOR MENTORS

The main downside for the mentor is the time it takes to mentor well. Managers need to avoid being overambitious when asked to participate in a mentoring scheme and restrict the number of people they mentor at any one time. Other potential risks are summarised in Table 17.3.

Table 17.3 **Potential risks for the mentor**

MENTOR
▶ Conflicting demands on time
▶ Mentees breaching issues of confidentiality
▶ Having to deal with a failed mentoring relationship

POTENTIAL RISKS FOR MENTEES

David Clutterbuck (2001) emphasised that the potential risks for the mentee generally occur when the mentor is poor or the programme is badly designed. Risks that have been identified are summarised in Table 17.4.

Table 17.4 **Potential risks for the mentee**

MENTEE
▶ Mentor cannot spare the time needed to mentor effectively
▶ Overbearing style of the mentor
▶ Having unrealistic expectations of the mentoring process
▶ The mentor going too far in giving advice that might not be correct

POTENTIAL RISKS FOR BOTH MENTORS AND MENTEES

Some of the potential risks are equally applicable to mentors and mentees. These are summarised in Table 17.5.

Table 17.5 **Potential risks for the mentors and mentees**

MENTORS and MENTEES
▶ Seen as special by other, uninvolved groups
▶ Behaviours are not conducive to fostering a good mentoring relationship
▶ Line managers feel exposed, not knowing what's going on
▶ Relationships don't 'gel'
▶ Lack of commitment (perhaps generated by 'I've been told to do this')
▶ Overcommitment to mentoring actions which infringes on primary job responsibilities or work–life balance

A concern expressed by one mentor illustrates the importance of setting the context for the scheme and ensuring that participants (and others) are properly informed.

> *I have one concern which is that the mentoring process gets confused with a sponsorship programme and cliques form.*
> Potential mentor

It is worth remembering that benefits will also accrue for line managers provided they are kept informed. As a result of the relationship:

▶ Mentors and mentees will see increased motivation and improved performance, helped by an increasing ability to identify and resolve issues early on

▶ Line managers often find they have a better relationship with their employee, who, in turn, may get on better with the rest of the team

▶ This can result in the line manager retaining valuable staff in an increasingly efficient team

▶ Where mentors are also line managers, they will be encouraged to use mentoring skills and approaches in the daily line management role.

Summary

Having clarified the benefits and risks, both mentors and mentees will be in a better position to build a positive relationship, avoiding some of the pitfalls highlighted. Mentors and mentees also need to help line managers to see that they will benefit from the process. The benefits far outweigh the potential risks and, with careful preparation and planning, some of the risks may be avoided.

From the mentor's perspective, he or she can expect to increase key people skills in a safe environment and have time to be more reflective. The mentoring relationship provides opportunities to learn about different parts of the business and gives an opportunity to influence managers. It does provide a challenge for the busy manager, adding additional time pressures to what are often heavy workloads. The mentor must also be prepared for breaches of confidentiality and relationships that fail to work.

From the mentee's perspective, the mentoring relationship provides an excellent opportunity to reflect on short- and longer term goals. The mentor offers a sounding board and the relationship provides access to a more senior manager able to reflect back ways of addressing key issues. The mentoring relationship is particularly helpful in today's challenging and changing environment. It provides support and the space to create action plans to address key issues. The risks involved for the mentee mainly depend on the mentor who may not have enough time to devote to the relationship. There is also a risk that the mentor may be too inclined to dominate the relationship rather than enabling the mentee to take charge of his or her own development. On balance, in most cases the benefits are likely to outweigh the risks.

18 Finding a Mentee or Mentor and the Matching Process

Introduction

This chapter will look at the process of finding a mentee and mentor from both perspectives. In most formal mentoring programmes the scheme manager takes responsibility for the allocation of mentors. In informal pairings the mentors and mentees will have more influence on the selection and, in some cases, the mentee will find their own mentor. A case study is included to help mentees to understand what it might be like to have a senior executive as a mentor.

The chapter will outline the main ways of finding mentors and mentees, the qualities needed for a mentor and mentee and how to decide whether to have an internal or external partner. This chapter will help the potential mentor to assess his or her suitability to be an effective mentor, having considered the knowledge, experience and qualities needed of a mentor. Mentors and mentees will also benefit by referring back to Part III Chapters 10 and 11. The chapter also revisits peer mentoring, previously discussed in Chapter 4, for those considering this type of mentoring relationship.

Finding a Mentor

Those looking to find a mentor need to explore all the avenues available to them. Many managers now recognise the value of a mentoring relationship and are more likely to be open to acting as a mentor. It is best for line managers not to mentor their own staff. A degree of separation is valuable for a mentoring relationship.

Part III addressed the selection and matching process for mentors and mentees. However, if a person wants a mentor and there are no formal mentoring schemes available in the organisation, then different approaches need to be used to find one.

As part of the process of finding a mentor, mentees can take the following steps:

▶ Decide what is wanted from the mentoring relationship.

▶ Study the qualities and attributes of mentors to help to identify a suitable person.

▶ Seek advice from others; check out their attitude to development and helping others.

▶ Approach a senior manager in his or her own organisation, having considered who might be suitable.

▶ Explore external networks for a suitable mentor.

▶ Consider having more than one mentor to achieve different goals.

English & Sutton (1999) have worked extensively in the NHS. They explored the extent to which mentoring can contribute to personal growth. They highlighted the need for both mentee and mentor to be aware of their own personal mentoring model. They found that, whilst mentees had a primary focus on personal development, some mentors were unable or unwilling to engage in this type of conversation. It is important, therefore, for those looking for their own mentor to be clear about what they expect from the mentoring relationship and check that a potential mentor can meet these expectations.

Those wishing to have a senior manager as a mentor may be interested to read the case study below of an experience of being mentored by a senior executive. Mentees need to decide whether they would feel unduly inhibited by this type of relationship.

BENG MENTORED BY A SENIOR EXECUTIVE

An interview with a mentee

Why did you choose such a senior mentor?

It was a lot to do with him as a person. I was given the choice of two very strong individuals so it was quite tough, but I went for this particular person as he's in part of the organisation that I have had very little to do with; also the challenge was for me to go that one step further.

How do you arrange your meetings?

One of the key challenges is that his diary is a nightmare. His PA and I have come up with a process to try and make sure we do early morning meetings because that seems to work better in his diary. We schedule more than one meeting at a time and most of the time these will happen. However, having a number of dates set in makes it OK when his PA rings and says she has to reschedule me. We meet about once every 4–6 weeks in a meeting room – not his office.

Does his PA understand what your relationship is?

Yes. She treats me no differently whether it's a mentoring or business context and is quite accommodating because she could so easily go 'Well, mentoring – let's push that one out'. At the end of the day, time is made available and it's just a case of planning in advance. My mentor ensures we have an hour of uninterrupted time and I really do appreciate this because I know his time is so limited.

How intimidating is it to have such a senior mentor?

It is quite intimidating going to someone at that level and talking through some of the issues – they left this stuff behind so many years ago. However, my mentor is the type of person who takes everyone's views on board; the fact that he has got a high position does not prevent him sitting down and listening to people.

The key thing about him is that he's a straight talker; don't waste his time and he won't waste yours. I know that I'd get the message very quickly if I were wasting his time because I've watched him in meetings. He also said to me at the beginning 'I don't suffer fools lightly', so that positioned it for me and I make sure I prepare for our meetings.

What might you not feel comfortable talking about with your mentor?

There are obviously things that I do feel reserved about, whereas with someone else at a lower level I might feel a little more that the gap's not so big. Mostly it comes down to the issues I'm experiencing which, in the broader scheme of what he's doing every day, are just minor issues – am I wasting his time by going to him with such petty things?

Do you make contact with your mentor outside the formal face-to-face meetings?

I have and haven't. I tried the other day because an issue had come up that I wanted to talk with him about; but he'd gone into another meeting, so I addressed the situation. However, I'll discuss it at our next meeting: this was the situation, I did try to find you and this is what I ended up doing; what could I have done differently? We have also exchanged voice and e-mails.

Did you discuss confidentiality at the outset?

We didn't do formal contracting, it's just kind of grown into what it needs to be at that point in time. He is very open with me in terms of some of the issues that the organisation is facing and the conflicts that occur and I really appreciate that: he doesn't treat me like someone who shouldn't know this information. He absolutely trusts me and knows I'm not going to walk out the door and go tell everyone that I know what's happening. I think that's a remarkable quality coming from someone so high up, who essentially has so much to risk.

Are there any 'no go' discussion areas?

Not that we've discovered at this point in time.

What upward mentoring takes place, if any?

He is exceedingly interested in what my views of the organisation are and takes things on board. I can take things to him and say 'actually I think we've got an issue in the company in these areas' and he'll often pick it up and take it to the next executive team meeting. As a result I've seen people taking more cognisance of certain initiatives than they had in the past, which is making a positive impact on the things I do.

So you're saying there is a direct two-way link?

Absolutely. He does take things seriously and so I know he is actively listening and it's not just a case of 'well who are you to tell me what's wrong?'

What have been the main benefits of the relationship?
It is interesting to get exposure to the way people think at this level and I do get insights into this. I've benefited in terms of career planning and one of my key skill development areas. My mentor previously had problems in the same area and so was able to use personal experience to help me along the way.

One of the key things he does is to make sure he's testing me and making me test myself as to what it is I'm trying to do: do I really understand how much of a challenge it is or how I'm really going to get there? It's been exceedingly beneficial.

How does your line manager feel about the relationship?
He's 100% supportive.

Do you talk to him about it?
I speak to him about it quite a lot. I'll say that we've met and gone through the development plan that he (my manager) and I were talking about and that my mentor identified x, y and z. My manager is quite happy for me to take anything into the meetings and discuss them. I know that if he thought I'd gone to speak to my mentor about how to address a specific issue with him, my manager, he wouldn't be unhappy because I think he'd know it was being done for a specific reason, to make sure that the approach was appropriate.

Would you recommend having a very senior mentor to other people?
I'm not sure. I would certainly recommend my mentor, but it's very much down to style. I'm quite an ambitious person and do want to know how they're operating. So for me, having someone like my mentor is an amazing experience because I'm tapping into someone who has a wealth of knowledge, who's well-respected and who I know will give me good guidance. I think you have to be clear about what it is you want out of the relationship if you're going to go with someone at that level, because it can be intimidating and it can be frustrating when you don't have access to them as often as you want. I'm lucky because his PA's very accommodating; others might not be.

How long do you see the relationship continuing?
We've been meeting for about a year now and I'd like to continue for at least the next six months – even if he no longer has time for a formal relationship, I would still very much appreciate being able to pop in and see him.

An alternative approach to having a more senior mentor is to consider peer mentoring, which was discussed in Chapter 4. This was recommended for a number of situations:

▶ Mentoring the mentors

▶ To reduce the feeling of isolation experienced by home workers/virtual team workers

▶ For specific skill sets, for example counselling

▶ To increase understanding across different divisions

▶ To facilitate change – peer mentoring is more easily available than hierarchical mentoring

▶ To smooth the path of mergers and acquisitions.

Peer mentoring can be a one-way or a reciprocal relationship, with both gaining an opportunity to be mentored and act as the mentor. The choice of a peer or a more senior person acting as mentor depends on the reason for wanting a mentor. Where the mentee is seeking help to progress his or her career, then a more senior mentor is more appropriate.

An Internal or External Mentor

The mentee may want to select a mentor who is external to the organisation.

The relative merits of internal and external mentors are summarised in Table 18.1.

Table 18.1 **A comparison of the benefits of internal and external mentoring**

Internal mentor	External mentor
Understands the culture of the organisation	Is more likely to have a broader understanding of the external environment and can give the mentee a broader perspective
Understands the politics and personalities within the organisation	May have specific skills as a developer and mentor
Can open doors for the mentee within the organisation	May be more able to offer support and challenge for senior managers
Is clear about the strategic direction of the organisation and strategies for the mentee to develop their career	Fewer issues around confidentiality
	There may not be a suitable mentor internally

The mentee needs to ensure that the chosen mentor is able to meet his or her objective for having a mentor and that they can build a positive relationship together. The mentee would benefit from studying the next section as part of the selection process.

Attributes and Qualities of a Mentor

Those thinking of becoming a mentor, or have been asked to be a mentor, need to assess whether they are ready to undertake the role and whether they have the right knowledge, experience and qualities to be a successful mentor.

Alred et al. (1998) suggested the following steps to assess readiness for mentoring:

▶ Identify any mentoring being undertaken already, by themselves or others in the organisation.

▶ Discuss the role with other mentors.

▶ Potential mentors should talk to people who they have mentored previously, either formally or informally.

▶ Reflect on the differences between mentoring and management and the skills that are needed in both situations.

▶ Consider other forms of development, for example coaching.

▶ Think about any previous experiences of mentoring and what they have learned.

Knowledge that could be useful for a mentoring relationship could include:

▶ Functional expertise.

▶ Knowledge of the organisation and its strategies and culture.

▶ Knowledge of people and access to people for networking.

▶ Knowledge of the context within which the business operates.

Experience that could be useful for a mentoring relationship could include:

▶ Being a manager.

▶ Working within the organisation and in other organisations.

▶ Working under pressure.

▶ Dealing with difficult people and situations.

▶ Being a mentor already or having been mentored.

▶ Working in particular functions.

▶ Dealing with success and failure.

The Focus Group at Henley discussed what they saw as the key attributes of a successful mentor and agreed on 12 attributes listed in Figure 18.1.

- *Drive and energy*
- *Commitment to the process*
- *Successful/business acumen*
- *Respect and values*
- *Trust and integrity*
- *Perceived approachability*
- *Willingness to share*
- *Individual's agenda is key*
- *Prepared to give the person space*
- *Ability to challenge*
- *Curiosity – non-judgemental*
- *Supportive*

Figure 18.1 **The top twelve attributes of a mentor**

Choosing a Mentee

The mentor also needs to be clear about his or her objectives for entering a mentoring relationship. This will have an impact on the matching process. A mentor also needs to know what to look for in a mentee and the qualities and attributes that will help the mentee to be effective. The qualities have been discussed in Chapter 10.

Just to recap, the Focus Group identified the qualities needed by a mentee as being those listed in Figure 18.2.

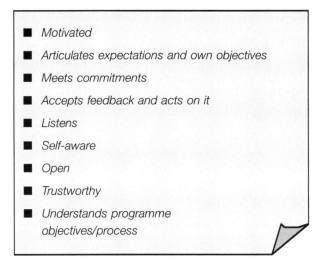

- *Motivated*
- *Articulates expectations and own objectives*
- *Meets commitments*
- *Accepts feedback and acts on it*
- *Listens*
- *Self-aware*
- *Open*
- *Trustworthy*
- *Understands programme objectives/process*

Figure 18.2 **The qualities of a mentee**

A Focus Group organisation also identified the skills attributes and knowledge that the mentor might look for in a mentee. These are summarised in Table 18.2.

Table 18.2 **The skills, attributes and knowledge of a mentee**

What a mentor might look for in a mentee

Skills	Attributes	Knowledge
Communication	Motivated	Preferred learning style
Influencing	Open	Expected outcomes
Time management	Committed	Roles within mentoring
Planning/organising	Trusting	Stages of the relationship
Objective setting	Empathetic	Cognisance of own strengths and weaknesses

The Matching Process

Whether the matching is conducted as part of a formal mentoring scheme or mentors and mentees are making a choice themselves, similar criteria apply. The critical issue is whether to opt for similarity or difference. In addition, both mentor and mentee need to assess whether they will be able to relate to one another: is the chemistry right? Potential matching criteria outlined in Chapter 11 were:

▶ Cross-functional

▶ Cross-cultural, that is, from different nationalities

▶ Gender alike or cross-gender pairings

▶ Similar or different experience/background

▶ Similar or different characters

▶ Knowledge wanted vs knowledge offered

▶ General 'wants' and 'offers' approach

▶ Profiling, for example MBTI®, emotional intelligence

▶ Learning styles

▶ Location, geography

▶ Tenure – long vs short

▶ Common interests (for example sports, hobbies).

Summary

In summary, the following views were expressed in *Business Week* (2001):

> Have realistic expectations when going into a mentoring relationship and the mentee needs to understand that they cannot expect the mentor to solve all his or her career issues. The mentor should be able to offer advice and be available for support in difficult situations. The mentee should find out whom, if anyone, has a good track record as a mentor. It must be remembered that mentors undertake the role for a variety of reasons. Some are seeking recognition, others for the incentives it might bring, but some do it for altruistic reasons. If mentees have mentors who seek to develop others, motives are more likely to be aligned. Finally mentors and mentees need to be prepared to invest the time and energy to make the relationship work.

The next chapter will help the mentor and mentee start to build a positive mentoring relationship.

19 Getting Started as a Mentor and Mentee

Introduction

This chapter will introduce the mentor and mentee to the first steps to be taken to build a successful mentoring relationship. Taking time in the early stages will lead to a far more satisfying experience and understanding the roles and responsibilities of the respective parties will ensure conflict does not arise between the mentor and mentee. By studying the models of the roles of a mentor, both mentors and mentees will be able to develop more realistic expectations of the mentoring relationship.

In the early stages mentors and mentees need to have a sound structure for their meetings. This chapter will provide topics for discussion, agendas and formats for developing a mentoring contract. It will also give guidance on how to build rapport, an essential element of a successful mentoring relationship. Finally a framework for setting mentoring goals and outcomes will be provided.

This chapter will also help those setting up a mentoring programme, and those developing mentors and mentees. It will give guidance on the type of briefing that mentors and mentees should receive before starting the mentoring process.

Roles and Responsibilities

For the mentoring relationship to be effective, the mentor and mentee need to be clear about their respective roles and responsibilities. They also need to consider the role of the mentor in relation to the mentee's line manager. Without this clarification, misunderstandings may occur that could impact on the effectiveness of the relationship. The role adopted will be influenced by the purpose of the mentoring relationship, which needs to be agreed at the start of the relationship, the seniority of the mentee and the context within which the mentoring relationship is being conducted.

Tables 19.1 and 19.2 summarise the roles and responsibilities as identified in schemes run by large organisations. The RWE Thames Water example also identifies roles and responsibilities which are not to be fulfilled by the various parties, thus helping to establish the boundaries.

Table 19.1 **Roles and responsibilities in RWE Thames Water's high-potential programme**

Mentors will	Mentors will NOT
▶ Meet with mentees for confidential discussions ▶ Prompt mentees to draw up their own development plans ▶ Prompt mentees to make contact with others who might be able to provide useful information or advice ▶ Prompt mentees to approach their line managers to seek specific support for developmental activities	▶ Take action on behalf of mentees ▶ Intervene on behalf of mentees ▶ Expect to act as role models except in terms of applying the corporate values in all they do ▶ Take part in any succession planning discussions that relate to their own mentee ▶ Discuss the mentee with the line manager
Mentees will	**Mentees will NOT**
▶ Meet with mentors for confidential discussions ▶ Access other sources of information and advice as may seem appropriate ▶ Share information about their strengths, weaknesses, ambitions and so on openly with their mentor ▶ Take responsibility for drawing up their own development plans ▶ Take responsibility for appropriate contact with their line managers about development issues ▶ Initiate their own development	▶ Expect their mentor to take any direction on their behalf ▶ Attempt to force their line manager into account by quoting their mentor

Line managers

▶ Will allow mentees time to attend mentoring sessions
▶ Will provide whatever support is feasible to the development of the mentee
▶ Will not attempt to talk to the mentor about the mentee

THE ROLE AND RESPONSIBILITIES OF THE MENTOR

Mike Pegg (2003) identified a number of distinct roles for the mentor showing the range of different mentoring relationships:

▶ *Classic mentors* – when the mentor is a 'wise and trusted adviser'. Giving an overview of a situation and the paths that people could follow towards achieving their goals. Their sharing of knowledge helps people to take greater control of their lives.

▶ *Models* – in business the mentor teaches the mentee about 'the things to do to be successful around here'.

Table 19.2 **Examples of roles and responsibilities defined in a Focus Group organisation**

MENTEE	MENTOR
Role:	**Role:**
Learner and developer and driver of the relationship.	One of guidance and teaching, focusing on the mentee's future performance in more demanding, more senior roles.
Responsibilities:	**Responsibilities:**
▶ Defining expectations and objectives for the relationship: having a planned outcome is critical to the success of the relationship. ▶ Agreeing and managing the 'working process' (mentoring contract). ▶ Commitment to completing agreed development tasks without neglecting other responsibilities. ▶ Being open and honest.	▶ To encourage and motivate the mentee. ▶ To agree and keep to a mentoring contract. ▶ To manage normal work objectives and the mentoring relationships – especially time commitments. ▶ To improve the mentee's breadth of knowledge and skills by providing a broader perspective of the organisation, its culture and strategies. ▶ To help employees realise their career plans through development and experiential learning. ▶ To ensure that the key skills of counselling, coaching, facilitation and networking are up to date. ▶ To ensure confidentiality of the relationship. ▶ To agree with the employee a debrief for the local and organisational Development Committee.

LINE MANAGER

Responsibilities:

▶ Setting out and reviewing day-to-day performance objectives. This includes the identification and support of development activities, for example coaching to rectify performance gaps.

▶ *Teachers* – a great teacher does three things: inspires others to want to learn, provides tools that work and helps the other person to integrate the learning into their everyday lives.

▶ *Advisers* – mentors can move into the role of giving advice but this is not the role of the mentor. If mentors do find themselves in a situation when they feel advice is necessary and they are able to give it, they must indicate to mentees that they are stepping out of role.

▶ *Coaches* – as was indicated earlier, people use the words 'coach' and 'mentor' in different ways. A mentor may find himself using coaching skills during a mentoring session. This requires the mentor to encourage the person to build on strengths, address areas for improvement and enable the person to achieve ongoing success.

▶ *Counsellors* – in this role the mentor is creating the right climate, practising listening and being non-directive, thus helping the person to find the answers to his or her own problems.

▶ *Buddies* – this occurs when an experienced staff member 'shows a new person the ropes'. There are occasions when mentors might develop this type of relationship when they become a buddy with their mentor but this is less common, except when the mentor is a peer.

▶ *Leaders* – great leaders encourage others to focus on certain values, pursue a clear vision and deliver visible results.

> *It's very difficult not to give advice – 'let me tell you what you should be doing'; if I find myself doing that then I quickly follow up with: 'It's your decision – go away and decide what's best for you to do.'*
>
> Avaya mentor

Clutterbuck & Megginson (1999) identified seven roles for executive mentors:

1 *Sounding board* – similar to the classic mentor in this role, the mentor is able to give feedback to the mentee by drawing on experience and wisdom.

2 *Critical friend* – the mentor fulfilling this role is able to challenge the mentee to question his or her own motivation and behaviour, and give honest feedback that would be more difficult for colleagues to give.

3 *Listener* – when the mentor is there to listen and give encouragement.

4 *Counsellor* – an empathetic listener able to use reflective and questioning skills. This helps the executive to analyse problems in a dispassionate manner without disregarding the emotional issues. Mentors effective in this role are able to help executives deal with dysfunctional behaviour.

5 *Career adviser* – helps the executive think through career options, plan personal development towards defined career goals and lessons learnt from previous careers.

6 *Networker* – provides access to people helpful to the executive for his or her career or development.

7 *Coach* – when the mentor is required to help the executive to make a personal change happen. This may occur when the executive is addressing a specific behavioural issue or needs to make a change to interpersonal behaviour.

In North America the role of the mentor and mentoring relationship is very different. The mentor is viewed as a sponsor for the mentee, more usually referred to as the 'protégé'. The mentor is more powerful, usually older and is able to give advice and help with making the right career moves. In contrast the European approaches place more emphasis on the greater experience of the mentor and guided learning and development. The European approach tends to be a more integrated approach across the different roles.

In summary, for those about to embark on a mentoring relationship in most situations, three key roles are likely to be needed to ensure that the mentoring relationship is a positive experience for the mentee:

1 **Support** – the mentor needs to give the right level of encouragement and recognition to their mentee. The listener role identified by Clutterbuck & Megginson is very important as part of this role. To give effective support, the mentor must:

   ▷ Listen actively and work to understand the mentee
   ▷ Question to help clarification of key issues
   ▷ Identify and build on strengths
   ▷ Disclose facts, feelings and opinions to help to build rapport and trust
   ▷ Encourage the mentee to set his or her own challenges
   ▷ Offer help and guidance.

2 **Challenge** – the mentor also needs to ask challenging questions and help the mentee to have stretching targets. This helps the mentee to take his or her development experience forward. This embraces the critical friend role identified by Clutterbuck & Megginson. To provide effective challenge, the mentor must:

   ▷ Question level of risk others are taking – too little or too much?
   ▷ Highlight possible avoidance or negative behaviour or thinking
   ▷ Set challenging targets for the mentee
   ▷ Offer alternatives – different opinions and approaches.

3 **Guidance** – finally the mentor needs to offer guidance, drawing on the experience they have to offer the mentee. This role combines the sounding board, career adviser and networker identified by Clutterbuck & Megginson. To provide effective challenge, the mentor must:

   ▷ Offer examples drawn from their own experience
   ▷ Give guidance on possible options
   ▷ Offer access to their network where possible to extend understanding of new areas and provide networking opportunities.

The role of the organisation may well be to provide visible support and recognition that the scheme is an important part of employees' development. An example of this might be the attendance of the key organisational sponsor at a final, closing event for the programme – particularly if they are able to speak briefly about its value and outcomes.

Certain companies in the Focus Group used mentoring champions mainly as an information source and local contact (see Chapter 9 for further information).

Managing the First Meetings

Mentoring is basically a relationship between two individuals and, therefore, it is essential that rapport be established. The first meeting between the mentor and mentee is crucial in terms of setting the tone of the relationship and establishing working principles. Individuals can sometimes experience difficulty in the early stages of the mentoring relationship as each person settles down to get to know the other and build rapport.

There are a number of different ways of managing the first meeting depending on the way the mentoring scheme has been set up in the organisation:

1 Meet during a training programme

2 Meet in an arranged, but social, context

3 Have a facilitator present to guide the pair through the first steps

4 Let the pair decide how the first meeting should be arranged.

Any of the first three approaches means that the organisation has some control over the 'starting' of the scheme and is able to ensure that the pairs meet within a reasonable timeframe. The fourth option allows the mentoring pair to organise themselves and take ownership. The risk here is that the meetings will not take place within a reasonable timeframe. The mentoring pair is more likely to arrange the first meeting when the mentoring relationship is not linked to an organised company scheme.

Whatever the approach, as much time as is needed should be set aside at the beginning of the partnership to develop the important ingredient of rapport.

At Smiths Group, the first meeting is facilitated by an external consultant and includes the mentee's line manager. Smiths feel that this is 'key to ensuring buy-in and commitment from all parties to the mentee's objectives for the mentoring. The line manager also learns about the scheme and is fully briefed by the consultant.'

Zurich also provides facilitation for the first meeting and at further meetings if additional support is requested – see Figure 19.1.

FACILITATING MENTORING MEETINGS   Zurich

The scheme at Zurich, where senior directors mentor high achievers, is relatively informal. However, once the pair has established that the relationship will work, they are offered a Facilitator for their contracting meeting. The Facilitator will help when required – for example mapping out how the relationship might work; alternatively, opening up a discussion about their MBTI® types, or acting as an observer and offering feedback. Zurich's Facilitators feel they generally have to begin by being prescriptive then gradually can back off, letting the pair take control.

Occasionally the Facilitator will be asked for advice, but their role is to encourage the pair to find solutions themselves – there are not necessarily any 'right' answers.

The provision of a Facilitator is a very positive method of getting relationships off to a successful start; so much so that Zurich is keen to make this a mandatory step. Where facilitation doesn't work is when the Facilitator is too prescriptive throughout and unable to adapt to the style and pace of the other participants – one size does not fit all.

Figure 19.1 **Facilitating the first mentoring meeting in Zurich**

The first meeting between mentor and mentee was usually more of a social meeting in most of the organisations in the Focus Group. It was more about getting to know one another, seeing if the chemistry worked, what the pair had in common and whether they enjoyed talking with each other, than worrying about formalising and contracting.

One scheme manager related how this approach had been adopted in his graduate mentoring programme and also, interestingly, told how participants underwent negative emotions at the beginning of the relationship – see Figure 19.2.

INITIAL IMPRESSIONS   A Graduate Scheme

At the mentor training workshop it was suggested that it may help build the relationship if the first meeting was largely an information-gathering/getting-to-know-each-other session and if it was held off-site. Many of the mentors took this advice, meeting in a pub over a drink and, in one instance, over a lunchtime meal, with the mentors paying out of their own pockets. The informal beginning helped to break down the barriers and get the relationships off to a good start.

During the relationship the mentors and mentees who were interviewed related how they experienced a larger number of negative emotions and feelings than positive. These feelings were expressed using the following words: uncomfortable, nervous, worried, shocked, lack of confidence, disappointed, surprised, wary, daunted, challenged, confused, overawed, insecure, pressured, difficulty, regretful, lacking, awkward, frustrated, inhibited, embarrassed, disheartened, miserable and failure.

Many of the relationships might not have progressed beyond the first meeting if they had not started the relationship with an informal agenda in an unthreatening environment, or would have drifted apart before both parties had established the necessary confidence. The mentors, most of whom had volunteered for the first time, had the same negative feelings and emotions as the graduates. Both parties found their new roles quite challenging and, surprisingly, not what they expected. This may help to explain why there were more negative emotions and feelings, than positive, experienced during the relationship start-up.

A positive outcome was that all the mentors interviewed volunteered to become mentors again, when mentors were being sought for the next year's graduate intake. In the end, the positives outweighed the negatives.

Figure 19.2 **Initial impressions gained on a graduate mentoring programme**

Common discussion topics at the first meeting of the graduate mentoring programme pairs tended to be respective degrees, business background, interests and what they were both involved in at present both inside and outside the business. Most pairs did not discuss expectations or objectives for the relationship, but some did cover what the mentee was hoping to get out of the relationship and what the mentor could, or was prepared to, do for the mentee. Generally, the objective for the first meeting was to get to know each other and build rapport. Most of the mentors and mentees interviewed saw this as a good way in which to start the relationship and found it helpful and non-threatening.

In summary, most of the first meetings outlined tended to be an icebreaker for the mentor and mentee. Establishing rapport and building a relationship with one another is an essential element of successful mentoring. Once this initial meeting has taken place, or sometimes at the later part of the first meeting, the mentor and mentee need to agree some ground rules and ways of working together.

> **First Meeting**   Yorkshire Water
>
> ▶ Mentors attend a lunchtime session during the graduates' Induction Week
>
> ▶ They meet informally over lunch
>
> ▶ The graduates then arrange the first meeting as required
>
> ▶ Graduates drive the on-going relationship and arrange all meetings.

Whatever the right approach, there are a number of topics/rules of engagement that are recommended discussion items at the first 'formal' meeting – see Figure 19.3.

AGENDA

◆ *Introductions:* that is, more detailed information about background, experience, motivation and so on. This helps to establish common ground.

◆ *Ground rules:* the boundaries or scope – what is acceptable, unacceptable to either party (see examples later in this chapter).

◆ *Objectives:* for the meeting and the relationship overall.

◆ *Working style:* expectations on meeting times, locations and frequency; responsibility for agenda-setting and note-taking and so on.

◆ *A formal (written) or informal contract:* representing what each party is committed to (examples can be found later in this chapter).

◆ *Actions:* things to be done by both parties before the next session.

◆ *Date of next meeting:* recommended to be within a fortnight or soon after the first one.

Figure 19.3 **Recommended agenda items generated by Focus Group members**

An agenda for the meeting allows the mentor and mentee to have a structure to follow. This helps the pair to prepare for the meeting, builds confidence and rapport and is particularly useful for those involved in a mentoring relationship for the first time.

Figure 19.4 outlines the topic headings given to mentors and mentees by one organisation to help make their early meetings more effective.

AGENDA FOR THE FIRST MEETING

Note down any points you want to raise during the first meeting. Below are some headings to remind you of topics to cover:

- Introductions
- Discuss the employee's career aspirations
- Review the employee's current situation, Leadership Programme output and personal SWOT
- SWOT analysis of the organisation
- Agree a Mentoring Contract
- Other issues; contact methods and timings
- Action points
- Date of next contact or meeting

Figure 19.4 **Agenda for the first meeting in a high-potential scheme**

EXPECTATIONS OF MENTORS AND MENTEES

Mentors and mentees need to be quite clear about what they expect of one another and their relationship for it to be a success.

Realistically, a **mentor** can expect:

▶ The mentee to be committed to the mentoring relationship.

We have established good, regular – but reasonably informal – contact with each other. We meet every other month, but if things happen (in terms of career and so on) he will pick up the phone and chat things over.

RWE Thames Water mentor

▶ The mentee to respect confidentiality issues.

▶ The mentee to take active responsibility for his or her own learning.

▶ To have an opportunity to develop key skills.

▶ To have the chance to learn more about another part of the organisation.

▶ The mentee to discuss issues openly.

▶ The mentee to respect their time constraints.

> *I've found that the mentor gets enormous benefits as well. The mentor gets to step completely outside his or her normal world and really think about what is important in terms of process and approach to real problems. ... Helping mentees think through their issues is just like going back to school for the mentor – it teaches us to stop, and think, and analyse, and assist with finding the RIGHT approach – not the politically or practically expedient.*
>
> Smiths Group mentor

Realistically, a **mentee** can expect:

▶ The chance to gain insight into the broader skills base and thinking patterns of more senior management.

▶ Increased self-awareness.

▶ The opportunity to consult with someone higher up the organisation about career options.

▶ New perspectives on the organisation.

▶ To be challenged and supported.

▶ To have someone to act as a sounding board.

▶ The benefit of contact with a highly respected person within the organisation.

▶ A better understanding of the informal culture of the organisation.

Glover (2002) reported on the work of Pegg at Microsoft: Microsoft recognised that people needed the chance to recentre and take a helicopter view of their options. Mentoring provided the time and space to reflect. Microsoft also found that mentoring helped to tackle the issue of effective teamworking when people were rewarded individually (see Chapter 20, Useful Structures and Models for Longer Meetings).

CREATING A MENTORING CHARTER

At B&Q a Mentoring Charter was defined during the training days, with input from both mentors and mentees. This not only built the commitment on both sides, but (together with the mentee's personal profile) provided areas for discussion, which helped to get the first meeting off to a good start.

The framework for the charter was adapted from Pegg (2003) – see Figure 19.5.

Our Mentoring Charter

What I *will* do

- Act with integrity & confidentiality
- Be honest, objective & impartial
- Honour time commitments
- Ask you challenging questions
- Listen to you
- Share knowledge as appropriate
- Provide information I have promised
- Work to the company values

What I *won't* do

- Do your work for you
- Talk at you all day
- Only give you 'nice' feedback
- Answer *all* your questions
- Intervene between you and your manager
- Allow you to ignore company values
- Take the place of your manager

Things I *can* do:

- Provide access & guidance to widening your network
- Help you learn from experiences
- Ask others for feedback about you
- Help you to identify goals
- Help you understand the business/ strategy
- Assist you to analyse problems
- Help you to work through resolving conflicts
- Support you when you have valid points

Things I *can't* do

- Nursemaid you
- Teach you everything
- Demand feedback from others
- Identify your goals
- Solve all your problems
- Realise your career aspirations
- Resolve all your conflicts

If you feel there are other things you would like me to do, let's talk about them.

Figure 19.5 **Mentoring charter developed by participants in B&Q's mentoring programme**

This approach again identifies not only what the mentor can, and is prepared to do, but also highlights what the mentor cannot or is not prepared to do. The items reflect the three key roles of the mentor identified earlier.

ESTABLISHING A LEARNING CONTRACT

So how important is it to have a learning contract? Mentors and mentees may or may not draw up a formal learning contract. According to Clutterbuck (2001), in an experiment within the National Health Service involving 100 pairs, the success of the relationship was not dependant on whether or not the pairs had a formal learning contract. Only about 20 per cent of the sample actually had a formal contract. Clutterbuck concluded that the most important aspects were that:

▶ Both sides had discussed the relationship objectives.

▶ Expectations of each other had been shared.

▶ An agreement had been reached as to how the relationship would be managed.

Avaya drew up a formal learning contract for mentors and mentees to complete. They also laid down certain rules for the mentoring process and supplied a checklist of issues that could be included as part of the contract. The rules are particularly helpful, offering a useful checklist for anyone embarking on a mentoring relationship. The documents are included in Figures 19.6 and 19.7.

AVAYA

The Mentoring Contract

This is a statement of commitment to a mentoring relationship between

_____ [mentor] and _____[mentee]

We agree to commit ourselves to the development of:

_____ [mentee]

_____[mentor] commits to supporting the agreed learning goals and to help meet the career objectives by accessing the appropriate learning resources and by personal support , working for a useful honest and confidential mentoring relationship

_____[mentee] commits to actively progressing the agreed learning goals and working for a trustful, confidential and honest mentoring relationship

Signed

_____ [mentor] _____[mentee]

Rules of the Mentoring Relationship

The mentor will only enquire or intrude into the mentees personal life by invitation

The mentor and the mentee will not make excessive demands on each others time

The mentee will only use the mentors authority with the mentors consent

The mentor will assist the mentee in achieving objectives but will let the mentee run his or her own show as much as possible

The agenda for each, meeting will be published and agreed before the start of the meeting this will be driven by the mentee

We will review each meeting for improvement and constructive feedback

The relationship will be reviewed to ensure we are on track and it is adding value every 3 months minimum

Figure 19.6 **Documentation for mentoring drawn up by Avaya**

Other areas which may be included in a contract depending on the individual circumstances:

❏ Boundaries of the mentoring contract

❏ Confidentiality – safe to say environment

❏ Agreeing objectives of mentoring contracts

❏ Structure of the meetings

❏ Easy exit criteria

❏ Whatever we discuss stays between us unless we agree otherwise

❏ We are here for our development in the business. Personal factors may arise but we will bring it back to a business objective

❏ We will not use each other's position for personal gain

❏ Our relationship is private and will not be abused

❏ Our time together will be mutually agreed and set in advance, we are both accountable for this

❏ I expect an agenda with any material pre-sent (7 days before), conversely I commit to prepare for that meeting

❏ We will not discuss hearsay or other people

❏ We will not allow these discussions to be based on emotion

❏ We will spend time at the start of the contract establishing a clear vision and clear objectives

❏ We will always review the last meeting and review our objectives on a quarterly basis

❏ No fault exit clause at any time

Figure 19.7 **Other possible areas for inclusion in a contract (collective views of several mentors within Avaya)**

A FRAMEWORK FOR THE MENTEE TO PREPARE FOR THE FIRST MENTORING MEETING

Initial meetings work best when the mentee has undertaken some preparatory work. One framework that can be used is the SWOT analysis. Completing this in advance gives some useful insights into the hopes and concerns of the mentee. It also provides a structured element for the first meeting.

An example of a personal SWOT analysis is shown in Figure 19.8.

Strengths	Weaknesses
Current competences Experience Core talents	Competences/knowledge needing development
Opportunities	Threats
Career aspirations Interests Possible job moves	Perceived obstacles

Figure 19.8 **Personal SWOT analysis**

Building Rapport and Establishing Mutual Trust

Whether a mentoring pair is able to build an understanding with each other and form some kind of bond is the make or break of their relationship. A natural rapport is not always easy to find and it is worth considering the great value of having a mentor who is 'opposite' in many aspects.

Rapport means that the two parties to the relationship are in tune with one another. Once rapport has been established, it is then possible to build a deeper relationship.

There are a number of ways rapport can be built. Some practical suggestions to help mentors and mentees include the following.

▶ **Informality** – if early meetings are held away from the office environment (for example in a pub, on the golf course, over lunch or dinner), this helps to break down barriers.

▶ **Self-disclosure** – revealing details of a more personal nature helps to engender trust. These need not be intimate personal details – more personal experiences of life or work, for example via a CV.

▶ **Early discussion of objectives and expectations of the mentoring relationship** – this will help to establish a common purpose and avoid misunderstandings. Having a clear developmental goal for the mentee helps to provide a shared focus of interest.

▶ **Complete and get feedback on a diagnostic tool beforehand** (for example Myers–Briggs Type Indicator®, Strengths Finder®, learning styles and so on). Share this information as an 'icebreaker' discussion topic.

Informality helps rapport building: by considering the location of the meeting: being away from the office immediately creates a more relaxed atmosphere.

Sharing personal information helps to build trust and deepens the relationship. It may also throw up common ground.

Through sharing expectations, both the mentor and mentee will increase mutual understanding and knowing the aims of the mentee will give a shared goal for the pair.

Finally, sharing data on selected diagnostic instruments will further help to build rapport by helping to develop mutual understanding of styles of working.

Hay (1999) identified seven aspects of the working relationship that the pair could usefully discuss to build the relationship further:

1 *Compatibility:* What opinions do we share? What do we have in common?

2 *Control:* Who will control what? How much do each of us like to control? How will we share control – the mentee over content, mentor over process, perhaps?

3 *Caring:* Do we have the ability to behave in a nurturing way towards each other? It is often assumed that only the mentor should be caring, but this creates a very one-sided dependency relationship.

4 *Closeness:* Real closeness occurs when both of us are able to be spontaneous – how will we show our emotions and let one another know how we really feel, genuine emotions such as anger, sadness and fear as well as happiness?

5 *Competence:* Two heads are better than one – working together in a logical mode will increase our mutual abilities to problem solve and get decisions made. How best can we do this?

6 *Cooperation:* How will we do this? What are our previous experiences of cooperation like? How flexible can we be?

7 *Challenge:* Two heads should be better than one – how will we challenge each other?

> The mentorship programme has been beneficial thus far in that my mentor has provided a perspective that has improved my ability to manage new projects. We have discussed initial project tasks, possible obstacles, risk management, and what is required to obtain 'buy-in' from all personnel involved. The mentor has been helpful with insight into project management methods and considerations as well as answering questions that I have.
>
> Smiths Group mentee

BUILDING RAPPORT THROUGH COMMUNICATION

People gather information and interact with others using the five senses:

Visual   seeing
Auditory   hearing
Kinaesthetic feeling
Olfactory   smelling
Gustatory   tasting

People tend to use some senses more than others and through the senses they represent the world to themselves internally. They are, therefore, known as representational systems. The language used by people offers clues to the way people are processing sensory information.

Table 19.3 gives some examples of words used by the different representational systems.

Table 19.3 **Examples of words indicating a visual, auditory or kinaesthetic preference**

Visual		Auditory		Kinaesthetic	
clear	focus	tune in	listen	feel	grasp
insight	perspective	sound	say	touch	pressure
reflect	highlight	hear	tone	handle	pushy
outlook	vision	clash	harmony	pull	firm

When mentors and mentees are building rapport, it helps to be aware of the representational systems their mentor or mentee is using. If the same representational system is used, they are more likely to build rapport. For example, if a mentee is using a lot of visual language, the mentor may want to present what they are talking about (auditory) in a diagrammatic format (visual). If people are operating in different modes, the relationship will not feel harmonious.

A MODEL FOR BUILDING RAPPORT AND TRUST

Human beings tend to operate at different levels. You may have heard people saying things like: 'On one level I am perfectly happy and yet on another I'm very uneasy.'

Anthropologist Gregory Bateson (1972) identified five basic levels of learning and change. Each level is more abstract than the level below it, but each having a greater degree of impact on an individual.

These different 'levels' indicate what may be important to a person in a particular context or as a general level of information that interests the individual. These levels, or 'logical levels' as they are referred to, are one of the models used in neurolinguistic programming (NLP) and are useful for mentors to understand when building rapport (see Figure 19.9).

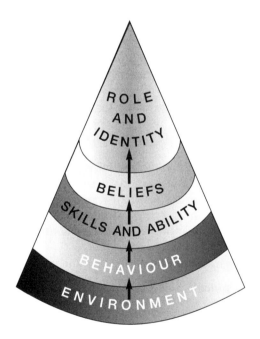

Figure 19.9 **Diagrammatic representation of logical levels**

At the start of the mentoring relationship when rapport is being built, this model can help to provide a structure for sharing information that will lead to a deeper relationship.

The model provides a way of understanding what is important to share and where the interests of the mentor and mentee lie. The levels at which people operate are mainly unconscious and this model provides a framework that enables people to become consciously aware of them.

Examine the statement: 'I can't do that here.'

Now, repeat it with the emphasis on each word in turn.

By doing this, one separates the meaning into an area of particular significance.

▶ Role/identity – *Who?*

▶ Beliefs – *Why?*

▶ Capability – *How?*

▶ Behaviour – *What?*

▶ Environment – *Where/When?*

By understanding the emphasis of a person's statement, you can identify what is important to that person, the level at which they are operating and, by responding at *that* level, create rapport.

Understanding these levels can help us to recognise the levels at which other people operate and to respond on the same level.

Level of environment – where and when

This is the context in which mentoring takes place and will include objectives for the mentoring relationship and the support the mentor and mentee may receive from the wider organisation. It refers to the place and time that the mentoring will take place.

The questions below help mentors and mentees to explore this level:

▶ Where and when have you been a mentor/mentee?

▶ Is this your first time?

▶ Have you done something similar?

▶ Where was that?

▶ How long ago was that?

Level of behaviour – the what

This refers to what people do, the physical actions people can see, but also cognitive behaviour in terms of specific thoughts and knowledge. It relates to specific behaviour that the mentor and mentee exhibit and the types of behaviour the mentor and mentee want to develop.

The questions below will help mentors and mentees to explore this level:

▶ What do you actually do as a mentor?

▶ What sort of things do you want to discuss?

▶ What do you want to do differently?

Level of skills and ability – the how

At this level, to produce a particular behaviour, people use a whole range of skills and abilities from motor skills to move different parts of the body to high-level metacognitive skills, including communication and analysis.

The questions below will help mentors and mentees to explore this level:

▶ What skills do you have that enable you to be a mentor/mentee?

▶ What training have you had?

▶ What experience have you?

▶ What skills and abilities do you want to develop?

Level of belief and values – the why

At this level, our beliefs and values are the motivators and principles that guide and explain behaviour. They can be very deeply held and will have an impact on the way people act as mentors and mentees. For example, this could include values and beliefs about learning in general and the process of mentoring in particular.

The questions below will help mentors and mentees to explore this level:

▶ Why are you a mentor?

▶ What do you think about people?

▶ What do you believe about sharing knowledge?

▶ What do you believe about learning?

Level of role and identity

At the level of role – what role

Some people identify very clearly with the role they are fulfilling. When asked who they are, people will reply in terms of their job title. In the case of mentoring, they will be seeing themselves as a mentor or mentee at this level.

The questions below will help mentors and mentees to explore this level:

▶ Is this your role all the time?

▶ What is your normal role?

At the level of identity – the who

At the level of identity people have a sense of who they really are. This level is closely linked with values and beliefs about themselves such as their sense of self-esteem and their ability to achieve the personal goals they have set themselves.

The questions below will help mentors and mentees to explore this level:

▶ What are you like as a person?

▶ What do you do when you're not working?

Mentors can use the Logical Levels model to challenge the mentee's world and enable him or her to gain additional information that may not be available to them at a conscious level.

We can become so focused that we give all our attention to certain aspects of projects, tasks and even life itself. Taking people through the steps of the logical levels gives them the opportunity to pause and consider the importance of each level: take the learning from that level and move to the next. Once each level has been visited, a metaphorical 'walk' through the levels allows one to assimilate the information quickly, thereby giving a possible new understanding.

Mentors may find that their mentees have already gone through this process in their own way but have not formalised it and they often find it a helpful method of seeking information for further professional or personal projects.

There are a few things worth remembering when using this model in mentoring:

▶ The 'normal' place to start questions at is at the 'lowest' level of the environment and progress to the highest level of identity. This is because 'normally' people need to get through the outer layers of the onion before revealing their innermost thoughts and feelings and you are, in effect, asking people to think deeply about themselves at the levels of their beliefs, values and identities.

▶ This does not necessarily mean that the most significant information gained may not be at the outer levels because environmental information (where we live, work and play, sit within an office or standard of hotel we stay in away from home) can directly affect us at higher levels (self-esteem).

▶ A mentor can either formally take a mentee through the process step by step, or ask the questions in a random fashion, noticing the different strengths of response to make a judgement on whether or not it might perhaps be useful to assist the mentee to consider this area more fully.

Agreeing Mentoring Goals

Mentoring relationships work best when the mentee is very clear about what he or she wants to achieve as a result. One way of achieving this clarity is to use a framework known as 'Well-Formed Outcomes', based on the work of Bandler & Grinder (1975). This framework not only gives clarity about the end goal but will also help the mentee to know if the relationship has been a success or not.

WELL-FORMED OUTCOME FRAMEWORK

This approach can be used in one of two ways:

1 The mentee answers the questions outlined below as part of the preparation stage and takes their answers to an early mentoring meeting for discussion.

2 The mentor asks the mentee to answer each of the questions during a mentoring meeting to help to build rapport between the two. In this case the mentor would record the answers for the mentee thus allowing the mentee to focus on the outcome they seek to achieve:

   ▷ An outcome is the ultimate reason for having a goal.
   ▷ A goal is a way of articulating something tangible that will enable a person to achieve his or her desired outcome.
   ▷ Goals need to be continually reevaluated to check whether or not they will still produce the same outcome.

MENTORING OUTCOMES

Desired outcomes or results are useful to have prior to undertaking a task, a project or a personal or professional training programme. Knowing what you want, *specifically*, is a valuable piece of information to have.

People tend to live in a problem-solving culture rather than one that is 'goal-oriented' or 'outcome-based' and, as a result, people can have a tendency to fix problems and miss noticing when they have got what they wanted in the first place.

In order to have a Well-Formed Outcome, or one that is achievable, a mentor needs to ask a series of questions that help the person to formulate a clear understanding of what is to be achieved.

The questions outlined below will help mentees to focus on what they specifically want to achieve by the conclusion of the mentoring relationship.

The eight focus steps are:

1 State what you want in the positive – What do you want?

   People often know what they don't want, but what do you want?

2 Find out what evidence procedure is in place – *How will you know when you have what you want?* The answer to this must be in terms that we as human beings understand, that is, they must be specific to the senses.

   As we take in the world through our senses (seeing, hearing and feeling) we need to give ourselves an evidence procedure that can be verified using these senses.

   How will you look, sound and feel – what will be the same or different?

3 Can you start and maintain the process to get what you want?

   What stops you from having it now?
   What do you need?
   What is your first step?

4 You presently do things which work, so what part of your present behaviour can you use to get what you want?

5 In what context do you want this?

   Everywhere or somewhere specific?
   When do you want it – all the time?
   When, where and with whom do you not want it?

6 What are the costs of what you want?

   Is it worth the cost to you?
   What will you gain?
   What will you lose?

7 Is it worth the time it's going to take?

8 Is what you want in keeping with your own purpose, your sense of self and identity?

Having completed this eight-stage process, the mentee should be much clearer about the final outcome for the mentoring relationship. It is well worth spending time on gaining this clarity if the relationship is to be successful.

Summary

Experience has shown that mentors and mentees who use the tools, techniques and frameworks suggested in this chapter are more able to build a successful mentoring relationship. The first stage of the mentoring relationship is to clarify roles and responsibilities. Mentors should be prepared to offer support and challenge and guidance. In return the mentee must be prepared to take responsibility for his or her development and draw up development plans. If the relationship is to be successful, mentor and mentee must be open and honest.

The first meeting is critical for setting the tone of the relationship. An agenda is helpful and various topics for discussion have been suggested in the chapter. Some organisations with formal schemes facilitate the first meeting to help establish the relationship.

Mentors and mentees need to have realistic expectations of one another. Ideally a learning contract should be established. This allows the mentor and mentee to share expectations, agree objectives and decide how the meetings will be managed.

Establishing rapport is important; two frameworks were suggested, representational systems and logical levels, to help the process. Finally mentors and mentees should establish mentoring goals. The next step is to deepen the relationship, which requires the mentor to use certain key skills. These will be covered in the next chapter together with strategies developed by members of the Focus Group.

20 Making the Relationship a Positive Experience

Introduction

A successful mentoring relationship depends on a number of factors and both mentor and mentee need to take an active part. In the previous chapter building rapport and contracting were discussed. This chapter will explore how to progress the mentoring relationship effectively, thus making it a positive experience. There are certain logistics that will ensure that the mentor and mentee meet on a regular basis and further guidance on how to structure the meetings. The organisations in the Focus Group developed certain helpful strategies and tactics to ensure that the meetings are productive.

Positive relationships also depend on the mentors having the necessary skill set to ensure that the relationship is satisfying for both parties. This chapter will give advice to the mentor on important skills including questioning techniques, active listening, giving and receiving feedback and using emotional intelligence to make the meetings even more effective. Recommendations on ways that the mentor and mentee can help to develop the relationship are also included.

This chapter has been primarily written for the mentor and mentee. Those acting as a scheme manager or who have responsibility for training mentors and mentees will also find this chapter useful.

Meeting Frequency and Venue

Once the initial meeting and formal contracting has taken place, participants often ask for guidance on how frequently they should meet. RWE Thames Water's guidelines state:

> **It is anticipated that mentor/mentee meetings will probably:**
> ► last a couple of hours
> ► take place every 3–4 weeks
> ► be spread over a period of about 12–15 months

Generally speaking, participants were encouraged to plan a frequency that suited the pair of them best – often every 6–8 weeks. From experience, when meetings occurred more infrequently, without a good reason, momentum was lost and the relationship faded.

The mentor and mentee also need to agree on the length of the meeting. Ideally the meeting should last for approximately two hours: this allows time for quality listening and reflection. The initial contracting around this area may need review if the process originally agreed is found not to be working.

In terms of venue mentors and mentees all found that the meetings worked best when they occurred in 'neutral' space such as meeting rooms, the office restaurant or cafeteria and so on, but not in the mentor's office. In the latter the mentor was too likely to be distracted or interrupted. Ideally meetings should take place away from the office completely, as this makes the meeting rather more special and enables the mentor and mentee to distance themselves from day-to-day issues.

For many mentors, finding time in a busy work schedule is challenging. Some 'multiple mentors' spoke of arranging mentoring days when they devoted the entire day to seeing their two or three mentees. However, one reported disadvantage of this approach is that it can be quite mentally draining by the time they see the final mentee.

It is also helpful to ensure that line managers understand the guidelines on meeting frequency – there will then be fewer problems for the mentee in managing reactions to their absence from the workplace.

Initial Assessment of the Pairing by the Mentor and Mentee

In the early stages of a mentoring relationship, there will be a raft of 'initial impression' reactions – some coming soon after mentors and mentees have been notified. The following three examples are drawn from Focus Group organisations:

1 In one organisation a mentee had never met the proposed mentor, knew nothing of him and so started asking around: he did not like what he found out and contacted the Scheme Manager to express discontent. After discussion, they agreed to wait until the first couple of meetings had been completed, to see if any action was, in fact, needed: it was not, the pair went on to establish a successful relationship.

2 In another example one mentee thought he had drawn the 'short straw', because the mentor he had been given had a reputation for being pretty obtuse and quite difficult. From their profile forms it was clear that they shared some common objectives and pastimes and, in fact, feedback after the first couple of meetings was 'Actually he is nowhere near as bad as I thought he was'. Popular opinion was proved wrong and emphasises the point that it is worth persisting at the beginning.

3   Another mentee was allocated a director of the organisation. Shortly after the mentoring relationship started the director resigned and a replacement mentor was found. Unfortunately the mentee had valued the seniority of the first mentor and was reluctant to accept a more junior one. The most important qualities of the mentor are having suitable experience, and the skills needed for mentoring. The more junior manager turned out to be just as helpful.

Inevitably, some pairs just do not gel. At this stage, it is best for the pair to continue for two or three meetings and see how things develop. Occasionally the relationship proceeds so badly that the best course of action is to discontinue it. Both parties are likely to experience a certain sense of failure. However, in most cases people go on to build a positive relationship in a different pairing.

During a Q&A session at Henley, David Megginson referred to the phrase 'no blame divorce'. This is a good way of describing the situation without attributing blame to either party and helps to avoid feelings of failure. David also addressed the issue of whether mentees should tell others that they have a mentor.

The replies are shown below.

Practitioners' Problem-solving

Questions and Answers with David Megginson and David Clutterbuck

What do you do when it goes wrong?

We use a phrase 'no blame divorce'. I think that this is a nice one and goes something like: 'If either of you decides that you don't want to continue, then just let us know and we can pair you with someone else.' Make it as easy as possible for people to get out.   **(DM)**

How open should people be about the fact they have a mentor?

If there is any question about whether you should disclose that you have a mentor, my answer is always yes. It strikes me that it is a bit like if you have an illicit affair and you think you've been really clever and nobody knows – when, actually everybody knows.

I expect it is the same with a mentor and so don't try and keep your mentor secret – encourage people to talk about it and get it out in the open. **(DM)**

Topics for Discussion

Each mentoring relationship is unique and, therefore, topics for discussion will vary from pairing to pairing. However, at the start of mentoring relationships, particularly if the mentor is acting as a mentor for the first time, people often ask what they should talk about.

Some suggestions are given in Figure 20.1.

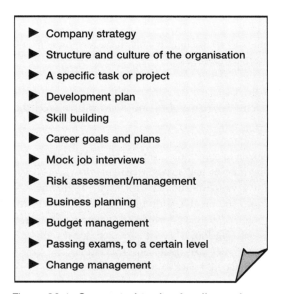

- ▶ Company strategy
- ▶ Structure and culture of the organisation
- ▶ A specific task or project
- ▶ Development plan
- ▶ Skill building
- ▶ Career goals and plans
- ▶ Mock job interviews
- ▶ Risk assessment/management
- ▶ Business planning
- ▶ Budget management
- ▶ Passing exams, to a certain level
- ▶ Change management

Figure 20.1 **Suggested topics for discussion**

However, if the mentee has been able to establish clear objectives at the outset, topics for discussion will be apparent.

Mentees are encouraged not to expect 'answers' to their problems – the whole focus of mentoring is for the mentor to guide them into finding the solution that best fits their circumstances. Later in this chapter there are a number of opening approaches and questions that mentors can use.

At one organisation a recurring question raised by the mentees on their graduate scheme is: 'If I haven't any specific problems why do I need to see my mentor?' It is important that the mentor is not just seen as a solver of problems, but rather a developer of unrealised potential.

Whatever is discussed during the meetings, it is between the two people involved and not usually the concern of anyone else. Each relationship varies in the way it works and in the subjects covered. The intent is to provide space, time and a safe environment within which ideas can be tested, options explored and the mentor is used as a sounding board.

A mentor is not generally seen as a day-to-day troubleshooter; that is the line manager's role – although the mentor may facilitate the learning that can be derived from setbacks.

It is, perhaps, inevitable that conversations move into more personal areas – this possibility should be discussed at the initial contract setting so that both parties understand the boundaries of the relationship. If the mentor feels that the conversation is getting beyond their capability to handle, they should back off and seek professional help. The scheme manager within the organisation could be a useful place to start.

Straying into areas beyond the mentor's depth can happen very easily. Whitmore (1996) commented on this issue:

> The boundary between coaching and counselling is only that coaching is mainly proactive and counselling is generally reactive.

When mentors are new to the role, issues can emerge early on that may need the help and facilitation of the scheme manager – one of whom related this story:

> One relationship suffered from an inappropriate intervention by the mentor early on in the relationship. The mentor had strong views on what he believed mentoring should be about; these views did not fit with what the mentee was looking for from the relationship. The mentor, although he participated in the mentoring training workshop, seemed to have formed or maintained a hierarchical, authoritative view of the relationship, where the mentee saw it (correctly in my opinion) as equal. Perhaps if they had discussed expectations and objectives early on in the relationship they could have resolved a situation which eventually became an obstacle to the building of an effective relationship.
>
> *(Focus Group scheme manager)*

The example outlined below further explains the nature of the mentoring relationship that can develop as part of developing the career of the mentee. In this case a mentor from one of the Focus Group organisations was fulfilling a coaching role within the mentoring relationship, on request for advice from the mentee.

MENTORING TO SUPPORT JOB MOVES — A mentor's perspective

Mentees contact you more frequently around career break points, where something's happening in their career that becomes very time sensitive. Sometimes it's a 10-minute conversation over a coffee, or a chat on the mobile – in one case that happened pretty much every day for a week. The mentoring arrangement then turns from 80% listening/20% talking to 80% coaching and giving advice on the lines of: *I've been through these situations before; this may be something you'd like to consider.* We then start to explore the situations where I've been at that career point and the benefit of my experience – for example: *You need to hot up the pace until a decision is about to be taken. If you leave it a week, the decision will be taken without your influence into the process.*

In one mentee's case it was: *I've heard this job's coming up and would like to go for it, but it's nearly closed and almost too late.* So I explained that it would become a selling job: *Have you met the director who's recruiting? ... Once ... What did he say? If you meet with him again before he makes a decision, what are you going to say to him? What are some of the topics?*

Then you start to give the mentee a bit more advice and guidance: *Who are the people that influence that director? Do you have relationships with the people who influence the director?*

Could you meet with any of them? Do you get on with any of them already? It would be easiest to meet with those ones first. Before you have that meeting, think through what you want to say to them.

In the end it worked quite well for her: she met firstly with one of the director's inner circle and we discussed beforehand what she was going to say: *make pleasantries, but get to the point quite quickly in case he is called away to an emergency. You don't want to be leaving it half an hour without making your point.* She explained that she was going for the job and wanted to ask what advice he would give her – what might she need to say to the director. As a result of doing this she was able to get both his support and his coaching; he also mentioned her interest in the job to the recruiting director. She gradually worked round the list of potential influencers and also had a meeting with the other person going for the job.

The end result was that, although it was pretty much a done deal that the other chap was going to be successful, the job was actually carved up into three parts and she got a third of the responsibilities. So she came away with a lesser role than she wanted, but a more substantial role than she would have got if she'd not had some coaching.

Strategies and Tactics for Achieving the Objectives

Certain strategies and tactics to achieve the objectives defined at the outset can be used to help progress and deepen the mentoring relationship. Actions are agreed and are aimed both at developing skills/knowledge and assessing how well they have been absorbed. During this stage, the feeling of mutual trust develops and intensifies, giving the mentee the confidence to challenge the mentor in a safe environment.

In practical terms, some pairs find it helpful to agree a formal structure for each meeting – for example agreeing the discussion topics in advance.

At Avaya, all participants are given a diary in which they can record progress (Figure 20.2).

Date	Objectives for Meeting	Notes on Outcome	Meeting Rating
			1 2 3 4 5
			1 2 3 4 5
			1 2 3 4 5

Figure 20.2 **Progress diary provided by Avaya**

B&Q take a similar approach with a Mentoring Session Record covering topics discussed and conclusions reached. Such documents could be developed further to include: agenda topics, issues covered, action items/timings and date of the next meeting. In the UK, Zurich is keen to make learning logs a key part of the process – for both parties; these can then be used to review and evaluate progress.

During a meeting with the Focus Group, Eric Parsloe advocated giving mentees Reflection Notes pages, covering:

> Event: what happened and why?
>
> My reaction (thoughts, feelings, behaviour)
>
> What did I learn/discover?
>
> What am I going to do about it?

PRACTICAL MEETING MANAGEMENT FOR SHORT MEETINGS

When meetings are to be relatively short, best possible use of that time can be made by, for example:

▶ proposing and agreeing an agenda/discussion topics beforehand, either by e-mail, fax or over the phone

▶ having only the briefest recap of the last meeting

▶ sending a brief progress/learning summary to the mentor in advance.

Clutterbuck & Megginson (1999) quoted the following experiences of Richard Field as an external mentor and described how he stays in contact with his mentees:

I ask them to send me a fax each week saying how they are going with the issues that they raised the previous week and anything else that concerns them. I fax back to them each Sunday, sending a common message from my learning during the week, and also a message unique to each of them. ... I must be totally dependable for them; I am always there. I do not miss a weekly fax unless I am away – in which case I let them know in advance.

USEFUL STRUCTURES AND MODELS FOR LONGER MEETINGS

Pegg (2003) offered the Five C Model for structuring a mentoring session:

1 **Challenges** – at this stage the mentor helps the mentee to view his various challenges within a broader context and a framework of longer term goals. The objective at this stage is to help the mentee gain a good overview of the challenges they are facing and any relationships between these challenges.

2 **Choices** – starting with the most important challenge, the mentee is encouraged to identify all the possible options for dealing with it. The mentor needs to draw out the mentee until she or he can think of no other alternatives. Mentees are always hungry for advice and solutions and so the mentor must guard against giving the 'perfect solution'.

3 **Consequences** – once all the options have been highlighted, the mentee is helped to look at each of the options in terms of advantages and disadvantages, and attractiveness on a scale of 1–10. At this stage the preferred option or combination of two options is identified. The choice must be left to the mentee; he or she must have ownership of his or her decision in order to follow it through to action.

4 **Creative solutions** – at this stage the mentor can be a little more active in helping the mentee to come up with the best solution. Creative techniques can be used, active listening or just talking and acting as a sounding board for the mentee. Once this stage has been completed, the mentee will draw up an action plan for addressing the chosen option.

5 **Conclusions** – this final stage confirms the action plan to be followed. The mentee turns ideas into reality.

Pegg used the Five C Model with mentors at Microsoft. Glover (2002) reported that Microsoft recognised the importance of giving people the time to recentre and take a helicopter view of their options. Mentoring provided that time to reflect and share ideas with an impartial person without a corporate agenda. More recently, Glover (2003) reported the view of Angela Knight, senior HR consultant at Microsoft, that mentoring was making a significant contribution to the high retention rate at the company. At this time the attrition rate was 5 per cent annually. Microsoft set up the programme to encourage cross-teamworking, realise individual potential and get more employees thinking outside the box.

Essential Skills for Mentoring

Mentors need to use certain key skills to help make the relationship a success. This section will provide a reminder of good questioning, influencing and feedback skills. To be effective the mentor must remember that the emphasis is on listening and helping the mentee to find answers to his or her issues, rather than telling and taking over the relationship.

OPENINGS AND QUESTIONING APPROACHES

Having decided on a structure for the meeting, mentors need to be skilled at asking the right questions to help the mentee:

▶ Gain fresh insights to their issues

▶ Develop different ways of thinking

▶ Rise above the day-to-day problems

▶ Look at issues from different perspectives

▶ Evaluate options

▶ Have a vision of the future.

> *To tell denies or negates another's intelligence*
>
> Coaching for Performance,
> John Whitmore (1996)

There are certain traps that must be avoided when questioning another person. These are listed in Table 20.1. Careful questioning, which avoids these pitfalls, will help mentors to build a more effective relationship with the mentee.

Table 20.1 **Questioning traps to be avoided**

Questioning traps	
Leading	Suggesting the expected answer: the effect of this type of question can be to encourage or possibly compel the respondent to say what the questioner wants to hear, rather than what he or she actually thinks. Leading questions might imply that you are trying to advise the person.
Multiple	A question with several parts, which tends to confuse the respondent as he or she does not know which bit to answer and possibly cannot remember all the bits.
Ambiguous	A question which is vague or has a double meaning.
Irrelevant	These are 'nice to know' questions, rather than ones which are directly related to the subject matter.
Closed	Asking too many closed questions shifts the balance of the exchange into one where you talk the most; the consequence can be that the speaker goes quiet and just waits for your next question.
Open	Questions starting with 'why?' can put people on the spot, with the implication that they should justify themselves. They can provoke a defensive 'because' reply, which doesn't encourage exploration of the issue and so should be used with care.
Too many	Can lead to the receiver feeling as if he or she is in a Spanish Inquisition! Also, remember the 80/20 listening/speaking rule.

Listed below is a range of questions or openings that can be used by a mentor.

How can I help?
Shall we start by recapping briefly on our last meeting?
What do you want to achieve?
Where do you spend most of your time … ?
Where do you want to get to?
Where are you now?
How do you learn best?

What patterns or themes are emerging?
What's the most important thing to work on first?
What would you like them to do?

Let's explore this some more.
Tell me about your experience of …
To summarise what you're saying …
You've said very little about … which seems central to the issue.

How do you think you'd feel if …?
What would you lose if …?
What else could you do?

What do you think is getting in the way/stopping you?
What problems is that creating for you?
Can you look at it from another angle?
What have you forgotten to do/haven't you done?
What stops you?
What do you think you're afraid of?
What would that mean to you/the others involved?
What led you to approach it that way?
What are you avoiding?

Can I ask you about … ?
It would help me to know about …
Is that a fair comment?

What do you think this means?
What is the learning point here?
How can you apply this learning in the future?
What will you do differently next time?
What's concerning you most out of all the things we discussed today?
What are the pros and cons of each option?
What do you need to do first?
What support do you need?
When will you get started?
Will this help you meet your goal?
Well done, that feels like a breakthrough!

A sequence of questions shared by Richard Field with participants at a European Mentoring Centre Conference can be particularly useful – whether used singly or all together.

What would happen if you did ...?

What would happen if you didn't ...?

What wouldn't happen if you did ...?

What wouldn't happen if you didn't ...?

> *The hardest thing has been the very direct and open questions: What do I think? Where do I want to go? However, it is probably a good thing as it makes me think in a different way.*
>
> Avaya mentee

ACTIVE LISTENING

The challenge for some mentors is to ensure the right balance of contribution between the mentor and mentee. This requires the mentor to be a good listener. If the mentor is a good active listener, he or she will pick up not only what the person is saying, but also will have insights as to what the person is thinking and feeling, at a deeper level. Listening is a major component of rapport.

Good active listeners:

▶ Focus their attention entirely on the other person.

▶ Are sensitive to non-verbal cues.

▶ Have a genuine interest in the other person and what they are saying, thinking and feeling.

▶ Maintain good eye contact with the other person.

▶ Ask good open questions, making the other person want to open up.

▶ Ask questions in a way that is non-evaluative and does not make the other person feel defensive.

▶ Encourage the other person to talk by nodding the head and having an open body posture.

▶ Summarise back what they have heard using the same words as the other person.

▶ Spend more time listening than talking.

▶ Encourage the other person to find solutions to their own problems.

▶ Are sensitive to the needs of the other person and find ways of satisfying these needs.

> *What I've learned most from the whole programme is the power of listening and the power of silence.*
>
> Avaya mentor

THE RIGHT STYLE OF INFLUENCING

Effective mentors use a good balance between the push and pull styles of influence.

The *pull style* is used to:

► Encourage the mentee to think through issues

► Support the mentee by acting as a sounding board

► Gain a greater understanding of the mentee

► Establish common ground

► Help build trust.

The pull style makes use of active listening and puts the onus on the mentee to solve problems or find a way forward:

What is your next step?

Tell me more about your plans?

What do you most enjoy about your current role?

The *push style* is used to:

► Challenge the mentee to think outside the box

► Provide the mentee with knowledge and experience

► Stimulate the mentee to move out of the comfort zone

► Make the mentee aware of what is expected of him or her.

Mentors need, from time to time, to use the push style to avoid the mentee feeling insufficiently challenged or when the mentee appears complacent:

How might you tackle the issue in a different way?

Have you thought of moving to a different area of the business?

How could you achieve even greater stretch?

GIVING AND RECEIVING FEEDBACK

The mentor can combine the influencing style with giving feedback as part of the development process. From the mentors' perspective the skills of giving feedback are very important if they are to build a positive mentoring relationship. Observing the following rules of giving feedback will help mentees to be able to take the feedback on board, rather than ignore it or become defensive and, in turn, will increase their self-awareness and development. There may also be occasions when mentees need to give mentors feedback. Giving good quality feedback is a skill that needs to be handled carefully. Certain rules apply that will help to ensure that mentors and mentees give useful feedback.

Characteristics of good quality feedback

▶ **It should be based on behaviour rather than the person** – the person giving the feedback should refer to what an individual has done rather than making generalised comments about the person. For example, the mentor might say: 'you have interrupted me three times in this meeting', which is more acceptable than saying: 'you have a rather aggressive style'.

▶ **It should describe specific behaviour** – broad general comments that are positive may help to build the relationship, but specific comments help to increase self-awareness. It is more helpful to tell the mentee: 'I like the report you have prepared for this meeting: it was clear and concise, well structured and you have clearly identified what you have learned'; rather than saying it was a 'good report'.

▶ **Feedback is more useful if it focuses on what the person could do differently next time** – adopting this approach encourages the receiver to focus on doing things better next time instead of dwelling on the past and getting discouraged and emotional and, therefore, unable to act on the feedback.

▶ **It should be based on observable behaviour rather than opinions** – observations are based on what the person sees and hears, while opinion is the conclusion drawn from what has been observed and this may or may not be accurate.

▶ **Feedback should be well timed** – the feedback should be as close as possible to the time when the behaviour is observed. It would be a poor strategy if a mentor waited until a final review to give their mentee feedback or vice versa.

► **It should be given in small amounts** – the mentee will have difficulty handling large amounts of feedback. The mentor needs to be very sensitive to the non-verbal cues about how the feedback is being received and the way the person is feeling.

► **The feedback needs to be of value to the receiver** – it is inappropriate for the giver to use the mentoring relationship as a chance to dump negative feelings.

► **Positive feedback is even more important then negative feedback** – it encourages positive behaviour and enables people to do more of what they do well. In many organisations the philosophy is that no news is good news; very little attention is paid to giving people positive feedback.

Giving negative feedback

This is the most difficult type of feedback to give, but it is sometimes needed to help the person to develop. Again, following a few key rules will increase the level of acceptability of the feedback.

► **The relationship between the giver and receiver must be positive** – particularly when giving negative feedback there must be a relationship of mutual understanding and trust. For this reason care should be taken to give the appropriate levels of feedback in the early meetings.

► **Appropriate levels of positive feedback should be given** – this helps to preserve the self-esteem of the person receiving the feedback.

► **Make it easy for the person to talk about any negative feedback** – the feedback needs to be put across in a way that presents the issue as a problem to people in general.

► **Use positive language when talking about problem issues** – it is easier to talk about areas for improvement than weaknesses.

Receiving feedback

Some people naturally have difficulty receiving positive feedback. Those who experience this problem will have greater difficulty in recognising and playing to strengths and are more likely to have low self-esteem.

By following a few rules people can gain the most benefit from feedback they receive.

▶ When offered positive feedback the best response is simply to thank the person giving it.

▶ The more actively a person seeks feedback, the more the person will learn.

▶ Listen carefully to feedback given and check understanding if necessary.

▶ Get clarification of the feedback by asking questions: ask for examples of specific behaviour to support the feedback and ask what might be done differently.

▶ Remain assertive when receiving negative feedback and focus attention on the future and what could be done differently next time. This stops the person becoming emotional and being unable to process the feedback.

Helping the other person give feedback to themselves

People are usually very aware of the feedback they should be receiving at any given time. A number of questions will help the person to review a situation and, as a consequence, they will be more likely to change.

▶ How do you think that went?

▶ How well do you think you did on ...?

▶ I liked the way you handled that situation; what did you think?

▶ Why do you think that didn't work as well as it might have?

▶ How do you think you might do that differently next time?

▶ What effect do you think that might have?

Using Emotional Intelligence (EI) to Deepen the Relationship and Deal with Feelings Effectively

In a well-rounded mentoring relationship both mentor and mentee need to be able to deal with emotional aspects within that relationship. Having an understanding of emotional intelligence and being able to access the elements when appropriate will greatly help the deepening of the relationship.

Higgs & Dulewicz (2002) investigated emotional intelligence to help clarify exactly what the term means and help people understand its impact on performance in the work environment. Having thoroughly researched the area, they suggested the need for a new definition of emotional intelligence as follows:

> Achieving one's goals through the ability to manage one's own feelings and emotions, to be sensitive to, and influence other key people and to balance one's motives and drives with conscientious and ethical behaviour.

(Higgs & Dulewicz 2002 p. 24)

They went on to identify seven elements of emotional intelligence, which are shown in Table 20.2.

Table 20.2 **Seven elements of emotional intelligence**

1	**Self-awareness** – awareness of own feelings and ability to control them. Self-belief in one's own ability to manage emotions and to control one's impact in a work environment.
2	**Emotional Resilience** – performing consistently in a range of situations under pressure and to appropriately adapt behaviour. It includes the ability to retain focus in the face of personal criticism.
3	**Motivation** – drive and energy to achieve results, to make an impact and balance short and long-term goals.
4	**Interpersonal Sensitivity** – being sensitive to the needs of others and their perceptions when arriving at decisions.
5	**Influence** – the ability to persuade others to change a viewpoint where necessary.
6	**Intuitiveness** – the ability to arrive at clear decisions and to drive their implementation when presented with incomplete or ambiguous information, using both logic and emotion.
7	**Conscientiousness** – the ability to display clear commitment to a course of action in the face of challenge and to match words with deeds.

Source: Adapted from Higgs & Dulewicz 2002 and reproduced with permission of the publisher nferNelson.

THE IMPORTANCE OF EMOTIONAL INTELLIGENCE FOR MENTORS

Mentors will benefit from accessing the elements as follows:

▶ **Self-awareness** – it is important that mentors are aware of the impact they have on mentees. They also need to have sufficient control of their

feelings, so that any negative ones do not get in the
way of building a positive
relationship.

> *I deliberately wanted to work with people I didn't know, because I could be more independent and more objective. I'd obviously get to know them through the meetings, but I would not be going in with preconceived ideas.*
>
> Avaya mentor

▶ **Emotional resilience** –
mentors need to be able to
perform at a consistent level
even when they are exper-
iencing extreme pressure.
Managers are often required
to act as mentors on top of an exacting workload. Successful mentors are
able to remain focused on the objectives of the task in hand even when
they are experiencing excessive demands on themselves.

▶ **Motivation** – mentors need to be able to help mentees to set challenging goals and stay focused, especially during difficult times. Mentors who
have high levels of motivation tend to believe in the potential of others.
They are also likely to set high standards of performance for themselves
as mentors.

▶ **Interpersonal sensitivity** – mentors able to access high levels of interpersonal sensitivity are likely to be good listeners and sensitive to the needs
of mentees. They are more likely to invest time and effort in ensuring that
they fully understand what mentees are saying to them. As mentors, they
are less likely to impose their own views on mentees.

▶ **Influence** – mentors need to listen to their mentee and, using their
influencing skills, change the mentee's perception of the situation if
necessary. Mentors who have high levels of influence tend to be able to
establish rapport more easily, and can more readily gain respect.
However, mentors with high influencing skills need to guard against
appearing too daunting to their mentee – especially if self-confidence is
an issue for them.

▶ **Intuitiveness** – mentors with high levels of intuitiveness are likely to be
able to understand the complexity of business decisions and be comfortable with balancing intuitive judgement with detailed analysis. They will
be able consistently to make decisions in difficult situations. However,
as mentors, they will need to be cautious of taking control and ownership of the situation, especially with a mentee who has a low level of
intuitiveness.

▶ **Conscientiousness** – mentors with high levels of conscientiousness are
likely to demonstrate a significant level of commitment to the mentoring
relationship and achieving the agreed goals.

THE IMPORTANCE OF EMOTIONAL INTELLIGENCE FOR MENTEES

Mentees will benefit from accessing the elements of EI as follows:

▶ **Self-awareness** – it is important that mentees are aware of the impact they have on mentors. Having self-awareness will help to create a positive outlook on life. This is particularly important for mentoring, as mentees are more likely to take ownership of their development and future career. They also need to have sufficient control of their feelings, so that any negative ones do not get in the way of analysing situations effectively.

▶ **Emotional resilience** – mentees also need to be able to perform at a consistent level even when they are experiencing extreme pressure. Mentees may well be at a critical stage in their careers, either new into the company, new in role, undertaking a difficult or challenging job or participating in a development programme. They need to be able to perform consistently under these pressures. Mentees also need to sustain a focus on goals and be able to deliver even when they are on the receiving end of criticism.

▶ **Motivation** – mentees need to set challenging goals and stay focused on these especially during difficult times. Mentees who have high levels of motivation are also likely to set high standards of performance for themselves as mentees.

▶ **Interpersonal sensitivity** – mentees able to access high levels of interpersonal sensitivity are likely to be good listeners and sensitive to the needs of the mentor and the demands they are facing in undertaking the mentoring role. They are more likely to invest time and effort in ensuring that they fully understand what is being said to them and taking the ideas of others into account when making decisions.

▶ **Influence** – mentees, like their mentor, need to listen to the mentor and, using their influencing skills, change perception of the situation if necessary. Mentees who have high levels of influence tend to be able to establish rapport more easily and can more readily gain respect. Mentees with high influencing skills will be able to use these skills when putting ideas into action.

▶ **Intuitiveness** – mentees with high levels of intuitiveness are also likely to be able to understand the complexity of business decisions and be comfortable with balancing intuitive judgement with detailed analysis. They will be able consistently to make decisions in difficult situations. As mentees, they will be in a better position to take control and ownership of the situation rather than defer to the mentor.

▶ **Conscientiousness** – mentees with high levels of conscientiousness are likely to demonstrate a significant level of commitment to the mentoring relationship and agreed goals. They will take the action planning process seriously and are more likely to deliver what they commit to deliver.

How Can the Mentee Contribute to a Positive Mentoring Relationship?

The mentee needs to remember:

▶ To prepare carefully for mentoring meetings in order to ensure that there is plenty to be discussed. This takes the onus off the mentor in leading the discussion.

▶ To have clear and realistic expectations of his or her mentor. The best mentors are probably the busiest.

▶ The most successful relationships are those that operate on a more equal basis, with the mentee being proactive and following through on agreed actions.

▶ To have the confidence to share difficult issues and areas of concern.

▶ To act on feedback given by the mentor and be prepared to give the mentor feedback if necessary.

Guidelines for Developing a Deeper Relationship

Dejovine & Harris (2001) identified a number of things that can be done by the mentor to help to deepen the relationship:

▶ **Create a safe environment** – the mentor should create the type of environment where the mentee can feel comfortable and able to be honest. Part of creating this environment is for the mentor to be open about some of the issues that he or she has faced. Self-disclosure, even talking about failure, is the first step to building trust. It is, however, important to emphasise that information shared is strictly confidential.

▶ **Listen without judgement** – while sharing information the mentor must put his or her own thoughts to one side and focus on listening to the mentee. The secret is to listen and resist the temptation to make a point, teach a lesson or offer a note of caution. This will make the mentee feel heard and valued.

▶ **Focus on learning** – mentors can gain knowledge from their mentees and the mentoring experience by bringing a learning attitude to the relationship. The mentor needs to take the attitude that both mentor and mentee can learn from the relationship, the mentor should not be perceived as the person having all the answers. In this way the mentoring relationship operates more as a partnership.

▶ **Agree on objectives rather than approaches** – the best approach to the mentoring relationship is to open up possibilities to explore with the mentee rather than being prescriptive and coming up with answers. In this way the mentee can be exposed to the best form of learning experience.

▶ **Appreciating differences** – mentors and mentees usually have different backgrounds, experiences and may also differ in age and personality characteristics. The greater the difference, the greater the scope for learning.

Summary

Mentors and mentees need to allocate sufficient time for meetings at intervals of six to eight weeks. They also need to be patient in the early stages of a relationship if they do not seem to be gelling together. Sometimes pairs do split up and both can go on to form successful mentoring relationships with other people. Topics for discussion will vary from pairing to pairing; ideas to help to build the relationship were included in this chapter. Mentors need to recognise when the agenda has moved into an area that is outside his or her comfort zone and seek appropriate advice. Various approaches have been included in this chapter for those liking a structure to follow in their meetings and strategies are included for those needing to be time-efficient.

The success of a mentoring relationship depends in part on the skills of the participants and, particularly, of the mentor. A recap on the essential skills of questioning, active listening influencing and the giving and receiving of feedback has been included in this chapter for those needing a quick refresher. Mentors and mentees need to access their emotional intelligence if they are to move the relationship to a deeper level. A summary of the model put forward by Higgs & Dulewicz, and the importance of the seven elements of EI, has been included in the chapter for those less familiar with the topic. By preparing well for meetings, having realistic expectations and the confidence to operate on an equal basis, the mentee can also impact on the success of the relationship.

21 Issues Impacting on Mentors and Mentees

Introduction

Poe (2002) quoted Larry Ambrose as saying: 'a bad mentoring relationship is worse than no relationship at all'. A negative relationship can affect morale, stress levels and even turnover rates. Those who have a bad experience with mentoring are often reluctant to take part in another relationship.

What are the pitfalls that can turn a potentially successful relationship into a failure? This chapter will discuss common concerns that are likely to impact on the mentor and mentee, covering relationship issues such as trust, confidentiality and gender. Issues related to mentors, and their competence to be a mentor, and the attitude of mentors will also be considered. Finally, the chapter will examine the impact of logistical issues such as the time available for mentoring and mentoring at a distance. This chapter is primarily written for the mentor and mentee, but the scheme manager and people training mentors and mentees will also find the chapter helpful in raising awareness of the issues likely to affect the mentoring relationship.

Establishing Trust and Mutual Respect

Mentoring has the most impact when it is based on trust. Building rapport is the most essential element of creating trust and respect. Early meetings are, therefore, critical to ensure an appropriate level of comfort exists to allow the mentor and mentee to trust one another with personal and sensitive information. Mentoring relationships are unlikely to succeed if the mentor and mentee feel unable to open up to one another and share feelings, insecurities and weaknesses.

Respect is closely related to trust. The mentor needs to respect that the mentee is a responsible adult who is able to think, solve problems and take decisions. Hay (1999) emphasised that true respect requires acceptance of the person 'warts and all', being realistic that everyone has weaknesses as well as strengths. Respect for one another is also based on the other person's view of the world. People have a range of different opinions and mentors and mentees need to respect and value difference. The level of mutual respect that develops may be threatened if opinions are widely different.

Mentors and mentees need to remember:

▶ Careful preparation at the start of the relationship will help build rapport.

▶ To seek data to establish the level of trust the person engenders generally.

▶ Trust is reciprocal, if the mentor trusts the mentee and vice versa the relationship is more likely to be built on trust.

▶ Once trust is lost it is very difficult to rebuild.

▶ The importance of valuing and respecting differences.

Issues of Confidentiality

Confidentiality is critical for a successful mentoring relationship and must be discussed at the start of the relationship; it certainly should be included in the mentoring contract. Concerns over confidentiality are likely to constrain both mentors and mentees from sharing more sensitive information and will, therefore, impact on establishing rapport and trust. Clutterbuck (2001) stated that although issues of broken confidentiality are remarkably rare, concerns over confidentiality remain one of the biggest limiting factors on relationships.

To help to address confidentiality issues:

▶ Ground rules should be established early in the relationship and be a part of the mentoring contract.

▶ Mentors should keep a good distance from the mentee's line manager, and HR, and not reveal anything discussed in the relationship unless by prior agreement with the mentee.

> *My mentor is extremely supportive, objective and doesn't give me the answers – he enables me to think about things in a different way and come up with solutions for myself. I know this is a confidential relationship – that really helps.*
>
> Yorkshire Water mentee

Gender and Other Diversity Issues

Research suggests that mentoring relationships, while important for men, may be essential for women's career development, as women managers face greater organisational, interpersonal and individual barriers to advancement. Linehan & Walsh (1999) focused on the role of mentors in the careers of senior female international managers. A total of 50 senior female managers were selected for the study based in Ireland, Belgium, England and Germany. All were part of a senior management team and had made at least one international career move. The findings showed that mentoring relationships helped female managers overcome barriers to advancement in organisations. Several had, in turn, facilitated mentoring in their own organisations to make the benefits received more widely available.

Many organisations are now using mentoring as a way of helping different groups, including women and ethnic minority groups, to progress. The issue then arises as to whether the mentor and mentee should be of the same gender or ethnic group. In some situations this is very important as it provides a role model. In the case of gender there will not be any detrimental sexual connotations that cross-sex relationships could elicit. The level of empathy that is possible when mentor and mentee are from the same group is greater. Some people will get the best of both worlds by having a formal mentor from a different group and adopt an informal mentor from the same group.

Practitioners' Problem-solving

Questions and Answers with David Megginson and David Clutterbuck

Same sex/opposite sex mentoring – what are the challenges and pitfalls?

I was in Brussels recently talking with a group of people from big companies who were interested in mentoring. A very experienced woman from a large Swedish company was in the group who were discussing the subject of mentoring, and how something everybody worries about is an older, more senior, man mentoring a younger, attractive woman. I have two things to say about this and the first is just to pass on this lady's advice which is 'when I am seeking a senior male mentor for a younger woman I look for one who is a father, with a daughter of similar age just starting out in business – because that man will be passionate about young women pursuing their careers and be single minded on that'. That is not to say that mentors need to be fathers to their mentees, but if you have concerns about the sexual dynamics that is a way to make it as safe as it gets.

What they say in the voluntary sector when mentoring young people where sexual dynamics is a really hot issue is that mentoring needs to be done in a private space in a public place and that seems simple and helpful. (DM)

Clutterbuck (2001) highlights the very positive developments in mentoring for diverse groups, particularly for international businesses, who are globalising their cultures. It benefits mentees by having doors opened for them and it benefits the mentor who learns to interact with, and get the most from, people from different backgrounds.

To ensure the mentoring relationship is successful:

▶ Both mentor and mentee need to be clear about the relationship's goals.

▶ Expectations of one another need to be discussed at the start of the relationship.

▶ Both mentor and mentee must be open to learning and valuing differences in the case of cross-group mentoring.

Competence and Attitude of the Mentor

For a mentoring relationship to be successful the mentor needs to be familiar with the various stages outlined in earlier chapters. Most formal mentoring schemes in organisations offer mentors and mentees the chance to undergo some form of training or attend a short briefing session. Whilst senior managers are likely to possess the various skills discussed in Chapter 20, most would benefit from an understanding of the mentoring process; unfortunately many managers are reluctant to take part in the training offered – sometimes for fear of revealing any weaknesses. Attending the briefing or training enables the mentoring relationship to get off to a far more confident start.

Mentors need to guard against the desire to keep giving advice to their mentee or being patronising, particularly with young mentees. Some mentors want to try and stop the mentees making the same mistakes they have made earlier in their own careers. Sometimes mentors may volunteer to be a mentor for the wrong reasons, like improving their CV, and are insufficiently motivated to help their mentee develop, or may not give the mentoring relationship a high enough priority.

Starcevich & Friend (1999) conducted a web survey of mentees via the home page of the Centre for Management and Organisation Effectiveness in the US. The mentees in the survey wanted a mentor to develop their potential and their career prospects. They were asked what was the most significant thing the mentor did for them. The following four responses captured 62 per cent of responses:

1 *Built my confidence and empowered me to see what I could do.*

2 *Stimulated learning with a soft, no pressure, self-discovery approach.*

3 *Shared experiences, taught me something and explained things.*

4 *Listened and understood.*

In order to ensure that the competence and attitude does not impact on the relationship:

▶ Both mentor and mentee should take advantage of any briefing or training available to them or follow the guidelines given in this book.

▶ The mentor should be mindful of the characteristics of a good mentor.

▶ Either the mentor or mentee should seek the advice of a scheme manager or HR if the relationship is part of a formal mentoring scheme.

▶ Establish a mechanism for reviewing the relationship on a continuous basis.

▶ Be prepared to walk away from the relationship if it is failing to meet the needs of the mentee and all other options have been explored.

Competence and Attitude of the Mentee

Clutterbuck (2001) reported that mentoring relationships are far more likely to be successful and mutually rewarding if the mentee is selected for having a reputation for hard work, enthusiasm and ability. Sometimes when mentees are given a mentor as part of a broader development programme, they do not see the benefits of a mentoring relationship and may not give it the time it deserves. If they are allocated a mentor who has limited time, faced with this type of mentee the mentor may lose commitment too.

Starcevich & Friend (1999) explored the role of the mentee in their survey of mentees. The mentees were very proactive, taking responsibility for their own development. Successful mentees take responsibility for keeping the relationship alive. When asked about the 'musts' of a good mentee, two-thirds of the group responded:

1   Listen.

2   Act on advice.

3   Show a willingness, desire and commitment to learn and grow.

4   Check ego at the door – ask for and be open to feedback and criticism.

5   Be open-minded and willing to change.

Lack of Time for the Mentoring Relationship

For the mentoring relationship to deliver real value, meetings must take place on a regular basis, according to Anderson (2003). There is little research to show that casual, unstructured conversations make a significant difference to leadership effectiveness. Mentors are often selected from a senior management pool with extensive demands on their time. The busiest people are likely to have the most to offer a mentee. Clutterbuck (2001) found that time was one of the top three issues likely to lead to a failed mentoring relationship. Sometimes people will say that there is a lack of time for mentoring, when the real problem lies with the mentoring relationship itself.

Those who are able to manage the demands of a job alongside managing a successful mentoring relationship follow a few simple guidelines:

▶ Mentors are clear from the start about the time commitment involved.

▶ Meet with the mentee away from their own office, sometimes off-site, to avoid endless interruptions.

▶ Schedule several meetings in advance so that if a meeting does have to be rescheduled, an alternative date is available.

▶ Encourage the mentee to take responsibility for the meeting schedule and to be persistent in getting time in their mentor's diary.

▶ Mentors and mentees gain the commitment of the line managers to allow the mentee time for the mentoring process.

Practitioners' Problem-solving

Questions and Answers with David Megginson and David Clutterbuck

A lot of mentees have trouble pinning down time with their mentors: how would you handle this?

Sometimes mentees read the wishes/intentions of their mentor very wrongly: they'll telephone the mentor or speak to their PA/secretary to book an appointment and are told: 'OK we'll get back to you' – but no one does. The mentee rings again or sends an e-mail and still gets no response, so they think 'Oh! they don't want me' and walk away demotivated. However, this may not be the case and it needs to be made clear in the training that mentees should be proactive in connecting with their mentor, as well as saying to mentors that it is absolutely fine for them to approach their mentee. Lots of relationships don't work because they have a stuttering start: by acting as facilitator for perhaps just one meeting and encouraging them to connect, you will help keep the relationship alive.   **(DM)**

E-mentoring

If geography has not been a matching criterion or the organisation is a European or global business, then alternatives to face-to-face meetings will probably need to be sought and e-mentoring may be the answer. It is particularly well suited to the stage of the relationship when contracts and rapport have already been established and progress is being made. This approach can also be used to supplement face-to-face mentoring when meetings become difficult to schedule.

What are the benefits of e-mentoring?

▶ Time and cost savings

▶ The opportunity to take time to reflect on responses

▶ More frequent exchanges than face-to-face meetings may allow

▶ The opportunity to have a mentoring relationship at a distance.

The 'geographic' challenge was one that faced a European division of a global business and, from the outset, the concept of e-mentoring was built into the mentoring programme – allowing greater flexibility in the setting up and management of the relationships.

Participants were, however, provided with cautions as to potential drawbacks (see Figure 21.1).

Precedents have been set for establishing relationships using electronic means: for example, 'internet marriages' and the use of the internet by the Samaritans. However when using these e-methods you should take time to consider how you will overcome:

▶ The lack of visual information normally provided through body language

▶ Potential misunderstanding of the written word – either through the inability to hear the tone or lack of understanding of colloquialisms

▶ The greater opportunity to seem insulting, blunt or inhuman

▶ The perceived lack of confidentiality inherent in using some of these methods.

Figure 21.1 **E-mentoring cautions given in guidelines for a pan-European scheme**

Methods by which e-mentoring could be conducted include e-mail, telephone, hard copy mail and video-conferencing. In the example of The Prince's Trust project featured in Chapter 4, hard copy mail and telephone were methods frequently used by the participants.

These e-mentoring methods are often resorted to in times of crisis, where a mentee urgently needs guidance from their mentor over an issue that has arisen in between the scheduled meetings.

When David Megginson was questioned by the Henley Focus Group about the effectiveness of e-mentoring, he focused, firstly, on the people taking part. He then commented on the issues related to e-mentoring, particularly the lack of non-verbal communication.

Practitioners' Problem-solving

Questions and Answers with David Megginson and David Clutterbuck

How successful is e-mentoring?

Some people feel happier having a phone/e-mail mentoring relationship, as they don't feel happy talking to people face to face about personal issues. The more disembodied the medium, the more the mentor needs to be able to express warmth and connectedness so that the mentee feels relaxed and that they are getting benefit/support from them. People who are naturally reflective seem to appreciate the opportunity to have time to respond. Of course, a disadvantage is that you are not able to get the subtleties of what someone is saying, their language, tone, body posture and so on.

We don't really know enough about the techniques we have to employ to compensate for the lack of face-to-face meeting. Some of the things that seem to be important are storytelling. When meeting face to face we tend to be more open about storytelling. Also acting – projecting yourself as you talk about something. It isn't easy and is an area we are still researching. **(DM)**

Summary

This chapter has given an overview of the potential pitfalls to building a positive mentoring relationship. In the early stages care must be taken to build respect and trust for the other person. As part of this process both mentor and mentee must recognise and value differences between one another. It is this diversity that is part of the value of a successful mentoring relationship. Confidentiality is an issue that is likely to influence the level of trust that can be built between the mentor and mentee and both parties need to be sensitive to this issue.

In recent years emphasis has been placed on the development of diverse groups, including gender and ethnic minority groups. Those entering a relationship need to consider whether they favour similarity and the benefits of having a role model, or diversity and learning from differences. One way to get the best of both worlds is to have a formal and an informal relationship running in parallel.

The competence and attitudes of the mentor and mentee can also impact on the success of the relationship. The mentors need to refrain from being too dominant in the relationship. The mentees need to listen, act on advice when appropriate and be open-minded and willing to change.

Time issues are high on the list of factors contributing to a failed mentoring relationship. The best mentors often have severe time constraints and mentors and mentees must be disciplined and give sufficient priority to the mentoring relationship. E-mentoring can be useful for addressing both geographical and time issues. It can take the form of e-mails, video-conferencing and telephone calls and is likely to be most successful after initial meetings have taken place and a contract and learning goals have been established.

22 Review, Evaluation and Closure

Introduction

Evaluation and review is not just a once-only activity and still less an after-thought. It is a continuous process that enables a mentor and mentee to check that they are working towards achieving their objectives and also responding to changing circumstances. It is also a part of the ending process, to enable both parties to understand and accept what has been achieved, seek closure for the relationship and move on. This process of understanding and acceptance needs to take place at both intellectual and emotional levels, that is, both thoughts and feelings.

Evaluation of any learning activity is not easy, but evaluating a mentoring relationship may be more complex and challenging than other training and development activities for a number of reasons:

▶ The confidential nature of mentoring relationships.

▶ Some outcomes from mentoring, such as 'soft skill' development, may take a long time to become clear.

▶ Some outcomes, such as 'coping with change' may be difficult to measure exactly.

▶ It may be difficult to disentangle the effects of mentoring from other potential interventions and experiences.

Chapter 14 discussed evaluation, review and closure from the perspective of the scheme manager. This chapter focuses on this stage from the perspective of the mentor and mentee. It will identify the how, what and when of evaluation and review.

Table 22.1 gives a helpful overview of the chapter.

Mentors and mentees will find referring back to the company checklists in Chapter 14 helpful in order to identify what to review when evaluating the mentoring relationship and lessons learned for both parties. The chapter will also expand on areas already covered in Chapter 14 and is therefore useful for scheme managers and those seeking to train mentors and mentees.

Table 22.1 **Outline of evaluation and review chapter**

How	
▶ Formal	
▶ Informal	

What	
▶ Different perspectives:	mentee mentor mentoring relationship mentoring scheme
▶ Different levels:	behaviour thoughts and beliefs emotions and feelings

When	
▶ During the meeting	
▶ After each meeting	
▶ At the end of the relationship	

How to Evaluate and Review

Evaluation from the perspective of the mentor and mentee may be formal or informal.

Formal

Those favouring a formal evaluation process may want to set aside time at each meeting to check progress or hold a periodic review session. The final review session is likely to refer back to the mentoring contract established at the start of the relationship. If the mentoring relationship is part of a company scheme, then there are likely to be links with the evaluation and review conducted by the scheme manager. This might involve the completion of questionnaires by both the mentor and mentee, as shown in Chapter 14.

Informal

Those favouring an informal approach are likely to conduct the evaluation and review on an ongoing basis. This may be more likely to occur when the mentoring pair has initiated the relationship themselves. However, in every mentoring relationship evaluation and review is an important part of the overall process and should not be overlooked.

What to Evaluate and Review

Mentors and mentees will need to carry out evaluation from a number of different perspectives and at different stages in the mentoring relationship, helping each other to focus on particular issues.

DIFFERENT PERSPECTIVES

Review from the mentor and mentee perspective

▶ *From the mentee perspective* – the focus will be on the achievement of agreed developmental or learning outcomes. It will also look at questions such as whether the mentee is taking ownership of his or her development.

▶ *From the mentor perspective* – issues may include the satisfaction being derived from the relationship, or what competencies have been identified for further development.

In both cases evaluation is likely to give a good insight into what has been achieved as a result of the mentoring relationship and what both parties have learned about themselves for the future.

> *I feel I am giving something back to YW – helping someone to understand YW and how it works – it challenges my thinking too; the scheme is very good.*
>
> Yorkshire Water mentor

Review from the perspective of the relationship

This aspect focuses on the nature and quality of the mentoring relationship. It is a critical aspect because of the impact that the quality of the relationship has on the achievement of desired outcomes. In addition, the quality of the relationship in itself can be a cause of satisfaction or dissatisfaction. The focus of attention will be on:

▶ The learning climate established

▶ The degree of trust and rapport

▶ The frequency and effectiveness of mentoring meetings.

Review from the perspective of the mentoring programme

The mentoring relationship may be part of an organisation-sponsored mentoring scheme. If it is, this aspect will focus on such issues as:

▶ The support being received for mentoring from the organisation.

▶ The degree of alignment between the mentoring activity and the programme objectives.

DIFFERENT LEVELS

In addition to these perspectives of evaluation, there are three interrelated levels of evaluation.

Level 1: Behaviours

Mentors and mentees would review:

▶ What individuals do and say and also patterns of behaviour and communication at the relationship or organisation level. For example, if the focus of evaluation is on the meetings between mentor and mentee, the individual aspect may explore what both the mentor and mentee do and say in the meetings – including who is doing the talking and who the listening.

▶ In terms of the relationship aspect, the focus may be on how easy it is to arrange the meetings, how frequently they take place and how long they last.

▶ From the organisational aspect, issues may include the degree of practical support that is given to facilitating mentoring meetings – do senior managers communicate their encouragement for mentoring relationships or do they actively discourage them by what they do or say to their people?

Level 2: Thoughts and beliefs

▶ From the individual aspect, the mentor and mentee could consider the issues discussed in the meetings and the extent to which the mentor has been able to help the mentee to explore his or her thoughts on that issue and consider possible consequences.

▶ From a relationship perspective, an issue could be the extent to which the mentor and mentee have a shared understanding of the purpose of the meetings.

▶ From the organisational perspective, the mentor will need to consider the culture of the organisation and what implications this has for mentoring meetings. For example, does the culture make it easy or difficult for mentors to be available for regular meetings, and are informal contacts between mentor and mentee outside the work situation expected or discouraged?

Level 3: Emotions and feelings

This final level is one that is often overlooked. It is extremely important as thoughts and feelings are so intertwined in everyday life and attitudes towards people and events.

▶ A mentor will need to be aware of both his or her own feelings, as well as those of the mentee and the patterns of emotional awareness and response within the relationship and the organisation more generally.

▶ In evaluating mentoring meetings, the mentor will need to consider how well the feelings of the mentee regarding specific courses of action or events have been explored, as well as his or her thoughts.

▶ Evaluation of feelings is probably most appropriate from the individual aspect, but there may be occasions when relationship or organisational issues may be important. For example, the mentor may notice patterns of response in the mentoring meetings which could suggest that the mentoring relationship may be coming to a natural conclusion, or even that the relationship is not working for one or other of the parties.

A key point to remember is that these three levels (the behavioural, cognitive and emotional) and the three perspectives (individual, relationship and organisational) are inextricably interrelated.

When to Evaluate and Review

Re-emphasising the point that evaluation and review is a continuous process, in order to get the best out of the mentoring relationship it needs to take place on three separate occasions:

1 During the actual meeting

2 Reflecting back after each meeting

3 At the end of the relationship to help capture learning.

At each of these times the purpose of evaluating and reviewing is different. If it is conducted during the meeting, it helps to ensure that the session is meeting the expectations of both parties and any immediate problems are rectified. Reflecting back after a session helps to capture both positive and negative aspects of the relationship and enables mentors and mentees to plan for the next one. The final review is important for sharing learning from the experience and setting an agenda for the future.

1 *Evaluation and review during the meeting*

The mentor may want feedback from the mentee on the following:

▶ Checking in: asking how are things going, what has been going on and sharing observations and happenings that are relevant to the mentee and mentor.

▶ Establishing the mentee's outcomes for the meeting and for his or her development – and checking whether these outcomes are SMART (Specific, Measurable, Agreed, Realistic, Time-bound).

▶ Asking for feedback on the meeting and the relationship. Possible questions include:

  ▷ How are you progressing towards your learning or developmental goals?
  ▷ What is going well?
  ▷ What challenges are you experiencing?
  ▷ What do you need to work on?
  ▷ What support would be helpful to you?
  ▷ How could we make our meetings as effective as possible for you?
  ▷ How could I make the meeting more effective?

> *Allowed me to talk, but shaped discussions with good, stretching questions.*
> RWE Thames Water mentee

2 *Evaluating and reviewing after each mentoring meeting*

After the meeting it will be helpful for both mentor and mentee to reflect on the process and outcomes of the meeting. Taking 5–10 minutes soon after the meeting to crystallise thoughts and feelings is a good time to do this while everything is still fresh in the person's mind. It may also be appropriate to reflect further at a later point, perhaps during preparation for the next meeting.

The following checklist may be helpful.

- ❏ What did I notice about my behaviour, thoughts and emotions in the meeting; was it what I planned; and what was my role?
- ❏ What did I notice about the mentee's/mentor's behaviour, thoughts and emotions in the meeting?
- ❏ How do I feel about the meeting?
- ❏ What do I think went well in the meeting?
- ❏ What do I think went less well in the meeting?
- ❏ How would I describe the mentoring relationship itself?
- ❏ How am I developing as a result of this mentoring relationship?
- ❏ Are there any particular problems or barriers being experienced?
- ❏ Do we need to revise the mentoring contract?
- ❏ Are we meeting the organisation's expectations in terms of mentoring?
- ❏ How could the support I am getting from the organisation be improved?
- ❏ What do I need to plan to do in the next meeting?
- ❏ Is there anything else I need to do as a result of this review?

This review process may confirm that the mentoring relationship is progressing well towards meeting the desired outcomes of both mentee and mentor, as well as those of the organisation in a formal programme.

It may, however, reveal that the mentee is having difficulties or has unfair expectations of the mentor. For example, the mentee may be placing excessive demands on the mentor's time or may be seeking excessive levels of advice or support.

The mentee could also have serious personal problems, which are impacting upon the relationship.

The review may reveal issues with the relationship itself, such as a lack of openness or focus. Sometimes the mentor may become aware that he or she is causing potential problems for the mentee, for example where there is jealousy or the mentor may be promising more than can be delivered.

> *Being able to discuss difficult issues openly has been worthwhile. Talking about my strengths and weaknesses, again openly, and in a confidential manner has been very useful.*
>
> RWE Thames Water mentee

Problems identified in the evaluation process need to be recognised and appropriate action taken. In the majority of cases these issues can be addressed openly within the relationship. On other occasions, the mentor may need to refer a mentee with personal problems to a professional counsellor. In some formal mentoring programmes, mentors have a confidential mentoring counsellor with whom they can discuss their issues and seek advice or a self-help group of mentors where generic issues may be discussed.

3 *At the end of a relationship – carrying out a final evaluation and review*

The final stage in a mentoring relationship is coming to closure. It would be nice to imagine that this will happen when the relationship has run its full course and that all the desired outcomes of the relationship have been achieved. When this is the case, there is a good chance that the relationship may transform itself smoothly into one of genuine friendship and equality.

Whether a mentoring relationship ends because an associated programme has come to an end, it is not working, the professional/vocational qualification has been achieved or the overall objective has been met, it is helpful for all parties involved to hold a review. This will help to establish:

> *I wrote out everything I had done and achieved over the last year. I was amazed I'd done so much.*
>
> YELL mentee

▶ whether the mentor/mentee achieved their objectives

▶ the way in which this was done (skills/behaviours/feelings/processes)

▶ how well the process has met the needs of those involved

▶ what the line managers think about the mentoring relationships

▶ the return the organisation has got on its investment, that is, have the immediate success criteria been met? How has mentoring contributed to the overall development process and therefore to the organisation as a whole?

▶ what improvements can be made

▶ whether mentors will mentor another person and the mentee will take on the role of mentor.

This transition requires that both mentor and mentee reach an agreed understanding that the learner has completed the journey. The mentee must let go and so, too, must the mentor. In the words of Daloz (1999, p. 18):

> The trip belongs, after all, to the traveller, not the guide – and the mentor has her own promises to keep.

However, not all mentoring relationships end in this way. Sometimes they may end prematurely because the mentor or the mentee has moved away, or because the mentoring scheme has ended. Where this is a sudden or unexpected event, it can lead to feelings of grief and sadness.

At other times the relationship may need to come to closure prematurely because it is not working for one or both parties and issues cannot be resolved within the relationship. The relationship may be uninspiring or have outlived its purpose, or it may have become dysfunctional. Mentoring contracts can contain a 'no-fault' conclusion clause. Where this is the case, and where the mentoring relationship is continuously evaluated, potentially destructive or dysfunctional relationships may be avoided.

As the relationship comes towards a conclusion the mentor should, therefore, pay particular attention to signals for closure – including boredom, or unwillingness to meet. Recognising feelings, whether of sadness or joy at what has been achieved, will be important, as well as noting signs that there may be difficulties in 'letting go'.

Developing a strategy to handle the closure process can be helpful. Of course this may be difficult when the relationship ends prematurely. The ideal scenario is to agree that there will be a 'closure meeting' to review achievements and look forward. Where this is not possible, the mentor may wish to carry out the final review on his or her own.

INDIVIDUAL PREPARATION FOR CLOSURE OF THE RELATIONSHIP

The proposed format is for individual preparation prior to the meeting in which both mentor and mentee ask themselves a number of questions. This preparation then forms the basis for a review in which both parties share positive feedback. Alternatively, the mentor and mentee could agree to consider all questions in their final review meeting. The questions are based on suggestions of Ann Holloway (1994).

1 *Looking back:*

   ▷ What were my outcomes?

▷ What were my mentee's outcomes?
▷ What have we achieved?
▷ What problems have we had?
▷ What successes did we have?
▷ What surprised me?
▷ What have I learned about myself, other people and the organisation?
▷ What support from the organisation has been particularly helpful?
▷ What other support would have been valuable?

2 *Looking forward:*

▷ What is my vision?
▷ What new goals and targets do I have?
▷ How will I get there?
▷ What support do I need?
▷ What is my action plan?

Sharing Positive Feedback and Success

The final meeting may then be based around sharing feedback on four topics:

▶ What have you valued most from the mentee or mentor?

▶ What have you learned from one another?

▶ What has he or she helped you to achieve?

> *The mentor/mentee relationship has provided me with a more focused advancement approach that seems obtainable and that I am enthusiastic about – for example this is real!*
>
> Smiths Group mentee

▶ What else do you want to say 'thank you' for?

When the relationship is part of a formal mentoring programme, there may also be scope for the organisation to recognise successes publicly, for example where the mentor has helped a mentee to achieve a professional qualification.

> *It has been really productive and given me an outlet for things I feel I can't discuss with my manager because he's too busy or maybe we don't have that kind of rapport.*
>
> Avaya mentee

Recognising Achievements and Ending the Relationship

The need to say goodbye presents a wonderful opportunity to acknowledge the relationship and celebrate what it has achieved, from the perspectives of all the stakeholders.

People may find this ending meeting difficult and false – rather akin to the feelings at their first meeting.

Mentors and mentees who are part of a formal scheme may have the opportunity to attend a closing social event with all the participants/stakeholders. This is an opportunity to give feedback on the overall outcomes and success stories of the scheme – perhaps inviting willing participants to talk about their experiences. This is a good way to end the relationship formally.

A review of mentoring relationships in a range of organisations showed that very often the mentee wanted the mentoring relationship to continue.

Smiths Group found a way to make this happen and still have enough people to mentor – see below.

Smiths Group *found that a number of mentees wanted to continue with a mentoring relationship at the end of the specified timeframe. This presented the scheme manager with an issue in that the Mentors would be needed for the next group of Mentees.*

A win/win solution was found where the Mentor either agreed to continue the relationship informally (provided s/he could commit to the time); or they helped the Mentee to define new objectives and then worked with them to identify who else might be a good Mentor to help them move forward and realise the new objectives – particularly where specific skills/knowledge were involved. The added advantage of this approach was that it brought new Mentors into the scheme.

In other cases when a strong relationship had been developed, the mentor and mentee decided to continue the relationship on an informal basis.

During the expert panel session with the Henley Focus Group, David Clutterbuck emphasised the importance of having a formal closing down of the mentoring relationship. Without formal closure, the relationship may continue long after it has served a useful purpose and vital learning is never captured.

David Megginson commented on the value of having the space and time to reflect that is provided by the mentoring relationship.

Practitioners' Problem-solving

Questions and Answers with David Megginson and David Clutterbuck

How important is it to end a mentoring relationship formally?

I had a very successful mentoring relationship for several years with a woman in a very senior position who went through a number of transitions in her job. What I failed to recognise was that in this relationship I had done most of what I could for her – but neither of us were prepared to acknowledge that. The meetings got longer and longer apart and eventually sort of drifted away. Doing research over the past few years into effective winding down or closing of relationships has stimulated me into getting back to her and having formal closure. It is a lesson I have learnt which I am in the process of implementing and am committed to doing. After I had made the approach, she is too. It was that neither of us had the time, thought or maybe the courage to actually say: 'We need to formally celebrate the end of this.' **(DC)**

What, for you, is the most valuable aspect of mentoring?

Creating/having time and space to reflect. At a hospital – the scheme was structured so that pairs had one hour a month for mentoring. People got such value from that one hour. It is being able to step back for a little while from that constant pressure of events and think. In Mentoring Executives and Directors *we talk about personal reflective space – having that space and holding it is perhaps the key role that a mentor performs.* **(DM)**

Summary

Evaluation, review and closure is an important stage of the mentoring relationship and should not be omitted if the mentor and mentee really want to benefit from the learning that has taken place.

It may be conducted formally or informally. If it is formal, it may link to evaluation being conducted by the scheme manager. In both cases it will embrace different perspectives and all parties will benefit. The mentor is likely to gain an insight into the level of satisfaction of the mentee with the relationship and the competencies he or she needs to develop to be even more effective as a mentor. The mentee will have a better understanding of the extent to which he or she is achieving learning outcomes and is taking responsibility for his or her development. In evaluating the mentor relationship, both mentor and mentee will become more aware of the effectiveness of the relationship and the meetings being held.

The evaluation process takes place at different levels with the different contexts, namely behaviour, thoughts, beliefs and feelings. The behavioural level is easier to explore but thoughts, beliefs and feelings are also extremely important and mentors and mentees need to ensure that feelings about issues are discussed.

Evaluation may take place during the mentoring meeting to help to ensure that it is effective and the relationship is achieving the expectations of both parties. They can further evaluate the relationship and the effectiveness of the meeting afterwards. This helps the subsequent planning for future meetings and captures any learning. Probably the most important time to review is at the end of the mentoring relationship to celebrate what has been achieved.

23 A Summary for Mentors and Mentees

This chapter is intended to give mentors and mentees a quick reference guide to things they may need to consider during the various stages of the mentoring relationship. Whilst not all points will be appropriate in every context, the following pages illustrate key areas that can usefully be discussed and thought about when: getting involved, starting the relationship, working and learning together, and ending and evaluating the relationship.

Getting Involved

These are some of the questions and points it was felt important to consider when thinking about whether to get involved in mentoring:

▶ *Organisational commitment* – is the organisation behind the scheme and committed to its success? What support is there and who is sponsoring it? What support will your involvement need from your line manager?

▶ *Definition* – what is meant by the term 'mentoring' within the context of the organisation or environment?

▶ *Information about the scheme* – are you part of a targeted group of mentors or mentees or is the scheme open to anyone? What information is available; where and with whom can you speak to learn more about it?

▶ *Organisational objectives* – what outcomes is the organisation expecting? What are the measures of success?

▶ *Benefits and risks* – what do you see as the main advantages, personally, of taking part; what are the potential pitfalls? What steps can you put in place to prevent pitfalls occurring and ensure that the advantages are realised?

▶ *Process* – how will the scheme be administered; what is the process involved? What skills and knowledge do you need to acquire? What training or information is available to you? Are there any forms that need completing?

▶ *Confidentiality* – what is the organisation's policy regarding confidentiality?

▶ *Finding a mentor or mentee* – will this be done for you through a formal programme or will you need to find your own? Will a hierarchical or peer relationship be best? What knowledge, experience and qualities will best serve your purpose? How will you pair or match up with someone?

Getting Started

Beginning a new relationship is always difficult. However, with forethought and planning, it is possible to achieve the best possible start. Questions that might be asked of a mentor or mentee at this stage include:

▶ *Roles and responsibilities* – how clear are you about what your own role and responsibilities are? Further, what about those of the other parties involved, such as line managers, the scheme manager and your potential mentor or mentee?

▶ *Mentoring objectives* – what are your personal objectives for volunteering to become a mentor or mentee? How will you express these to the other person?

▶ *Expectations* – what do you expect from your mentor or mentee in terms of behaviours and actions? Be clear about these before going to your first meeting.

▶ *First meeting* – where and when will you hold this? What will you discuss? Have you prepared your thoughts on objectives for the relationship and your expectations of the other person?

▶ *Contracting* – what ground rules and boundaries need agreeing? Will a formal contract be appropriate? What do you both understand by the term 'confidential relationship'? Will it be appropriate to contact one another outside the normal working day?

▶ *Establishing rapport* – what personal information will you share with your mentoring partner? What other ways are there of establishing trust and creating a positive connection? Will it help to gain an understanding of the other person's values and beliefs?

▶ *Agreeing goals and outcomes* – is there clarity on both sides about what you each want to gain from the relationship? Are the goals or outcomes well-formed, realistic and measurable?

▶ *Initial assessment of the relationship* – how and when will you check out whether you will be able to work together and that the relationship is 'gelling'?

Working and Learning Together – Making the Relationship a Positive Experience

Once the relationship has progressed beyond the initial meetings, there are a number of ways in which the mentoring pair can maintain momentum and progress towards achieving the established goals. Questions that may be asked include:

▶ *Meeting management* – have you agreed a 'working practice' for your meetings, for example their frequency, duration and venue? Who will arrange the details and outline the agenda? Will aspects of e-mentoring help to overcome issues which prevent meeting face to face? For mentees, is the line manager aware of the meeting plans? Are your plans for meeting actually working or having to be changed regularly? What can be done about this?

▶ *Discussion topics* – what areas might be open for discussion during the meetings? Have you agreed a mechanism for handling 'crises' should they arise?

▶ *Are we making progress?* – how and when will you assess whether the relationship is working well and is on course to achieved the desired outcomes? What steps will you take if things are not going well?

▶ *Mentoring skills* – whether you are mentor or mentee, are you comfortable that your listening, questioning and giving/receiving feedback skills are up to scratch? How can you be sure? Where can you get help or training if it is necessary?

▶ *'I'm out of my depth'* – as a mentor, what will you do if you feel you do not have the necessary skill or that matters have gone beyond the boundaries of mentoring? What access is there to specialists, such as professional counsellors and help lines, that you can suggest to your mentee?

▶ *Reviewing progress* – what process will you put in place to review learning and progress throughout the life of your mentoring relationship? What opportunities are there to share experiences with other mentors or mentees?

Ending and Evaluating the Relationship

As the mentoring lifecycle draws to a conclusion, the mentoring pair will need to consider a number of areas:

▶ What will be the best way to say 'goodbye' and end the relationship? Will the organisation be holding a formal event to conclude the lifecycle? If the ending is because the relationship has broken down, how will you formally end it?

▶ What will be your course of action if the other person does not wish to end the relationship?

▶ Will the organisation be asking you to participate in a formal assessment of the relationship and the mentoring scheme? How will you then do your own informal review? What preparation do you need to do for this?

▶ What has been achieved during the relationship? Were expectations met and agreed outcomes realised?

▶ What have been the main learning outcomes for both parties?

▶ What outcomes are there for the organisation and other stakeholders?

▶ Will you continue to be involved in mentoring – either with another mentor, carrying on in the role of mentor with someone else or becoming a mentor for the first time?

▶ What key learning points from the relationship can be taken forward to improve your next mentoring relationship in terms of:
  ▷ Behaviours
  ▷ Skills and knowledge
  ▷ Thoughts, beliefs and emotions?

▶ How will you celebrate and recognise the successes you have achieved together?

Having a successful mentoring relationship is a positive and rewarding experience. It needs careful forethought and regular assessment and review to check that everything is on track. As important is the final evaluation which allows the mentoring pair to realise exactly what has been achieved and celebrate that success.

PART V

Lessons Learned and Conclusions

24 Lessons Learned and Conclusions

This book offers an insight into the world of mentoring from the perspective of a range of different participants. These include the mentors and mentees themselves and also the organisation scheme manager. Other organisational stakeholders, such as line managers, are also represented and all of this is through the experience of actual practitioners. This means that the lessons which can be learned from this book are ones which others have been through for themselves and, more than this, the scheme managers at the heart of the process have had the opportunity, through the Henley Focus Group, to reflect upon their learning with each other. This has resulted in access to a unique collection of material, which is far more than simply inferences from case studies.

This chapter summarises the key themes about mentoring that have emerged during the Henley Focus Group meetings. It complements information contained in the summaries in Chapters 15 and 23 by drawing out the lessons that resulted in scheme managers and participants making improvements to their next scheme or relationship. There are examples of lessons learned by some of the Focus Group organisations and also a case study of what went wrong in a mentoring scheme.

Finally, the chapter explores conclusions that may be drawn as a result of reading this book. Linking back to the contexts for, and benefits of, mentoring, this section points the way to the continued use and future of mentoring as a development initiative.

Key Lessons of Mentoring

As each of the Focus Group organisations progressed their mentoring schemes, the key learning points were pulled out and changes made for the next cycle.

The following are what was felt to be important from the perspectives of mentoring scheme organisers, mentees and mentors. The points represent the most commonly recurring themes and have been structured to follow the mentoring lifecycle model referred to in Chapters 10 and 16.

Stage of the Lifecycle	Lessons Learned
Gaining commitment	▶ Understand the business context in order to be able to put the business case and gain agreement from key stakeholders.
	▶ Senior management sponsorship is crucial, as is the identification of all the potential stakeholders.
	▶ Have a clear understanding or definition of what mentoring means within the organisation and how it differs from coaching.
	▶ Ensure that the purpose of the mentoring scheme is clear to all.
	▶ Accurately anticipate the resource levels required. This is critical: a great many of the Focus Group organisations under-estimated this aspect and struggled to support their participants effectively.
Getting involved Planning and launching the scheme	▶ Voluntary participation by mentors and mentees is essential to building a successful relationship.
	▶ Defining a timescale for the scheme or relationship provides a focus for the mentoring pairs: it helps them plan their time and be realistic about what can be achieved.
	▶ Having a line-based mentoring champion works and eases pressure on the scheme manager.
	▶ Training is a critical factor for all involved; include mentors, mentees, line managers, other stakeholders and, if relevant, executive-level mentors' secretaries or assistants.
	▶ Spend time making the right match and involve participants as much as possible, for example by giving them a choice. Let people know how the matching has been done and complete it as soon after the training as is possible.
	▶ Avoid selecting mentors who are within six months of starting a new job or project – they simply will not have the time, however good their intentions.

Getting together **Getting to know each other**	▶ Preparation is key to a successful first meeting.
	▶ It may be helpful to provide a facilitator for the first meeting.
	▶ Using diagnostic tools provides an aid to understanding difference and so builds rapport.
	▶ Ensure that sharing and agreement of expectations occurs.
	▶ It is essential to have a 'get out clause' for situations where the relationship does not gel.
	▶ Scheme managers need to be available, while giving sufficient time for things to bed in.
	▶ Cultural differences in mentoring pairs may have little impact in organisations where the corporate culture is strong.
Working and learning together **Building a positive relationship**	▶ The mentee must take responsibility for driving the relationship.
	▶ A formal structure for meetings may help in the early stages of the relationship.
	▶ The mentor must avoid taking over and solving problems for the mentee.
	▶ Mentors may find it useful to have 'top-up' training midway through the cycle.
	▶ Review progress towards goals as often as possible, both formally and informally; also look at how the relationship is working.
Review and evaluation **Saying goodbye**	▶ A scheme will work better with a framework, not rules! The participants, not the scheme manager, should own it.
	▶ Ensure there is a formal ending of the relationship and the scheme.
	▶ Celebrate success – this is not done often enough in any sphere of business.
	▶ Evaluate the scheme on a number of different levels, not forgetting to include stakeholders other than the mentoring pair, for example line managers.
	▶ A successful scheme will attract interest and more volunteers.

Lessons Learned – Case Studies

LEARNING POINTS

Yorkshire Water

- ▶ Don't underestimate the success of the scheme – be prepared for others to want to have a mentor too.

- ▶ Training for both parties is necessary, with a short timescale between training and the first meeting.

- ▶ Experience is equally, if not more important, than seniority in matching.

- ▶ The mentee needs to drive the relationship – based on their needs.

- ▶ Matching using learning styles worked well.

- ▶ Regular reviews for both mentors and mentees are an essential part of evaluation.

REFLECTIONS FROM A SMITHS GROUP MENTEE

When I was invited to join the Mentoring Scheme I found it difficult to understand exactly how it would relate to me and benefits that it might have. At the end of the introductory training course things were a little clearer, but I was still to be convinced. I have now been in contact with my Mentor for nearly a year and the benefits that it has brought me personally are many.

The process of Mentoring has led me to recognise and overcome the small hurdles that you may encounter at work. Previously I had not realised that some of them existed or the effects that they may be having on my career progress.

Having said that, Mentoring is not about providing answers; it allows you to find solutions to problems by using information that you already have to hand. The skill is in leading the Mentee towards resolution. It's helping you to learn, not teaching.

The advantage that the Mentor has is that he/she is divorced from the problem. They can 'step back' and assess the situation. They may have encountered something like it before. All they need from you are the local details that they cannot possibly know. The rest is down to the Mentor process. Using someone as a sounding board, receiving feedback, testing new ideas, these are all activities that happen during 'a session'.

After each session, I always return to work feeling 'good'. If you were to ask me to write down why, I would have difficulty with that. If you are well matched with your Mentor, it's just something that seems to happen.

LESSONS LEARNED FROM A PRIVATISED UTILITY

1   There is great value in selecting or establishing a definition of mentoring, and a clearly defined purpose, which are universally understood by all the stakeholders.

2   To be effective, the design of the mentoring scheme needs to fit with the culture of the organisation.

3   If possible, all stakeholders should be involved in the programme in some way.

4   A formal scheme seems to work better if it has a defined duration.

5   Making participation voluntary is more likely to lead to enhanced commitment and buy-in from both mentees and mentors – which will help with achieving a successful relationship.

6   Ideally training/briefing should be an essential ingredient for both mentee and mentor groups. The training should reinforce the purpose of the programme and help mentees and mentors understand their responsibilities within it.

7   Where possible the mentees should be involved in the matching process.

8   Geography needs to be taken into consideration when matching mentors and mentees. For the relationship to be effective, they need to be near each other.

9   Everything practically possible should be done to help with the building of effective relationships between the mentees and their mentors. The programme manager should plan on bringing the relationship to an end and starting another with a new mentor, if the relationships are not working.

10   There needs to be a short timescale between the end of the training and the first contact between mentor and mentee.

11   There should be a plan to review progress and share experiences of mentees and mentors at the halfway point of the programme.

12   The mentee should be encouraged to take on the primary responsibility for managing the relationship, that is, establishing their objectives and expectations for the programme (mentoring is their agenda).

13   Mentors and mentees should be encouraged to discuss their own, and their partner's expectations and the relationship objectives early, that is, during their first or second meeting.

14   Two mentees to one mentor is all that managers felt they could take on during a mentoring programme.

15   The mentors need to be experienced managers.

These lessons have become principles that are being used for new mentoring programmes in the organisation. They form part of a continuous improvement process.

BENEFITS AND LEARNING POINTS

▶ Both parties benefited – they learned from each other, particularly in sharing experience and knowledge about their different industries.

▶ Mentors found the different perspective very useful in their own approach to work and their personal development – the questions and preparation for the mentee were as useful to themselves as self-analysis.

▶ Mentoring is challenging and a great learning opportunity for growth.

▶ The mentors gave an external and different perspective to the mentee, enabling them to be developed in a very practical way. Previously, attending training courses, which are sometimes difficult to evaluate into real and tangible outcomes, was considered the normal development option.

▶ The process is rewarding and motivational for both parties.

▶ The matching process ensured that the relationships could work. The mentoring was structured in terms of the framing of the scheme and initial meeting contracting. Thereafter, the relationship became as flexible as required to achieve the overall goals.

▶ Mentoring says something very strongly about the company culture and its commitment to developing and promoting its people.

▶ Mentoring fits with today's challenges in organizations, where we are competing for the human capital available.

During meetings of the Henley Focus Group, members shared instances where particular approaches had not worked, for example expecting senior managers to attend a day's training programme. In the sharing spirit of the Group, the following case study outlines a scheme that did not work the first time round. However, the lessons were learned and the organisation has now gone on to have a successful scheme which is spreading its wings further and further.

A MENTORING SCHEME THAT DIDN'T WORK

Background

In this example, six middle managers were identified as high potential and it was agreed that they would be offered the opportunity to have a mentor, who would be a senior manager. As there were only six senior managers available, the matching needed to take account of existing reporting lines and, so, was done very simply.

The scheme was launched partly via a Development Centre, at which the mentors acted as assessors. Having been matched prior to this happening, it meant that discussion at one of the early meetings could revolve around how things had gone for the mentee at the Development Centre and feedback from the mentor on their observations.

Following the Development Centre, the scheme was left very much to the mentees to drive it and access their mentor when they needed to. No training was given to either party – partly driven by a sense among the senior management mentors that they knew how to go about it. Interestingly, no training or help was requested by the mentees themselves, perhaps because they had little or no expectations of what the process would involve.

The problems

▶ There was a lack of clarity about what mentoring was supposed to do for the participants.

▶ Some mentees felt threatened by the outputs from the Development Centre and, not surprisingly, did not want to start a mentoring relationship based on the thought that they had not performed very well.

▶ Another issue was that the mentees felt they should not bother their (senior manager) mentor as they had nothing to talk about or nothing major that needed discussing. There was a sense of: 'The mentor's very busy and I don't want to be seen as a drain on their time.' Therefore, leaving it in the laps of the mentees to make contact when they needed to did not work.

▶ Matching was done simply by ensuring that no one was mentored by a manager in their direct reporting line. The mentors had input but a limited number of options for a choice of mentee.

Lessons learned and implemented in the next programme

▶ Comprehensive training was needed for both mentors and mentees, covering organisational and personal objectives, benefits, 'rules of engagement', roles, skills and so on.

▶ Participation for all needed to be on a voluntary basis and matching was based on a much broader and informed basis than avoiding reporting lines.

▶ Starting off with a Development Centre did not work and was not repeated.

Final Lessons from the Expert Panel

David Clutterbuck reminded people that mentoring has already been used as a learning intervention for several years and is not just a fad. It meets some fundamental needs. David Megginson emphasised the timing of mentoring and the fit it has with today's approach to development.

Practitioners' Problem-solving

Questions and Answers with David Megginson and David Clutterbuck

Is mentoring likely to replace other forms of management/executive development?

People sometimes ask: 'Does mentoring work?' One smart reply is 'do you have any friends?' If they say 'yes', you can say: 'Well, does friendship work?' This kind of helping relationship is absolutely fundamental to what it means to be a collaborative human being, so it doesn't seem to be a fad. When David and I started working together on this we felt it was important. That was 12 years ago and it is still going strong because it responds to a fundamental need we have in organisations and a need we have as people.

Does it replace other forms of management development? Absolutely not. It is crucial that if people want to develop specific skills, they have the opportunity to do so. Then there are lots of developmental things that aren't inherent to the individual at all; they are about the team or about relationships between teams or relationships with suppliers or customers which aren't the direct business of mentors. **(DM)**

One of the reasons mentoring has become so popular, particularly at senior level, is because it is actually 'just in time' learning as opposed to 'just in case' learning. Traditional learning is 'just in case', but mentoring fits with the evolution of learning, is focused on the individual and is customised. So it is a genre that actually matches with the needs of individuals – which is why we're seeing so much growth in this area. It is not going to replace other forms of learning – it just complements them. **(DC)**

Conclusions

In final conclusion, today's world is changing, turbulent and competitive, and requires people to change and grow if they are to stay ahead of the game. A key driver for mentoring is its ability to support the individualised nature of personal development. With the changing psychological contract and the growth of portfolio careers, any approach that stimulates individuals to take personal responsibility for their own development has to be worthwhile.

As mentoring grows in its popularity it can start to move towards the centre of an organisation's development strategy and not simply remain as a marginal activity for a few selected groups. However, for mentoring to become embedded into an organisation's strategy, it needs to be recognised in performance management terms as being a part of the role of a manager.

Scheme managers should be very clear about the context for any mentoring scheme, and establish clearly defined boundaries, if the scheme is to be a success. The Focus Group members also stressed the importance of a realistic assessment of the resource implications in running a mentoring scheme, particularly as the scheme gains in popularity.

From a mentor perspective, most mentors gain as much from the mentoring relationship as the mentee. Whilst there is obviously a time commitment for the mentor, it does provide a welcome opportunity for the mentor to step back, become more reflective and actually see things from a different perspective. It also provides an excellent opportunity to hone important people skills.

Mentoring is an outstanding development tool for the mentee. It provides the space to develop a longer term perspective on careers and gives access to a wealth of knowledge and experience not always possible in normal day-to-day relationships. The mentee must, however, guard against overdependency on the mentor for providing all the answers. It offers a level of self-reliance that is critical in today's changing world.

The Mentoring Focus Group continues to meet, sharing good practice and learning together. As new companies have joined the Group, new people are able to bring fresh perceptions on the topic and learn from the wealth of experience that exists within the Group. The journey never ends, it just enters a new phase.

> *It's helped me stand back and look at how I get things done.*
> B&Q mentee

> *It's made me think differently about my day job!*
> B&Q mentor

25 Reading, Websites and Networking

Reading

The Art of Mentoring, Mike Pegg
ISBN: 1–85252–272–0, Management Books 2000

Coaching for Performance, Sir John Whitmore
ISBN: 1–85788–170–2, Nicholas Brealey

Everyone Needs a Mentor (3rd edn), David Clutterbuck
ISBN: 0–85292–904–8, IPD

Implementing Mentoring Schemes, Nadine Klasen & David Clutterbuck
ISBN: 0–7506–5430–9, Butterworth Heinemann

Learning Alliances, David Clutterbuck
ISBN: 0–85292–741–5, IPD

Making Sense of Emotional Intelligence (2nd edn), M. Higgs & V. Dulewicz
ISBN: 0–78087–0367–4, NFER-NELSON

The Manager as a Coach and Mentor, Eric Parsloe
ISBN: 0–85292–803–3, IPD

Managers as Mentors, Chip R. Bell
ISBN: 1–57675–142–2, McGraw-Hill Education

Mentoring and Diversity: an International Perspective, David Clutterbuck &
Belle Rose Ragins
ISBN: 0–7506–4836–8, Butterworth Heinemann

Mentoring Executives and Directors, David Clutterbuck & David Megginson
ISBN: 0–7506–3695–5, Butterworth Heinemann

Mentoring in Action, David Megginson & David Clutterbuck
ISBN: 0–7494–2394–3, Kogan Page

The Mentoring Pocketbook, Geof Alred, Bob Garvey & Richard Smith
Management Pocketbooks Ltd

Mentoring Students and Young People, Andrew Miller
ISBN: 0–7494–3543–7, Kogan Page

Mentoring at Work, Kathy E. Kram
ISBN: 0–6731–5617–6, Addison Wesley

Transformational Mentoring, Julie Hay
ISBN: 0–9521–9647–6, Sherwood Publishing

Websites

Whilst not exhaustive, this list provides a plethora of links and routes for finding out more about mentoring.

http://www.emccouncil.org/

The European Mentoring and Coaching Council exists to promote good practice, and the expectation of good practice, in mentoring and coaching across Europe. It is working to provide a number of common standards and, in 2003, introduced ethical standards for its members. There is an extensive library of materials on coaching and mentoring and a discussion forum for members. The trustees and executive board are drawn from leading experts across the UK and Europe. Publishes the *International Journal of Mentoring and Coaching*.

http://www.mentorsforum.co.uk/

The Mentors Forum is an interactive site hosted by Business Link Hertfordshire, looking not only at individual mentoring schemes, but studying mentoring as a 'generic' subject. Contains a section of useful information, mentoring tools and case studies, as well as a mentors' forum where you can post an issue you might have to contribute to existing discussions. Comprehensive list of other mentoring web sites.

http://www.oscm.co.uk/

The Oxford School of Coaching and Mentoring, has expanded the organisation with the formation of the OSC&M Total Learning Group. Links here to OSCM's qualifications and conferences.

http://www.clutterbuckassociates.co.uk/

David Clutterbuck's site which has helpful information and downloads about coaching, mentoring and mentoring schemes; includes International Standards for Mentoring Schemes in Employment.

http://www.nmn.org.uk/

The National Mentoring Network aims to promote the development of mentoring; offer advice and support to those wishing to set up or develop mentoring programmes; and provide a forum for the exchange of information and good practice.

http://www.cipd.co.uk

The Chartered Institute of Personnel and Development's site in the UK. Putting 'mentoring' into the search field will bring up numerous results, including information about the Certificate in Coaching and Mentoring.

www.businessmentoringscotland.org

This is a scheme set up by the Scottish Executive to create a pool of skilled mentors offering support and experience for selected growth companies in Scotland. Can apply online to become one of their mentors.

www.coachingnetwork.org.uk

An independent site, with all sorts of ongoing discussions about coaching and mentoring which you can join in with and search as well as a resource centre containing information on recent events and publications.

www.mbamentors.com

A network of professionals with the specific aim of helping those thinking about or already undertaking an MBA course.

www.mentor-cafe.com

You need to become a member and sign in (free) to use this website – it is split into sections for mentees and mentors. It can match you up to a mentor, and if you are already a mentor you can apply to join the mentor database.

www.MentorGirls.org

This is an American grass-roots, community outreach programme connecting women in industry with girls in schools. The newsletter and recommended reading sections may be useful.

www.mentoring.org

Website of the American National Mentoring Partnership, some helpful information on running a mentoring programme.

www.mentors.org.uk

Big Brothers, Big Sisters is a scheme, which matches young people aged 6–16 to volunteer mentors. You can read about the success of the scheme and find out how to apply to become a volunteer mentor.

www.mikethementor.co.uk

Mike works as a professional mentor and you can subscribe to his helpful 'Mentoring for Change' newsletter.

www.princes-trust.org.uk

Information about the work of The Prince's Trust which provides mentors for young people leaving care and for those starting up in business. Look out for its publications on mentoring – including a standardised toolkit.

Networking

Finding other people who have implemented a mentoring scheme (or are planning to do so), or have participated in one as mentor or mentee, can be done by joining networks, attending conferences, participating in focus groups and so on. Below are a few suggestions for conferences and networking.

▶ *Annual Coaching and Mentoring Conference:* normally held in the UK over two days during June or July and aimed at providing 'practical perspectives' (see the OSCM website).

▶ *European Mentoring and Coaching Council* has held an annual confer- ence since 1993 – normally in October/November (see the EMCC website in the previous section). Run over two days, it offers participants three types of workshop: research, case studies and hands-on, as well as keynote plenary sessions by international figures.

▶ *Coaching Congress:* run by Linkage International in London during the autumn. Brings together a large number of professionals and experts. Has included mentoring in the past.

▶ *Henley Learning Partnership:* member companies in the partnership can nominate people to attend a variety of focus groups, including the mentoring one which has now evolved into a Mentoring and Coaching Focus Group (for further information, see www.henleymc.ac.uk).

▶ *Networks:* exchange information with like-minded people by joining a mentoring network – see the website listings in the previous sections.

References

Alred, G., Garvey, G. & Smith, R., *The Mentoring Pocketbook* (London: Management Pocketbooks, 1998).

Ambrose, L., 'Mentoring Diversity', *Healthcare Executive,* Sept/Oct 2003: 60–1.

Anderson, H., 'Why Mentoring Doesn't Work', Harvard Management Communication Letter, June 2003.

Bandler, R. and Grinder, J., *The Structure of Magic*, vol. 1 (Science and Behaviour Books Inc., 1975).

Bateson, G., *Steps to an Ecology of Mind* (New York: Ballantine Books, 1972).

Bennetts, C., 'Mentors. Mirrors and Reflective Practitioners: An Inquiry into Informal Mentor/Learner Relationships', M.Ed. dissertation, Division of Adult Continuing Education Library, University of Sheffield (1994).

Bhatta, G. & Washington, S., '"Hands up": Mentoring in the New Zealand Public Service', *Public Personnel Management*, 2003, **32**(2): 211.

Business Week online, 'The Hidden Pitfalls of Mentoring' (McGraw-Hill www.businessweek.com, 17 April 2001).

Carrington, L., 'Global Game Plan', *Training Magazine*, June 2003: 22–5.

CIPD, www.CIPD.co.uk.

Clutterbuck, D., *Everyone Needs a Mentor – Fostering Talent at Work*, 3rd edn (London: CIPD, 2001).

Clutterbuck, D. & Megginson, D., *Mentoring Executives and Directors* (Oxford: Butterworth Heinemann, 1999).

Cowan, L., 'Weathering the recession (and protecting your job) by managing change', *San Diego Business Journal*, 2002, **23**(9): 21.

Daloz, L., *Mentor: Guiding the Journey of Adult Learners* (San Francisco: Jossey-Bass, 1999).

Dejovine, B. & Harris, E. R., 'Developing the mentor/protégé relationship', *Healthcare Executive*; Chicago, July/August 2001.

Eby, L., 'The Hidden Pitfalls of Mentoring', *Business Week online* (McGraw-Hill Companies, 17 April 2001).

Eisenhardt, K., 'Has strategy changed? The powerful forces of globalization are fundamentally changing the nature and dimension of strategy', *MIT Sloan Management Review*, 2002, **43**(2): 88.

Ellis, C., (2000) 'The flattening corporation', *MIT Sloan Management Review*, 2003, **44**(4): 5.

English, P. & Sutton, E., 'Working with Courage and Failure', European Mentoring Centre Conference (November 1999).

Fair Play Consortium, Fair Play Consortium Enterprising Approaches to Equality fair=play in 2002, www.eoc.org.uk/cseng/abouteoc/eaelealfet.pdf. Accessed 13/10/2003.

Glover, C., 'Good for the Soul', *People Management Online*, 11 July 2002, www.peoplemanagement.co.uk/pm/archive/2002-07/7023. Accessed 15 August 2003.

Glover, C., 'Staying Power', *People Management Online*, 9 April 2003, www.peoplemanagement.co.uk/pm/archive/2002-07/7023. Accessed 15 August 2003.

Guest, A. B., 'Organisational Mentoring', *Professional Women International Newsletter* (Spring 2001).

Hamel, G., Nonaka, I. & Prahalad, C. K., *How Organisations Learn*, Starkey, K., (ed.), (London: International Thompson Business Press, 1996).

Hay, J., *Transformational Mentoring* (Watford: Sherwood, 1999).

Health & Safety Executive, *Tackling Work-related Stress Issues; A Manager's Guide to Improving and Maintaining Employee Health and Well-being* (Sudbury: HSE Books, 2001).

Henley Management College, *E-business Management in the New Economy* (Henley Management College, 2000).

Higgs, M. & Dulewicz, V., *Making Sense of Emotional Intelligence*, 2nd edn (London: nferNelson, 2002).

Holloway, A., (1994) *Mentoring: The Definitive Workbook* (Manchester: Development Processes (Publications), 1994).

Horn, C., 'Keeping it in the family', *Bookseller*, (5091): **22** (22 August 2003).

IBM, www.MentorPlace.com.

Kellam, S., 'Try mentoring', *Last Word Indiana Business Magazine* (July 2003).

Kirkpatrick, D. L., 'Evaluation of Training' in Craig, R. L. & Bittel, L. R. (eds) *Training and Evaluation Handbook* (New York: McGraw-Hill, 1967).

Linehan, M. & Walsh, J. S., 'Mentoring relationships and the female managerial career', *Career Development International* (Bradford: MCB, 1999).

Megginson, D. & Clutterbuck, D., *Mentoring in Action* (London: Kogan Page, 1995).

Merrick, L. & Stokes, P., 'Mentor Development & Supervision: "A Passionate Joint Enquiry"', *The International Journal of Mentoring and Coaching*, 2003, **I**(1).

Mockler, R. J., 'Prescription for Disaster: Failure to Balance Structured and Unstructured Thinking', *Business Strategy Review*, 2003, **14**(2): 17–26.

Neuborne, E., 'Mentors as Motivators', *Potentials*, 2003, **36**(3): 16.

Oracle, One Team: Many Individuals, www.oracle.com. Accessed 13/10/2003.

Oxford English Reference Dictionary, Pearsall, Judy & Trumble, Bill (eds) (Oxford: Oxford University Press, 2002).

Parsloe, E., *The Manager as Coach and Mentor*, 2nd edn (London: CIPD, 1999).

Pearn, M., Honey, P. & Clutterbuck, D., 'Learning from the good, the bad and the ugly mistakes', *People Management*, **43** (November 1995).

Pegg, M., *The Art of Mentoring*, (Kemble: Management Books 2000, 2003).

Personnel Today, 'Battered Britain', (21 October 2003).

Poe, A. C., 'Establishing Positive Mentoring Relationships', *HR Magazine* (February 2002).

Starcevich, M. & Friend, F., 'Effective mentoring relationships from the mentor's perspective', *Workforce; Costa Mesa* (July 1999).

Starck, K. & Kruckeberg, D., 'Ethical obligations of public relations in an era of globalisation', *Journal of Communication Management*, 2003, **8**(1): 29–40.

The Work Foundation, 'Work–life balance policies are working yet a third of employees are failing to get the message', www.theworkfoundation.com (3 September 2003).

Tyler, K., 'Mentoring programs link employees and experienced execs', *HR Magazine*, 1998, **43**(5): 98.

Weinstein, G. & Schuele, K., 'Practitioners as Mentors', *Journal of Accounting*, 2003, **195**(6): 39.

Whitmore, J., *Coaching for Performance*, 2nd edn (London: Nicholas Brealey, 1996).

Wilson, J. A. & Elman, N. S., 'Organisational Benefits of Mentoring', *Academy of Management Executives*, 1990, **4**: 88–94.

Yudd, R., 'Real-life mentoring lights way for future leaders, nation's restaurant news', www.nrn.com, (28 July, 2003).

Index

Numbers appearing in **bold** type denote whole chapters